Scarring
the Black Body

Scarring
the Black Body

Race and Representation in
African American
Literature

Carol E. Henderson

University of Missouri Press
Columbia and London

Copyright © 2002 by
The Curators of the University of Missouri
University of Missouri Press, Columbia, Missouri 65201
Printed and bound in the United States of America
All rights reserved
5 4 3 2 1   06 05 04 03 02

Library of Congress Cataloging-in-Publication Data

Henderson, Carol E., 1964–
    Scarring the Black body : race and representation in African American
literature / Carol E. Henderson.
        p. cm.
    Includes bibliographical references and index.
    ISBN 0-8262-1421-5 (alk. paper)
    1. American literature—African American authors—History and criticism.
    2. Wounds and injuries in literature.   3. African Americans in literature.
    4. Body, Human, in literature.   5. Race in literature.   I. Title.

PS153.N5 H46 2002
810.9′355—dc21
                                                                        2002073957

⊗™ This paper meets the requirements of the
American National Standard for Permanence of Paper
for Printed Library Materials, Z39.48, 1984.

Text designer: Stephanie Foley
Jacket designer: Jennifer Cropp
Typesetter: The Composing Room of Michigan, Inc.
Printer and binder: The Maple-Vail Book Manufacturing Group
Typefaces: Techno and Goudy

For permissions, see p. 184

FOR MY BROTHER BOBBY

Definitions

scar *n* [1] a mark left on the skin or other tissue after a wound, burn, ulcer, pustule, lesion has healed; [2] a marring or disfiguring mark on anything; [3] the lasting mental or emotional effects of suffering or anguish; *vt* scarred, scarring; to mark with or as with a scar; *vi* to form a scar in healing

Synonyms
n. injury, stigma, trauma, reminder, memento, brand; v. hurt, blemish, wound

Contents

Scars are a map to one's past . . .
        proof that even the worst wounds heal.
                —Vincent of *Beauty and the Beast*

Acknowledgments

The writing of this book has been a profound journey. Along the way, the kindness of strangers and friends alike has influenced in innumerable ways this offering placed before you. To name them all would require a book in and of itself. Yet I cannot, in all good conscience, complete such a journey without acknowledging, at least in part, the names of those most essential to its completion. To my son, Kelsey, who provides a wonderful balance between "Mom" and "Dr. Henderson" and who handles the challenge of a working mother with dignity and grace—I love you. May this small token in some way help make this world a better place for you to grow and mature as an individual and person. To my mother, Barbara J. Henderson, who is my best friend and confidante and has always told me "she gave birth to genius"—thanks, Mom, for the love, the support, the unwavering belief that your daughter would complete this journey. In you I have a wonderful example of hard work, perseverance, and true grit; as any good genius knows, you are only as good as the root. To my brother, Willie "Bobby" Henderson Jr., and my sister, Latonya Johnson—your faith in your big sister has been my sustaining grace; I thank you for always welcoming me home. To my father, Willie Henderson Sr., who made intimate the process of wounding and its aftermath—I offer you this book as a gesture of understanding, for in it I have come to recognize the complicated sojourn of the black man in this country. To my church family at Bethel AME, my pastor Rev. Silvester S. Beamon, and my godparents Reverends Eloise and James Wilmore Sr.—thanks for the many prayers, the pep talks, the hours of sustained ministering. You know the depths of our pain as Christians, as black people, as human beings. Thank you for providing me a space to rejuvenate when the journey got tedious. To you I will be eternally grateful.

I also wish to thank those individuals whose contributions are reflected in the very inspiration behind this project. To my extended family, both here and abroad, I acknowledge your spirit of struggle and compromise. Your fortitude nurtures me; your courage inspires me. To the community of artists, critics, authors, and activists who continue to lay before the nation the wounds of our people, I salute you. Keep your eyes on the prize and keep "keepin' on." To the many colleagues who listened to partially articulated ideas, read earlier drafts, and offered spiritual and intellectual encouragement, I honor you here. Special thanks go to Carla Peterson, Ed Guerrero, Cheryl Wall, and Dolan Hubbard. I am particularly indebted to Emory Elliott. As mentor, confidant, nurturer, and safe harbor, you have shepherded me through the murky waters of academia with humility and grace. Your wonderful wisdom and keen intellect will always be a constant source of strength. And to "the Sergeant," whose unabashed belief in the spirit of *yemoja* set the stage for a new generation of scholars, thank you. I could not have made it without you, girlfriend!

My colleagues in the English Department at the University of Delaware were also helpful during the time I was completing this project. Alvina Quintana and Barbara Gates have sustained and inspired me in countless ways since my arrival in Delaware. I am grateful for their invaluable friendship and intercollegiate spirit. Special thanks go to Ron Martin, who took time out of his busy schedule to read and comment on more than one version of this manuscript. He went beyond his normal responsibilities as colleague and provided unfailing support during the final stages of this project. To Ann Ardis, Jeannie Pfaelzer, Mckay Jenkins, and numerous others who offered words of encouragement, a needed hug, or a kind gesture—thank you. You continue to make the English Department a unique place to be. To my students of African American and American Studies—you never cease to amaze me. Your boundless energy and passion for learning prove that the classroom is a wonderful space of intellectual exchange.

As well I would like to thank my writing group at the University of California, Riverside, who inspired me in the early stages of my research. Geoff Cohen and Marilyn Mehaffy proved to be stimulating company, both as colleagues and as faithful readers of my dissertation chapters. The gems gleamed from those discussions provide the impetus for many of the dialogues set forth in this current study. Over the intervening years, this dialogue has continued to grow in interesting ways as we accept the challenges of our demanding careers. But it is their enthusiasm, along with that of teachers like Katherine Kinney and Carol Anne Tyler, that has continued to expand the exciting possibilities of "body" scholarship.

Debts of another kind are owed to Carol Rudisell and William Simpson in the Morris Library at the University of Delaware, Donna Wells and Joellen ElBashir at Moorland-Spingarn Research Center, Mary Markey at Maryland Historical Society, and the unnamed dedicated staff at Delaware Historical Society, who gave of their time and expertise at crucial junctures during the completion of this project. Similar gratitude is extended to the generous editorial staff at *Modern Fiction Studies*, who graciously allowed me to reprint portions of my article "The Walking Wounded: Rethinking Black Women's Identity in Ann Petry's *The Street*" in this current study. I particularly want to thank the journal's editor, William J. Palmer, for his interest in my work and his confidence in my scholarship. He and the anonymous readers were pivotal in helping to shape the tenor of this essay.

Last, I want to acknowledge the wonderful people at the University of Missouri Press. Clair Willcox—what can I say? You are the reason this book has an audience. Thank you for your patience, your passion, and your vision. You saw the light at the end of the tunnel and encouraged me to see it also—even in those darkest moments. Thanks also go to the manuscript reviewers who, anonymity notwithstanding, aided me in pushing the boundaries of my scholarship in ways I have only now come to appreciate. This final product is a credit to their keen eye and scholarly intuition. Jane Lago, Beverly Jarrett, Karen Renner, and Jennifer Brown helped give finer shape to this project as it moved from "idea" to production. Thank you. Thank you. Thank you. And a special thanks goes to Jane Lago, who served as copyeditor for this manuscript as well. You know this project as well as I. Thank you for walking in my shoes with exceptional grace and wit.

And finally to those who will read the humble offerings of this author. May the ancestors help you find peace in the time of storm, courage in the heat of battle, and purpose in your daily walk. And may you come to know the struggle and your place in it.

Scarring
the Black Body

Introduction

Bearing Witness

Reading the Narrative of the African American Body

> I know why the caged bird beats his wing
> Till its blood is red on the cruel bars;
> For he must fly back to his perch and cling
> When he fain would be on the bough a-swing;
> And a pain still throbs in the old, old scars
> And they pulse again with a keener sting—
> I know why he beats his wing!
>
> I know why the caged bird sings, ah me,
> When his wing is bruised and his bosom sore,—
> When he beats his bars and he would be free;
> It is not a carol of joy or glee,
> But a prayer that he sends from his heart's deep core,
> But a plea, that upward to Heaven he flings—
> I know why the caged bird sings!
>
> Paul Laurence Dunbar, "Sympathy"

Sneaking in late one Sunday morning to the services of a very prominent Baptist church in San Bernardino, California, I took a seat in the
rear of the church next to a woman and her two children. Generally, I
try to make it to church services on time, but trying to convince a pre-
cocious (yet adorable) four year old to put on a suit and tie presents challenges of its own. Needless to say, I arrive at church when I can, and this
particular Sunday I took a seat on the pew with all those other individ-

1

uals who either arrived late or were too shy or too intimidated to move up front, or who simply found solace in sitting close to the door (presumably for a swift exit). As the minister proceeded to the part of the service that acknowledges visitors—when all eyes visually interrogate those individuals brave enough to stand and endure the scrutiny—I noticed that the woman next to me was starting to doze. Initially I thought, Why isn't this woman at home? Surely she could find a more comfortable place to sleep—one unburdened with the noise of a church choir and the monotonal droning of the announcement clerk. However, as I began to look at her more closely, I noticed that she had very deep scars on her leg facing me. For those of you who don't attend traditional black Baptist churches regularly, it is common knowledge that coming to church bare-legged is against "church protocol." This woman's legs were bare. Also, the marks visible on her legs—what appeared to be large cigarette burns—seemed to have been inflicted on her person with extreme force. There were actually small crevices, potholes (in the terminology used to describe damage to the surface of a street), on her body.

I was quite moved by the language of this woman's body—I felt I knew her story. I considered her life in terms of other women—abused, neglected, punished by the circumstances in their lives. This woman's physical form seemed to embody that narrative. Her clothes were disheveled, her hair unkempt. She seemed tired—her body postured in a resigned way. She appeared seasoned, as if aged by years of existing under circumstances that are inclined to make the young quickly old. Her children looked worn, and they also slept; her daughter had her head in the woman's lap, and her son dozed in the seat in front of her. I cannot recall the sermon for that Sunday because my thoughts drifted toward my interest in bodies and their ability to tell stories: vividly, subtly, powerfully.

I should note here that not every "body" moves me. Coming from the inner city of Los Angeles, I have seen all kinds of bodies in various states of disrepair: wasted bodies seduced by the promises of the street; wounded bodies enslaved to the vices of crack, cocaine, alcohol, and sex; displaced bodies in need of hope, direction, and some sense of security. There must have been something in this woman's demeanor, in her unspoken disposition, that drew me to her. To this day, she has remained an elusive part of my memory, an ever-so-present image in my investigation of scars and bodies, an unsolved mystery in life's ever-evolving riddle. I now realize I may never know the "real" story of the woman I observed that day. In retrospect, it may not have been the intimate details of her life that interested me; it may have been the story *implied* through her body's language—and *signified* by the presence of those scars on her legs—that piqued my curiosity and made me want to pursue this line of inquiry in greater depth.

On a larger scale, my interest in bodies has primarily centered on the ability of the body to alter certain historical moments in any given social milieu. Our historical record is replete with examples of the body being used successfully by various ethnic groups as a tool to challenge the stifling conditions of economic and social oppression or, at the very least, to challenge our understanding of those historical moments that revolve around the issue of social and political control of subjugated groups. In each of these instances, the body has functioned as a walking text, a fleshly reminder of the paradoxical nature of an American citizenry built around the ideology of difference. In the "bodily" history of the African American community, the civil rights movement of the late 1950s and early 1960s consistently used the African American body to show television audiences the harshness of the systems of segregation and racism. Etched into the minds of most individuals who witnessed the politics of that era are images of African American men, women, and children being attacked by water hoses and dogs. My reflection at this point is not to rehash that which is already known but to demonstrate the nuances of a historicity based on the signs of the body as text. As Paula Cooey maintains, the body is an important resource for understanding cultural ways of knowing "as these are informed by the relations of and struggles for power."[1] I want to suggest that these "cultural ways of knowing" provide a setting for the examination of African American bodies in the larger social context of struggles for power, an examination that centers on the ability of these bodies not only to "speak" into existence their own humanity but to do so in a way that resists racist or sexist paradigms of subjugated embodiment.

The corporeal body has continually served as an emblem for the conceptualizations of national identities. As sign, the body's narrative prowess stems from its contentious development as an ambiguous social entity. That is the body's identification. The very way we assess and contextualize social, political, and ethnic representations within the national public sphere revolves around the rhetorical fluidity of the Amer-

---

1. *Religious Imagination and the Body: A Feminist Analysis,* 9.

ican body politic. This politic, framed around what Karen Sanchez-Eppler calls "the bodily biases of the state," creates a political and legal climate that solidifies white male privilege through the repetitive reinvention of those public discourses that shape our understanding of the national subject. Within this context, the African American body has been viewed more or less as a conglomeration of social meanings, meanings that, in the end, *mark* this body as Other or "bodiless" according to specific cultural and national mandates that objectify the African American body so much that black identity is formed in relation to the split between mind and body. According to bell hooks, we live in a culture "where racist colonization has deemed black folks more body than mind. Such thinking lies at the core of all the stereotypes of blackness . . . which suggest we are 'naturally, inherently' more in touch with our bodies, less alienated than other groups in this society."[2] This focus within the dominant culture on the African American body testifies to the ways in which national authority—social, political, or otherwise—is derived from the interchangeability of "real" and "imagined" bodies.

This phenomenon can be more readily seen in the context of some highly publicized incidents of the past decade where false accusations were made against "imaginary" black men who were said to have committed offensive and even horrific crimes. The egregious manner in which these allegations were made reveals a startling cultural narrative in which African Americans are characterized by a disturbing pattern of phantom criminology. Consider, for example, Susan Smith's claims in November 1994 that she had been carjacked by an armed black man who drove off with her two young children. Smith garnered national sympathy, and prime-time media coverage, in her attempts to locate her missing sons. However, her story turned out to be a complete fabrication, and Smith was subsequently arrested and convicted of the murders of her two young sons. A similar and equally bizarre incident occurred in Boston in October 1989 when Charles Stuart alleged that a black man jumped into the backseat of his car demanding cash and jewelry before fatally shooting Stuart's wife, Carole, who was seven months pregnant, and seriously wounding Stuart in the abdomen. This case riveted the nation, and the television media went so far as to broadcast portions of Carole's funeral, dramatically overlaid with the reading of a letter Charles Stuart had written to his wife and deceased child, who

2. Sanchez-Eppler, *Touching Liberty: Abolition, Feminism, and the Politics of the Body*, 3; hooks, "Feminism Inside: Toward a Black Body Politic," 129.

lived only seventeen days after his mother's emergency cesarean section. This national interest only served to heighten racial tensions in Boston as police officers expended all available manpower to catch this elusive killer. Months later, Charles Stuart's brother Matthew confessed to authorities that the entire incident was a hoax. Charles Stuart had hoped to cash in on his wife's insurance policy and had solicited Matthew's help in disposing of the murder weapon. The following day, after learning of his brother's decision to go to the authorities, Charles Stuart apparently committed suicide by jumping from the Tobin Bridge. Matthew Stuart later pleaded guilty to conspiracy to commit insurance fraud and obstruction of justice and was sentenced to three to five years in prison.

Each of these incidents demonstrates with relative ease the national perception of African Americans as venal and inhuman beings. That some members of the public unhesitatingly accepted the validity of these stories is troubling in and of itself. That other members of the print and visual media fueled these national fears by devoting an enormous amount of coverage to them only serves to underscore the point that some criminal narratives within the context of America's social and legal systems are more believable (or should I say more acceptable) than others. It should be noted that a number of African Americans expressed disbelief that a black man would carjack a vehicle with children in it, proving that the oral culture (the word-of-mouth grapevine that is so powerful in certain segments of this community) offers a legitimate yet underappreciated counterculture to the printed word. Moreover, an investigation of the processes by which these cases were incited and quickly disposed of in the dominant culture lends credence to Toni Morrison's claim that America's written (and I would add visual) culture derives much of its "Americanness" from a real or fabricated Africanist presence that serves both as "a way of talking about and a way of policing matters of class, sexual license, and repression, formations and exercises of power, and meditations on ethics and accountability."[3]

The question then becomes, How does one disrupt those processes that mold the social meanings of the black body? What are the ways in which one can restructure those social discourses that are built on this body as sign/language? How does one regain agency in a system intent on destroying one's motive will? The answers to these questions can be found in the literary criticism and fictional and personal narratives of

3. *Playing in the Dark: Whiteness and the Literary Imagination*, 6.

African American writers. It is through writing that African Americans empower themselves. According to Kimberly W. Benston, self-creation and the reformation of a fragmented historical past are infinitely intertwined for African Americans. Therefore, African American literature should be viewed as "one vast genealogical poem that attempts to restore continuity to the ruptures or discontinuities imposed by the history of black presence in America."[4] Given the cultural dynamics regarding the meanings of certain bodies in the national public sphere, society is in a constant state of *rewriting* the cultural significance of the African American individual through the use of his or her body. Much of the methodological figurings of the systems of oppression consistently silence the voice of the subjugated using the body as their vehicle. I argue that African American culture, when taken as a whole, confronts this silencing by creating moments of resistance or "loopholes of retreat" that not only speak to the resilience of African American people but also allow for the *reconceptualization* of literal and figurative bodies within certain delimiting social structures. It is the gap between the literal and the figurative that allows for the possibility of speaking a counterdiscourse of the black body. Cultural expressions such as dance, jazz, and the visual arts provide an alternative method of reclaiming the body as voice. Yet the African American literary tradition is distinct in that writers can fashion a public "self" in language that protests their dehumanizing conditions. This impulse to testify, to map out the contours of one's journey from bondage to freedom in some cases, undergirds the potency of African American writing and its ability to transform delimiting systems of critical interpretation through creativity and innovative ways of thinking. This in turn provides the most stimulating view of cultural *re*-creation as the quest for dignity and selfhood becomes the impetus for a restructuring of African American subjectivity. Moreover, this persistence in acquiring a voice through the assertion of writing creates an emancipatory spirit that fuses feeling into action and helps the disempowered see their circumstances differently and act to change them.

"One of my most specific theoretical assumptions," writes Dana Nelson, "is that literature is symbolic action with reference to a real world, and as such, should not be abstracted from its material and cultural con-

4. "I yam what I am: The Topos of (Un)naming in Afro-American Literature," 152.

texts."[5] Nelson's comments provide an appropriate entry into my discussions of the methodological approaches in this study. Of key concern to me are the *variety* of ways African American writers respond to their larger culture and, more specifically, their struggles in that culture, and how these encounters in turn shape their *strategies* for addressing societal ills. Inevitably, as I will suggest, those discussions lead back to the formal and informal ways the black body is defined and, for the purposes of my argument, "written" upon in American culture. My intent is to understand the *markings* of the body, their literal and metaphysical meanings. I have made a conscious effort to particularize my literary investigations. By this I mean my deployment of certain theoretical and critical paradigms is juxtaposed with historical and social moments that present an opportunity for the consideration of what Sandra Gunning calls *national memory-making*. As Gunning explains, historical and cultural memory functions as a site of "endless exchange, intervention and reinvention, where what passes as national or communal or individual 'truth' becomes a dense composite of social and political desires in constant power play."[6] To this end, I have chosen to analyze literary materials that use the body and its inscriptions as an active metaphor for the reinvention of African American subjectivity within certain cultural moments. My contention is that all black bodies in America are marked or scarred in some way. However the manner in which these marks are critically viewed and interpreted allows for a reading that takes into consideration the dual functionality of scars as simultaneously signs of wounding and signs of healing. My choices reflect those works that were pivotal in determining my understanding of the scar, both as an actual bodily wound and as a rhetorical narrative device. This allows me to fully explore how scars become inscribed with contradictory and multiplicitous meanings. My purpose here is not to develop an exhaustive survey of literature on the subject, or to enumerate which authors have presented a more realistic portrayal of African American suffering in this country. Rather, I hope to examine the discursive ways in which African American writers recoup the African American body through a literary evocation of its physical trauma, thus reclaiming the essence of a selfhood fragmented under the weight of the dominant culture's gaze.

5. *The Word in Black and White: Reading "Race" in American Literature, 1638–1867*, ix.
6. *Race, Rape, and Lynching: The Red Record of American Literature, 1890–1912*, 138.

Scarring the Black Body owes its genesis to the proliferation of scholarship on the African American body. Critics such as Toni Morrison, Homi Bhabha, bell hooks, and Lauren Berlant have shaped in one way or another my theoretical and philosophical understanding of the conventionality of the national subject. Their keen analyses enabled me to develop my own ideas about the African American body politic and its place in African American literature and criticism, particularly as it relates to the critical and imaginative ways in which the disfigured body functions in our fields of interpretation both individually and culturally. I develop a critical paradigm centered around "body woundedness," a state of being that carries with it a complex doubleness that allows me to use the body's substance to investigate the richly textured field of scars and wounds. As Dennis Patrick Slattery aptly determines, scars and wounds are coterminous entities. Thus, "when the wound becomes a scar, there is always present the 'afterthought' of the original violation." In examining the substantive history of African American letters, this need to return to the site of the "original violation" redirects critical attention to the wounded body and the ways it is used as metaphor within the African American literary imagination. My critical response to the historical and brutal reduction of African Americans to "mere flesh" is to insist on the body and on embodiment. While others may exclusively focus on the soul or the spirit or intelligence or humanness to undo this wounding ideology, I perform a counteranalysis of the multiple ways bodies can speak historically and in literature. An investigation of the one (bodies) does not necessarily negate the presence or discussion of the other (wounds or scars). As Slattery concludes, "we might say that the scar is the wound that has matured and taken on its own shape on the body; from there it signals a greater level of psyche wholeness."[7]

African American literature has responded to this threat to the body in ways that reveal its psychological toll on this community's racial memory. To this end, writer W. E. B. Du Bois has influenced the way in which I read the African American subject—as a split self "unreconciled," a cultural manifestation of "two warring ideals in one dark body."[8] My book seeks to understand this split self, *disembodied* and *reembodied* in the African American literary imagination. Thus I focus on the ritualistic manner in which authors "reconcile" their views on

7. *The Wounded Body: Remembering the Markings of Flesh*, 54.
8. *The Souls of Black Folk*, 3.

double consciousness in the images they create in their narratives. In many instances, these conciliations become a catalyst for healing the body's wounds, as verbalizing the body's pain enables them to predetermine the margins from which they speak, thereby facilitating a communal healing in the borderland of the scar. Although writer Gloria Anzaldúa defines the borderlands as any physical space or territory where two or more racial, cultural, or economic groups edge each other, in my study the borderland consists of the intimate space that exists between the figurative and literal uses of the scar in the literature of African American writers. I argue that in this site, where the psychological and physical meet, there is an effort on the part of these writers to holistically reassemble a three-dimensional being that sees the marks on the body not as a delimiting factor but as a source of unlimited possibility.

My critical formations regarding the tropological uses of the scar owe much to those cogent conversations initiated by cultural theorists such as Hortense Spillers, Saidiya Hartman, and Mae G. Henderson. My analysis continues their discussions, positing alternative ways to view the psychosociological and literary contexts for what Hortense Spillers terms "high crimes against the flesh." These offenses, committed under the pretense of "severing the captive body from its motive will," utilize the "flesh" as primary narrative (that is, the wounds are signifiers of language registered on the surface of the body in the form of lacerations, tears, fissures) in order to reduce the captured individual to a thing. It is in this severing, as Spillers contends, that the "body" and "flesh" are made distinct. I am less concerned here, however, with the disjunctures Spillers initiates pertaining to the "body" and "flesh" than with what this tension illustrates about African American subjectivity. Slavery's gradual degeneration of the body, and its effacement in the political and legal arenas, had African American writers restoring African Americans' humanity through a constant restructuring of the written and social symbolic orders. My focus is primarily on these activities as I hope to add another apparatus through which we may read "the hieroglyphics of the flesh."[9]

In Part I, "The Call," I begin with a historical and literary overview of the cultural conditions under which the African American body and its scars were framed as text. Certainly any consideration of the naming

9. Hortense J. Spillers, "Mama's Baby, Papa's Maybe: An American Grammar Book," 67.

and framing of this body and the writing of its social meanings must begin at the origins of interaction, or at least at the nexus where American social subjectivities were formed. For me, this origin rests in the cradle of slavery. Slavery's own ambiguous inauguration proves fertile ground for discussions of bodily texts as these became the template upon which America would *narrate* its own moral, racial, and economic histories. As scholar A. Leon Higginbotham Jr. has stated elsewhere, the first Africans to land on American soil under bondage came as indentured servants in 1619. Within a year, the social and legal parameters of that servitude were unexplainably changed. It is this slippage from indentured servitude to slavery that I speak of as auspicious and "ambiguous." Thus one could argue that America's inaugural period of developing racial and gendered subjectivities is abstractly conceived in the intimate confines of the borderlands and inextricably tied to the precepts of "black" and "white" cultural markers embodied in the flesh of its citizenry. In analyzing how the bodies of African and African American slaves were violently expropriated for the purpose of facilitating this national agenda within the body politic, it is important to articulate the double relation between bodies and their representations. In marking the black body, these systems simultaneously acknowledge the significance of an American political identity fashioned around the corporeal oppression of subjugated people. This volatile exchange within the national public sphere over "real" and "imagined" bodies is what gives American social discourse its ever-changing currency. Yet it is the semiotic relationship between the "natural body" and the "abstract political/social body" that emphasizes the *instability* of embodied national identities. As Karen Sanchez-Eppler concludes, "what we take to be a 'natural body' proves instead [to be] a socially constructed 'political anatomy.'"[10] While I do not deny this claim, I feel it is important to remember that what is at stake for most African American writers and critics *is* the reclaiming of the "natural body" for the purpose of the development of specific epistemological frameworks that reshape our understanding of American cultural identities as these are directly tied to the ways in which we read the inscriptions of our own bodily texts.

Thus, in Chapter One, "Imag(in)ing the Body Wounded," I sketch (with broad strokes) the process by which African bodies were "Americanized" through the practice of scarification. My analysis incorporates various materials, from legal cases to slave advertisements, in an effort

10. *Touching Liberty*, 7.

to understand the cultural practice of "writing" the body in nationally printed materials. My interest in reading these documents is twofold: in interpreting these materials, I hope to elucidate the practices of everyday life—especially those acts of bodily inscription that sought to inscribe black bodies with particular meanings in the nineteenth century—and to examine the dynamic by which the body (and its scars) develops rhetorical meanings within the ideological mappings of America's complicated history.

In Chapter Two, "Whip-scarred and Branded," I trace—through those acts of resistance, modes of self-fashioning, and figurations of freedom—the formations of the black subject as seen in the narratives and personal histories of Frederick Douglass, Olaudah Equiano, Harriet Tubman, and Sojourner Truth. These examinations reveal the process by which these writers and social activists develop a "call" centered on the body and its scars. This "call" demanded that people of African descent be given equal rights and protection under the law. Their efforts spurred many individuals into action as black and white abolitionists and civic leaders used slave narratives as the basis for arguing for the elimination of slavery altogether. I also contend that these narratives provide a useful countertext to the glaring absence of African American voices in America's written social histories. As Henry Louis Gates Jr. reiterates, "If the individual black self could not exist before the law, it could, and would, be forged in language, as a testimony at once to the supposed integrity of the black self and against the social and political evils that delimited individual and group equality for all African Americans."[11] Slave narratives became a testament of the will *to be*, and the sentiments expressed by these writers would reverberate for generations to come as others would heed the "call" to speak into existence the black self.

The process of call and response is an integral part of communication in the African American community. Its roots go back to Africa, and its influence was retained in the way slaves communicated with each other as they worked in the plantation fields. What I find fascinating about this form of dialogue—the "conversation" that exists between the "caller" and the "respondent"—is the individuality of the response. There is no one particular response to a call; it varies and is based primarily on individual experience and one's willingness to acknowledge

11. *Bearing Witness: Selections from African American Autobiography in the Twentieth Century*, 4.

"the call." In considering the literate invocations of the "call and response" system within the African American literary tradition, critics and creative artists alike have engaged in a complex cultural interchange that reveals the continuous intersections of the "lived" and the "recorded" African American experience. My use of the "call and response" aesthetic reinforces this dynamic as I feature African American writers who engage in cultural discussions with their contemporaries or with predecessors of a different era, sounding the responsive but repetitive chords of a people's ongoing struggle for freedom and social equality. I demonstrate here that writers such as Frederick Douglass and Harriet Jacobs focus on the scarred black body intentionally, seeking not only to call attention to the social abuses of African American people in chattel bondage but also to rescue the African American body from its inanimate position as "thing" and "property" and give it a three-dimensional character.

Yet, in many respects, these writers were limited in their efforts to fully depict the physical and psychological suffering of African American people. The constraints placed on the written testimonies of runaway slaves have been well documented by scholars such as Frances Smith Foster, P. Gabrielle Foreman, and William L. Andrews. I will not repeat those findings here. What I will point out is that contemporary representations of the conditions of slavery by authors such as Sherley Anne Williams and Toni Morrison seek to signify on those silences imposed by publishers and editors of the eighteenth and nineteenth centuries. In particular, Williams and Morrison extend the efforts of their predecessors by developing creative responses to those calls centered on the wounds of the African American body.

An analysis of these efforts forms the basis of the second part of this study, "The Response." In Chapter Three, "Bodies of Texts," I explore Sherley Anne Williams's reinvention of the whip-scarred body in her 1986 novel *Dessa Rose*. Williams offers a provocative way to view the written histories of the slave body, both as a written-upon text and as a written-about text. Her novel frames a struggle of wills between Nehemiah, a white male author who seeks to write a book on "the roots of rebellion in the slave population," and Dessa, a runaway slave whose discursive contest with Nehemiah rests on her ability to keep hidden the story "writ about her privates."[12] This novel focuses on the obvious tensions inherent in claiming ownership of one's body and inner

12. *Dessa Rose*, 14.

essence in a system bent on destroying them through word and deed. In inserting Dessa's voice into her fictionalized representation of slavery, Williams provides another vision of the bonded female slave, not as a meek participant in the system of slavery, but as a willing catalyst in her own efforts to secure her freedom.

In Chapter Four, "Dis-Membered to Re-Member," I explore the tropological uses of the scar in Toni Morrison's *Beloved*. Morrison's novel is uncanny in its ability to place the psychological wounds of slavery next to those physical scars each of her characters bears. Set in the period of Reconstruction, this novel poignantly considers the formation of an African American identity in the aftermath of slavery. The presence of the ghost Beloved, which I argue is the fleshly manifestation of the wounded slave psyche, ensures that this process will not be an easy one as each character learns to view his or her scars differently through individual soul-searching and ritualistic healing. One comes away from Morrison's novel feeling that the scars of African American people run deep but, at the same time, that these wounds can be healed through a communal acknowledgment of their presence and a national recognition of their viability.

Morrison's consideration of the literal and metaphysical presence of unhealed wounds in the African American community provides an effective transition into my critical investigations in Chapter Five. Here, Hortense Spillers's "Mama's Baby, Papa's Maybe" proves useful in establishing a link between those scarred physically by the system of slavery and those scars systematically inflicted upon the African American psyche through the social landscape of the body. It is through this landscape that we are "marked," according to Gloria Anzaldúa, "written all over . . . carved and tattooed with the sharp needles of experience."[13]

For African Americans, this experience has historical significance as the *phenomenon* of marking and branding "actually 'transfers' from one generation to another," according to Spillers, "finding its various symbolic substitutions in the efficacy of meanings that repeat the initiating moments."[14] The "initiating moments" might well be found in the "Middle Passage," but its systematic transcription lies in the symbolic rearticulations of the black body found in the American body politic, and it is this volatile combination of ideas and energies that affects the

---

13. *Making Face, Making Soul, Haciendo Caras: Creative and Critical Perspectives by Women of Color*, xv.
14. "Mama's Baby," 67.

marking of the urban body and the role it plays in altering the personal experiences of city dwellers. Thus, in Chapter Five, "'Walking Wounded,'" I explore Ann Petry's references to the cultural marking of the female body in her 1946 novel *The Street*. Petry's analysis moves the critical optic away from the traditional practice of slavery and instead considers the reconfigurations of this scheme—commonly known as neo-slavery—within the multiple systems of oppression that continually stigmatize the black woman within her urban environment. While the term *neo-slavery*, by its very nature, connects the historical trajectory of my discussion to the previous analyses in the book, it affords me the opportunity to demonstrate how the urban environment and its contemporary concerns incorporate some of the same oppressive conditions as existed in the chattel system of the previous centuries.

Petry's novel moves the discussion of the disfigurement of black bodies to a rhetorical level, showing that unmarked bodies can be marked in interesting ways, sometimes more insidious than those marks visibly present on the flesh. As in each of the previous discussions, the female body has proved fertile ground for cultural and theoretical considerations of the scarred black body, perhaps because of the black woman's precarious position as a raced and gendered subject, or perhaps because the black woman gives birth to culture, both literally and figuratively. As Laura Doyle reminds us in *Bordering on the Body*, "the racialized mother figure harbors a knowledge and a history rooted in the senses of a racially and sexually specific body." Thus, "twentieth-century narrative tells its way around, through, and past her in its determination to reconfigure the phenomenal self." In order to get to this phenomenal self, a self that is constructed, in this study, through the generational "begetting" of cultural wounds, one must return to the figure of the black mother, both as a way to understand "group history and bodily grounded identity" and as a way to understand the "cultural vehicle for fixing, ranking, and subduing groups and bodies."[15]

Both Williams and Morrison consider these propositions in their narratives, Morrison going so far as to *embody* the cultural figurations of the histories of African American people in the form of a female ghost who "gives birth" to the wounds of her people. In Petry's narrative, the black mother functions as the poetic embodiment of urban identity. Petry's portrayal stands in stark contrast to Richard Wright's *Native Son*, a novel whose central character abhors the figure of the black mother and

15. *Bordering on the Body: The Racial Matrix of Modern Fiction and Culture*, 4.

subsequently self-destructs under the weight of economic and environmental racism. While critics have been quick to applaud Wright's adept portrayal of the challenges of urban living, particularly for African American men, few, if any, have examined the ways in which Petry's novel responds to and reinvents Wright's naturalistic rendering of the mutilated black body. Petry herself is quoted as saying her characters are the "walking wounded," marked, I would argue, by the prejudices of race, class, and gender, and bruised by the various social practices that relegate them to poverty, obscurity, and even death. I explore the crevices of these simultaneously open and closed wounds, sketching a journey that delineates not only how one identifies those "unseen" offenses committed against the body but also how one envisions the self as a complete being, irrespective of the marks on the flesh.

Petry's exploration of the embodied experiences of African American women in *The Street* points up the cultural realities and spatial dynamics of body woundedness in the urban setting. As Dennis Slattery reminds us in his study, the gestural body, in its woundedness, is an essential metaphor in establishing a critical system of the corporeal inscription of the body. While many of Petry's characters display maladies that disfigure them beyond the surface of the flesh, their "disabilities," be they economic, social, physical, or emotional, nonetheless lay bare the social isms that belie their oppression. Thus, it is through the landscape of the body, and more specifically its bodily imperfections, that we view the changing topography of African Americans' quest for selfhood—and view the disfiguring manifestations of America's racist principles. As Cornel West reiterates in *Race Matters*, the ideological current of white supremacist thought forms its discourse around the subjugation of black bodies. Nearly two hundred years of slavery and a century of racial and sexual terrorism insidiously institutionalized in segregation, lynching, and second-class citizenship have been instrumental in carrying out these horrid intentions. Such endeavors, according to West, have taken their toll on African Americans, and their manifestations can be found literally and physically "in the psychic scars and personal wounds now inscribed in the souls of black folk."[16]

West's observations prove useful in the considerations of the embodied experiences of African American men in Chapter Six. In "Fingering the Fissures of the Black Male Psyche," I examine the ritualized forms of bodily marking and disfigurement that serve as an ever-present

16. *Race Matters*, 123.

threat to black men. Historically, this threat has centered on the act of lynching, which has played a significant role in the psychosexual drama of masculinity in this country. Within the context of racist ideology, however, lynching subtends, as Robyn Wiegman has argued, the circuit of relations that marks out "a topos of bodies and identities . . . , defines and circumscribes social and political behavior, and punishes transgression from its wildest possibility to its most benign threat."[17] African American male writers have responded to these threats in a multitude of ways at various moments in our social history. I consider these responses in this chapter and demonstrate that the rhetorical legacy of writers such as Ellison and Wright speaks to these concerns vis-à-vis the inscribed black male body/psyche. Their examinations inevitably influence the creative processes of writers such as John Edgar Wideman and Michael S. Harper, who answer "the call" of their literary predecessors.

Through this discussion I hope to demonstrate that the creative acts of these authors bind that which has been wounded literally and figuratively as they invite those who hear the voices of the ancestors to connect to that part of themselves where the shadow of the past's wounds carries with it a self-knowledge that can alter the experiences of the present. The doubleness of these acts foregrounds the overall argument posited in this study: that the disfigured body as cultural metaphor and social invention is struggling to come to terms with its humanity and its embodiedness.

17. "The Anatomy of Lynching," 445.

The Call

One

Imag(in)ing the Body Wounded

Bodily Inscriptions and Initiation Rites
in America's Social Discourse

> Narrative, as a process of representation, provides a
> powerful tool for conceptualization.
>
> —Dana Nelson, *The Word in Black and White*

> The Libian dusky in his parched skin,
> The Moor all tawny both without and in,
> The Southern man, a black deformed Elfe,
> The Northern white like unto God Himselfe
>
> —Thomas Peyton (1620)

It is difficult to be sure of how or when, but there is no question that the superficial and metaphoric differences between various groups of human beings adversely affected the ideological figurations of "race" in the Americas. As Dana Nelson notes, "'race' has never been a fixed concept," but an evolving idea intimately connected to the cultural, moral, metaphysical, and biological landscape of America's history. The instability of the concept, as Nelson sees it, "reminds us that before notions of different races could become 'common sense,' the idea of 'race' had to be invented, described, promulgated, and legislated by those who would benefit as a group from the concept." Nelson's observations prove useful in that they direct attention to the arrant manner in which America's developing legal and political systems were based on the imaginative tropes of racial difference—particularly for people of African descent. According to law historian A. Leon Higginbotham Jr., Africans provided the perfect image against which the Europeans could favorably contrast themselves. "From the time the Africans first disembarked in Virginia," Higginbotham contends, "the colonists seized upon two obvious characteristics as the basis for distinguishing whites from blacks: physiological attributes and culure [*sic*]. African Americans were 'different,' because physiologically they were different: the color of their skin was different, the texture of their hair was different, and the shape of their facial features was different."[1]

Ronald Takaki similarly argues that, as early as 1611, Africans were not only viewed as savages but were summarily considered "deformed" due to the blackness of their skin. This initial "naming" of African bodies not only laid the groundwork for racializing the developing labor force in the new colonies; it also helped to precipitate the gradual shift from indentured servitude to slavery for individuals of African descent and to recontextualize the notions of class within these same parameters. As Ira Berlin contends, "the transition from societies with slaves to slave societies" distinguished the early Republic's labor concerns. In short, slavery allowed the creation of a planter class that was able "to command the region's resources, mobilize the power of [each] state, and vanquish" its more threatening competitors. The struggle over labor, therefore, created economic expectations that spurred commercial wars, which then created individual societies that separated black and white servants based on the premise of "*de facto* slavery—chattel bondage in practice," as Takaki contends, "if not in law."[2]

This polarization of black and white bodies would serve a crucial function in the burgeoning colonies as evolving social attitudes about inferior and superior characteristics of African and European people framed the context for racial interactions among various ethnic groups in the coming decades. These beliefs would similarly manifest themselves during the inception and subsequent institutionalization of chattel bondage in various regions and cultural spaces as public policies and social mandates sanctioned the vile behavior of white slaveholders and their mistresses toward their slaves. "Perhaps no more damning example of . . . the utter contempt in which whites held black life can be of-

1. Nelson, *Word in Black and White*, viii–ix; Higginbotham, *Shades of Freedom: Racial Politics and Presumptions of the American Legal Process*, 33.

2. Takaki, *A Different Mirror: A History of Multicultural America*, 52, 57; Berlin, *Many Thousands Gone: The First Two Centuries of Slavery in North America*, 11.

fered," claims Higginbotham, "than that of a statute first enacted in 1669 . . . in the slave codes of Virginia." This statute, in short, stipulated that it was not a crime for a master to kill a "recalcitrant black slave" because the slave was the master's property, and a master could not (and in all probability would not) form the requisite malice to destroy his own property. The 1705 draft of this same document "neatly disposed of any potential legal problems surrounding the killing, by stating that if a master killed his slave, the 'accident' would be treated as if it 'had never happened.'"[3] Statutes such as these introduced the notion of a racially distinct citizenry into the American legal system. Likewise, I would suggest that these laws concretized, in glaring fashion, the split between the body and the soul (that is, the mind and the inner essence, the spirit) of the bonded American slave. The inner lives of these individuals—their spiritual, mental, and psychological well-being—suffered immensely under this pretense of the law as slaves, even while not recognized as human beings, were summarily convicted as murderers.

No more striking an example of the paradox of the judiciary system presents itself than in the case of *State of Missouri v. Celia*. Celia was an African American slave girl who, in 1850, was purchased by Robert Newsom, a prosperous Missouri farmer. Celia was fourteen years of age when she came to live with the Newsoms, and Robert Newsom between sixty and seventy. For the next five years, Celia was cruelly and repeatedly coerced into sexual relations with Newsom, "even on the way home after he had purchased her." In June 1855, Celia, sick and pregnant for the third time, told Newsom that she would hurt him if he did not stop sexually abusing her. Unmoved by her threat, Newsom came to Celia's cabin that night to perform his "customary duty."

What happened next is unclear. We do know from trial testimony that the two exchanged words. During this confrontation, Newsom demanded sex from Celia, and Celia refused him. As Newsom approached Celia, she "retreated into a corner of the house" and retrieved a stick she had placed there for the sole purpose of protecting herself against Newsom's advances. As he reached for her, Celia struck him once. Newsom fell to the ground, dazed from the blow. Afraid that he would harm her should he recover from his injury, Celia struck him again. He appears to have died immediately. Unsure of what to do with the body, Celia burned Newsom's remains in her fireplace. The next morning, she spread the ashes on the pathway.

3. Higginbotham, *Shades of Freedom*, 30.

Celia's defense attorneys mounted an admirable counterattack to the charge of murder in the first degree. They argued that "the rape of a slave woman was not a property right of the master, that the master's economic privileges did not include the right of sexual molestation of his slave, and that the right to force her to work in the fields did not include the right to sleep in her bed and violate her at his whim." In claiming self-defense, her counsel had hoped to give Celia the same rights as white women had under Missouri state laws. These efforts were, however, to no avail. The trial judge rejected her lawyer's request and instructed the jury as follows:

> If Newsom was in the *habit of having intercourse* with the defendant who was his slave and went to her cabin on the night he was killed to have intercourse with her *or for any other purpose* and while he was standing in [sic] the floor talking to her she struck him with a stick which was a dangerous weapon and knocked him down, and struck him again after he fell, and killed him by either blow, it is murder in the first degree.

Celia's fate was sealed with these instructions to the jury. She was found guilty and sentenced to hang. Her counsel appealed all the way to the Missouri Supreme Court, but the trial judge's decision was upheld. And on December 21, at 2:30 P.M., Celia fell to her death at the tender age of nineteen.[4]

Celia's case reveals, in vivid fashion, the legal and political perils of African American life during the antebellum period. It similarly illustrates the law's treatment of African American women during slavery. While Celia's case is by no means isolated, it exemplifies the perpetual distortion of African Americans' inalienable rights. Celia's case is one in a long line of historical "incidents" that served to legitimize, through practice and intent, the ideological concerns of America's political and social elite. Through the creation of fictionalized bogeymen (the rapist, the murderer, the thief) and the perpetuation of a de facto citizenship that denied women like Celia the right to protect their persons, the elite reinforced the social dictums that named African Americans as inferior. These biases were affirmed in scientific and theological "investigations" of that era and justified in the political and legal writings of the same period. The Great Chain of Being Theory represents but one of

---

4. Melton A. McLaurin, *Celia, a Slave*, 35–37; A. Leon Higginbotham Jr., *In the Matter of Color: Race and the American Legal Process: The Colonial Period*, 100.

the many ways people of African descent were marked. Charles Darwin's theory of the "survival of the fittest," as well as Cotton Mather's assertions that Africans were the offspring of Satan, created a scientific and theological landscape of hatred unmatched anywhere in the world. As early as 1638, some critics argue, epistemological shifts from "actual" differences to "superficial" and "metaphorical" differences can be found in the textual and artistic representations of colonial writers, painters, scientists, and politicians.

With this said, I want to stress that these *imagined* anxieties concerning the corporeality of American personhood resulted in the *physical* marking of bonded Africans and their progeny by way of branding (a sign of ownership and possession) and whip-scarring (a sign of punishment). These signs became the *signatures* of slavery and crystallized, in vivid fashion, those assumptions maintained in the social systems of that age that held black life in such low regard. This violence framed the context for understanding African American subjectivity during slavery. According to Saidiya V. Hartman, "the slave was only considered a subject insofar as he was criminal(ized), wounded body, or mortified flesh."[5] If Hartman's assertions are valid (and I believe they are), then the *reading* of these wounds not only allows for a critical examination of the social systems that transfigure these signs upon the surface of the body; it also creates an occasion for the simultaneous reading of the figurative use of the scar in African and African American literature.

Among the most readily available and curiously underused documents that enable a textual reading of bodily scars of African and African American slaves are postings for fugitive slaves. While it is true that oral and written black slave testaments offer a perspective on spiritual and physical scarification that is both intimate and personal, slave advertisements underscore the intricate and complex ways in which slavemasters sought to indemnify the flesh. This effort was not only instrumental in maintaining the dominance of the slaveowning class; it was crucial in regulating the *material* interests of slaveowners as well. It should come as no surprise that slavemasters who sought to reclaim their "property" would list any distinguishing marks or characteristics that would make capture easier. But these "designations" also served another purpose: they developed categories for the recognition of black

5. *Scenes of Subjection: Terror, Slavery, and Self-Making in Nineteenth-Century America,* 94.

personages vis-à-vis the imperfect markings of the flesh. In the reward posting for fugitive Harriet Jacobs, for example, there is mention of a "decayed spot on [her] front tooth."[6] This seemingly benign characterization goes a long way in distinguishing Jacobs's mulatto body from the Caucasian population into which she could so easily assimilate. As her master, Dr. Flint, makes clear in the posting, Harriet is an intelligent and well-spoken individual who can read and write, and her physical appearance—her hair and her bodily features—do not clearly reveal her ethnic heritage. Still, Jacobs's decayed tooth makes her "different." It not only makes her status as a fugitive slave more visible, it makes her ethnic designation more visible as well, for placing these distinctions within the context of a fugitive slave posting makes the black body's minimal imperfections hypervisible, and therefore hyperethnicized (and in some cases hypercriminalized) within the social and political discourse of slavery.

The fugitive slave advertisement for Jacobs offers a more paradigmatic and seemingly complicated version of the marking of the black body. Other postings document more visible scars of bondage. These listings testify to the injurious and often abusive treatment of African slaves. Ralph, a runaway from Maryland, is listed as five feet six inches high, "flat nose[d] and very thick lip'd, and wide mouth'd. He has been scalded on the Back of his left hand, and up his arm, by which the scar thereof appears. . . . He has also a great many Dents in the Top of his Head, which seem to be the Ward-end of a key."[7] This posting presents an extreme example of the boldness with which some slavemasters sought to reclaim those they had abused, even going so far as to document those abuses in print. Other slavemasters were subtler. Their postings list anything from "a scar on the forehead from the kick of a horse" to mention of certain individuals being "a little lame in one ancle [sic]" or crippled. These representations, when read symptomatically, draw attention to the central practice of pathologizing the black body and accentuate the abject status of slaves as commodified flesh.

In *Blacks Who Stole Themselves*, editors Billy G. Smith and Richard Wojtowicz speak directly to the cultural significance of fugitive slave postings in their analysis of approximately three hundred advertise-

6. See the back cover of Linda Brent's *Incidents in the Life of a Slave Girl*, ed. Walter Teller.

7. Graham Russell Hodges and Alan Edward Brown, eds., *"Pretends to Be Free": Runaway Slave Advertisements from Colonial and Revolutionary New York and New Jersey*, 77, #172.

ments for runaway slaves in the Mid-Atlantic region that appeared in Ben Franklin's newspaper, the *Pennsylvania Gazette*, between 1728 and 1790. As a germane source, these documents "contain considerable information about a group of people who left behind few other personal records." Given the nature of slavery, and the lack of legal documentation afforded some enslaved African Americans (such as birth, death, and/or marriage certificates), these "portraits," on the whole, "offer extensive vignettes of individual runaways, sketching their fortunes, revealing their perceived idiosyncrasies, and suggesting the complexity of their relationships with other slaves, white servants, and their owners." Of particular interest to my study are the conclusions that Smith and Wojtowicz draw from their systematic analyses of these texts: "the physical aspects of runaways—including their age, sex, height, color, scars, and bodily markings—as well as the type of clothing they wore are exquisitely detailed. . . . The runaway's name, primary language, ritualistic African markings, religion, literacy, and connections to friends and family offer clues to the culture and values of many slaves."[8]

Although Smith and Wojtowicz admit that as historical records these advertisements are biased and limited in their perceptions of the past, these materials are nonetheless useful in highlighting the ways the body was used to both absorb and textualize the racial imaginings of that era. Consider for example the following advertisement that appeared in a Maryland newspaper for the capture of the fugitive slave Isaac:

$50 Reward
Ranaway from the subscriber living near Upper Marlboro, Prince George's county, Maryland, on Thursday, the 23 inst., Negro man,
ISAAC,
he is of black complexion, five feet eight inches high, stamers very much when spoken to, no marks recollected, except his heals sets in very much, he is no doubt lurking about the neighborhood.
  I will give the above reward for his apprehension no matter when taken, provided he is brought home to me or secured in jail so that I get him again.
  August 24, 1860   WM. P. Pumphrey

The codifications of the slave body in this instance are obvious. The references to Isaac's "black complexion," along with the cryptic suggestion

8. Billy G. Smith and Richard Wojtowicz, eds., *Blacks Who Stole Themselves: Advertisements for Runaways in* The Pennsylvania Gazette, *1728–1790*, 2.

that he may be "lurking about the neighborhood," indicate that Pumphrey not only sought to feed into the national paranoia about black men stalking "their prey"; he likewise sought to *authorize* (through socially sanctioned edicts) the *re*enslavement of Isaac by criminalizing his fugitive status through such a depiction. After all, how could one *truly* justify the reenslavement of an individual who desired to escape a system that denied him basic human rights? How could one also assure the economic viability of a system built on tenuous suppositions of difference if it didn't criminalize—socially malign—its workforce?

Pumphrey's behavior is by no means isolated. His advertisement mimics those of other slaveowners who hoped to recover what they considered "valuable property" through the use of public documents. These primers similarly convey that within the system of chattel bondage, appearance and personality were subjectively construed, and a perusal of these notices likewise reveals that no single quality or group of characteristics captures the anxieties slavemasters experienced regarding their fugitive slaves. However, analyzing the contents of these materials can establish other patterns of bodily framing. For example, in the subject index of the advertisements included in Smith and Wojtowicz's volume, "African markings," "branded," "whip-scarred," and "smallpox-pitted" are just a few of the terms used to categorize the distinguishing marks present on the bodies of fugitive slaves. Taken as a whole, this terminology may seem nominal. But when scrutinized more closely, the phrases can imply the *manner* in which these wounds were inflicted *on* the body and the *purpose* for inflicting such trauma *to* the body. There is a big difference between a "branded" mark (a mark slaveowners placed on their slaves to show possession of them, as one would do with cattle or other property) and a "whip-scarred" mark (a form of punishment, a wound inflicted on the person of a slave as a reaction to an act of defiance committed by the slave on his or her own behalf, usually in response to a slave's attempt to run away or to challenge the slavemaster). In the advertisements themselves, slaveowners often reference these marks differently. An illustration of these distinctions can be seen in the following postings:

April 4, 1745
Maberrin, in Bertie County, North-Carolina, March 13, 1745.
RUN away from the Subscriber, in *Bertie* County, *North-Carolina*, a likely Negroe Slave, named *Tony*, *Virginia* born, about Thirty Years of Age, middle sized, well set, short Neck, and somewhat

round Shoulder'd, yellow Complexion, and scarr'd on his Shoulders by Correction. He pretends to making and burning Bricks, and is a good Sawyer. He ran away the 18th of *June*, 1743, and has been heard of in *Pennsylvania* Government. Whoever takes him up, and brings him to the Subscriber, in *North-Carolina*, shall be Paid Ten Pistoles, or if delivered to Mr. *Hugh Parker*, in *Philadelphia*, shall receive Five Pistoles. *Benjamin Hill*.

June 27, 1734
RUN away on Thursday last from the House of John Richardson, Shoemaker, a new Negroe Girl about 16 or 18 Years of Age, short Stature, branded upon the Breast N R mark'd around the Neck with three Rows like Beads, suppos'd to be a Whedaw Negroe; had on a check'd Cotten Petticoat and a Seersucker Jacket. Her Name is Rose.

    Whosoever takes up the said Negroe, and brings her to John Richardson aforesaid, or B. Franklin Printer, shall have Twenty Shillings Reward and reasonable Charges paid by John Richardson.[9]

These advertisements unmask the teleological uses of "scarring" and "marking" within the system of slavery. In some instances, these symbolic indicators framed a context for national and international "discussions" of the ownership of the black body as America's "language" of slavery often competed for space on the same body that held African tribal markings. These discursive battles emphasize the significance of embodied (inter)national identities as bodily disfigurement within the system of slavery became a way for some slavemasters to "reclassify" African tribal marks as "hideous," "primitive," "ugly." Similarly, I would suggest that terms such as "small-pox pitted" (found in the posting of a runaway named Ned, for example) belie a whole host of national idiosyncrasies inferred from the use of a medical term that describes "an acute, highly contagious virus disease."[10] By quarantining "ethnic undesirables" to rhetorical spaces where they will not disturb the dream of a racially homogeneous nation, the state assumes the power to act in its own best interest. And although poor medical care and poor living conditions were a staple of slavery (and these marks were visible indicators

    9. Ibid., 18, 23.
    10. Ibid., 28; *Webster's New World Dictionary of the American Language*, 2d College ed. (1980), 1344.

of those conditions), these eruptions on the skin become another tool used to separate "diseased" individuals from the "general" population despite the fact the virus is no longer active.

It is not an understatement that diseases such as smallpox were of grave concern to slaveowners who wanted to protect their interests. Critics such as Michael A. Gomez and James Rawley have argued that this threat of disease was an extension of the hazardous conditions experienced by Africans during the Middle Passage. Notwithstanding the psychological impact of this transatlantic journey, these scholars attribute the high incidence of death to a variety of causes such as poor hygiene, inadequate food and water, medical neglect, and melancholy. According to Rawley, Isaac Wilson, a surgeon aboard the ship *Elizabeth*, estimated that of the 155 slaves who died on board, two-thirds of the deaths resulted from melancholy. "Without doubt," notes Rawley, "disease was a relentless killer of slaves on shipboard." Other illnesses found aboard ship include dysentery, measles, scurvy, ophthalmia (a condition leading to blindness), and yaws. This latter disease, evidenced by dark swellings on the skin, was widespread and in some cases fatal. In other instances, as Gomez reminds us, whole ships were quarantined at North American ports to allow some diseases the opportunity to run their course.[11]

Once the slaves were on shore, health care management became a considerable enterprise. "Duty, interest, and humanity require that you should make yourself acquainted with the diseases that prevail among your slaves," wrote one Mississippi planter. This planter's sentiments were echoed in a number of southern agricultural journals and newspapers devoted to the business of slave management. According to James O. Breeden, slaveholders and their allies expended much intellectual energy in search of the *ideal* in slave care and governance during the four decades preceding the Civil War. These efforts were, no doubt, self-serving, and as Breeden makes clear, "personal gain would be enhanced, and consciences eased . . . if, first, an awareness of the importance of effective slave management was instilled in the minds of the South's slaveholders. . . . [T]hey [slaveholders] repeatedly laid their case before their neighbors and colleagues." This media campaign, when coupled with the racist paternalisms of slavery, reinforced the ideological prac-

11. Rawley, *The Transatlantic Slave Trade: A History*, 291; Gomez, *Exchanging Our Country Marks: The Transformation of African Identities in the Colonial and Antebellum South*, 163.

tice of medical bias among some southerners and fueled the ritualistic debasement of African and African American people among the slave-owning community. Wrote one Georgia physician:

> So notoriously filthy are Negroes that many persons will doubtless smile at the very mention of cleanliness when used in connection with a people closely allied to *hogs* in their nature and habits. But while it is admitted that Negroes may have a natural antipathy to soap and water, and especially to *cold* water, their neglect of personal cleanliness is, at the same time, largely due to the nature of their occupations, to the circumstances by which they are surrounded, and the indifference of masters in this particular.[12]

Admittedly, this physician's reprehensible views can be easily dismissed, but these public depictions of African slaves in runaway advertisements and medical journals speak to the multiple ways the black body is distorted, "rewritten" within the public discourses of the American body politic. These mythic representations institute the illusionary world of race difference to which African and African American writers responded, rendering through their artistic allegories of natal alienation and transculturation a collective social practice of historical and memorial recovery. Likewise these literary endeavors altered the metaphorical attitude of an entire nation, reconstructing the parameters from which to view the embodied narrative of African and African American people.

Tribal Markings

Contrary to the ways slaveowners represented the bodies of Africans in their postings, Africans viewed their tribal markings as an extension of their *native* selves, a fleshly embodiment of tribal customs and histories. In some cases, the process of scarification marked a coming of age, a part of the ceremony in which a young man or woman ascended into the ranks of adulthood. In one of the rare literary pieces written by a former enslaved African, Olaudah Equiano speaks of the ceremonial significance of tribal marking:

12. Breeden, ed., *Advice among Masters: The Ideal in Slave Management in the Old South*, xvii, 157, 163.

> My father was one of those elders or chiefs I have spoken of and
> was styled Embrenché, a term as I remember importing the high-
> est distinction, and signifying in our language a *mark* of grandeur.
> This mark is conferred on the person entitled to it by cutting the
> skin across at the top of the forehead and drawing it down to the
> eyebrows, and while it is in this situation applying a warm hand
> and rubbing it until it shrinks up into a thick *weal* across the low-
> er part of the forehead. Most of the judges and senators were thus
> marked; my father had long borne it. I had seen it conferred on
> one of my brothers, and I was also *destined* to receive it by my par-
> ents.

This ceremonial tradition, passed down through patriarchal lines,
frames the scar as a mark of eminence, "a *mark* of grandeur." Within
the African context, particularly among the Ibo people, this scar indi-
cated the highest distinction among governmental personages, and it
separated royalty from the commoners. In this context we see the scar
differently, as a mark conferred not as a form of punishment but as a
symbol of national pride. As Equiano describes, "The manners and
government of a people who have little commerce with other coun-
tries are generally very simple, and the history of what passes in one family or village may serve as a specimen of a nation."[13] Thus one can infer
from Equiano's comments that the mark itself became a representative
of one's tribal customs, "a specimen of a nation," a signifier of the language of that country—it told who someone was, where he was from,
and to what tribe he belonged. In this respect, the scar functions as a literal history of one's life, a visible symbol of one's national heritage.

Useful to an investigation of the significance of tribal markings in the
slave community are the findings of a provocative ethnographic study
conducted by Capt. Cecil Hamilton Armitage in 1921 entitled *The
Tribal Markings and Marks of Adornment of the Natives of the Northern Territories*. This study cataloged the various cultural meanings attached to
tribal markings found on the bodies of the inhabitants of three provinces
in the northern territories of the Gold Coast Colony. The project grew
out of a need to understand the various patterns of scarification and to
ascertain the differences, if any, among the natives of these communities. As one British official laments, "a complete list of the tribal markings would be of considerable interest, but so far little attention has been
paid to the subject, and photography fails to reproduce the different

13. *Equiano's Travels*, ed. Paul Edwards, 1–2.

lines with accuracy. This is the more to be regretted, because the custom will probably die out as the tribes become civilized."[14]

The results of the survey not only speak to the issues raised in this project but also shed light on the customs of certain tribes within each province. For example, the tribal marks of the Dagomba, a tribe located in the southern province of the Gold Coast, seem to have originated from the Hausa and Grumah. One ethnographer suspects that "after the conquest of Dagomba, the aborigines adopted the tribal markings of their rulers." The four facial markings in general use among the Dagomba seem to vary based on one's location in the region in which one lives. The *Bali, Chista-ta, Chisa-nahi* (chisa = cut; ta = three; nahi = four), *Kallam-Chehilla*, and the *Zangwa Cheha* all wear variations of the marks of Dagomba. One's occupation also has a bearing on the tribal marks one wears. According to Armitage's study, the *Grumah* mark, a tribal mark in use all over Dagomba, consists of three rows of seven vertical cuts in horizontal lines on either temple, one row on either cheek, and one on either side of the mouth. A variation of this arrangement consists of five rows of thirteen vertical cuts on either side of the face. These latter marks are worn by all Grumah blacksmiths. Also, the inhabitants of the southern province each wear three vertical cuts above either breast, and four groups of three around the navel to ward off sickness.

Armitage's study also uncovered gender specificities among certain tribes with respect to bodily markings. Dagomba girls, for example, carry cuts all round the neck that are called "beauty marks." These are the commonest forms of marks found among this group in this province. The Mohammedan Mamprussi or the Tampali, in the North-Eastern province of the Gold Coast, do not wear these marks, or if they do, they are not arranged in the same order as those used by the Dagomba. Also, Armitage's study reveals that certain tribal markings are worn by soldiers, and when individuals are captured, the mark of the conquering tribe is superimposed upon that of the losing tribe, along with certain other scars.[15]

It is difficult, if not impossible, to obtain trustworthy information with regard to the establishment of these practices in North America. Very few records exist that discuss the importance of African tribal markings among slaves in the American chattel system. Even fewer

14. *The Tribal Markings and Marks of Adornment of the Natives of the Northern Territories*, 2.

15. Ibid., chap. 1, p. 1.

records exist that indicate how Africans viewed their ritualistic markings once their bodies became disfigured as a result of branding or whip-scarring. Recently, historians such as Daniel C. Littlefield and Michael Gomez have suggested that tribal markings—or "country marks" as they term them—denoted in the travel logs and letters of slaveowners and buyers of the eighteenth century are key in determining the patterns of slave exportation along the Eastern seaboard. This information provides a context not only for discovering which Africans slaveowners preferred but also for determining which Africans were "presumed" to commit mass suicide, escape in groups, or, as one South Carolinian planter put it, "be fit to work immediately." This interrelationship among land, crops, and people supported a cultural matrix based on misconceptions and half-truths. "Whatever the validity of the early ethnic characterizations," Littlefield concludes, "it is clear that they were taken seriously and acted upon, for slaves from particular geographical regions and of certain specifications sold better in one colony than another."[16]

Given these advances in the study of African practices and their transmission to America, it is now possible to push beyond perfunctory discussions of slave communal life to more clearly assess how Africans interpreted their slave reality, and how they communicated this reality to their descendants. The idea that Africa's cultural influences can be traced to the North American slave population is by no means novel. There is a body of historical and anthropological scholarship available from critics such as Sterling Stuckey, Sidney Mintz, and Richard Price that concerns itself with the acculturative process of African people. These studies are helpful in that they provide models for the investigation of certain processes through which people of African descent attempted to reconstitute their collective identity and were, likewise, reconstituted by that identity. As Gomez aptly points out, for one to understand the manner by which the African American identity was framed "it is essential to recover the African cultural, political, and social background, recognizing that Africans came to the New World with certain coherent perspectives and beliefs about the universe and their place in it."[17]

This same philosophy holds true for investigations of the cultural sig-

16. *Rice and Slaves: Ethnicity and the Slave Trade in Colonial South Carolina*, 10, 19.
17. *Exchanging Our Country Marks*, 4.

nificance of tribal markings in the slave community. As is evident in the advertisements for runaway slaves, ritualistic markings on the cheeks, the forehead, and the belly and arms of certain runaways were classified by some slaveowners according to regional affiliation (port of embarkation), distinct cultural "peculiarities," skills, and languages. This information, as Littlefield reminds us, is highly suspect because slaveowners were imprecise when it came to identifying particular groups—that is, "terms such as *Ibo, Calabar, Bonny,* and *Bite* were sometimes used interchangeably and are therefore vague if not inaccurate: the first designates an ethnic group, the next two refer to political entities, and the fourth refers to a geographical area."[18] The same can be said for the term *Mandingo,* which was based on appearance and not place of origin.

In addition, Africans who were named after the region or port of embarkation might not have originated from the same place. In some cases, they were sold thousands of miles inland and brought to the outer coast of Africa to be loaded aboard slave vessels, and the "agents" aboard those ships were unsure of the individuals' point of origin. The inability (or unwillingness) on the part of some slaveowners to specify tribal origins in slave advertisements is essential to understanding the process by which these diverse groups were indoctrinated into slave life. In general, slavemasters in the nineteenth century paid little attention to African ethnicities, leading this critic to speculate that although the flesh of the slave "spoke" of a cultural and racial existence prior to enslavement vis-à-vis the tribal markings of the body, slaveowners could not distinguish the meanings of these "country marks." The runaway advertisement for Tom, for example, states that he is a "surly ill natured fellow, hath some scars in his face, customary to Guinea Negroes."[19] The obvious reference here is that "Guinea Negroes" are "surly" and "ill natured" (assuming the stereotype had any validity). However, closer examination of such postings reveals a struggle between the social and embodied meanings of the black body and, through inference, a struggle over the cultural meanings of scars such as those found on Tom's face. Because slaveowners could not "translate" tribal markings into what Hortense Spillers terms "American grammar," they violently rewrote the language of the African body—figuratively and literally— by branding and superimposing their own marks onto the bodies of Africans through beatings, mutilations, and other forms of inhumane

18. *Rice and Slaves*, 23.
19. Smith and Wojtowicz, eds., *Blacks Who Stole Themselves*, 30, #29.

treatment. During this process, ethnic and national origins were simultaneously obscured as Africans were renamed *slaves* and "assigned" certain personality traits and behavioral distinctions that reflected a national disregard not only for their humanity but for their culture and individuality as well.

Two

Whip-scarred and Branded

The Ancestors Speak on the Slave Condition

And Shall Afric's sons be silent any longer?

—Maria Stewart, *Religion and the Pure Principles of Morality*

I say let him be placed in this most trying situation . . . then, and not till then, will he fully appreciate the hardships of, and know how to sympathize with, the toil-worn and whip-scarred fugitive slave.

—Frederick Douglass, *Narrative in the Life of Frederick Douglass, an American Slave*

The forced dispersement of Africans from their native land calcifies, for many, the indelible mark of cultural wounding prominent in the African and African American racial memory. The Middle Passage—that heinous voyage from Africa to the Americas in the belly of slave ships— lays bare the intricate mechanisms that facilitate not only the ruptures of a spiritual and cultural wholeness but also the formation of a linguistic system of suffering framed in the borderlands of the scar. As Sterling Stuckey suggests, "During the process of their becoming a single people, Yorubas, Akans, Ibos, Angolans, and others [who] were present on slave ships to America . . . experienced a common horror—unearthly moans and piercing shrieks, the smell of filth and the stench of death, all during the violent rhythms and quiet coursings of the ships at sea."[1]

1. *Slave Culture: Nationalist Theory and the Foundations of Black America*, 3.

Thus the psychological and physical wounding of the black body in transit—in the watery space between the African and American coastlines—added an additional layer to the reading of, and a whole new dimension to the marking and scarring of, the black body in the context of America's chattel bondage system. Unlike Equiano's familial context wherein the scar was bestowed with national and communal pride, in the North American context the scar became a signifier for the rebellious African slave. During the public selling of Africans, potential buyers "checked out" the "merchandise" by looking for bruises or marks that would lower a slave's market value. As is explained in *Many Thousand Gone*, the auction-block process was a humiliating one for the slaves. "Those who bought slaves showed no reticence in examining the merchandise," notes Charles H. Nichols. "They scrutinized their chattels as if the Negroes were horses or cattle. They looked at hands, arms and legs, felt limbs for muscularity, inspected back and buttocks for marks of the whip. The customers did not hesitate to put their fingers into the slaves' mouths, to look at their teeth, to test their sight and hearing. The men and women were stripped, thumped and pinched to determine their soundness." Any scars found on a slave's body during this process would let the potential buyer know the "temperament" of the slave— if the slave was a "problem" slave, one with a rebellious tendency. Amputated limbs, disfigured body parts, welted backs—all were read as manifestations of a rebellious spirit. Moreover, the slave's body served as a billboard in another way, a "visual aid" if you will, within the social structure of slavery, with these same marks serving as reminders to the black slave community of the consequences of rebellious action. Frequently, "whippings" or "beatings" were performed in public for this reason. Henry Bibb, for example, relates an incident in which he was flogged for not asking permission to attend a prayer meeting and for attempting to run away to escape his punishment. His master and overseer summoned the entire slave community as Bibb was forced to lie on the ground with his face to the earth and his hands and feet tied to four stakes driven in the ground. He was lashed fifty times by the overseer as his fellow bondsmen and his master looked on.[2]

Former slaves including Frederick Douglass, Olaudah Equiano, and Mary Prince speak of witnessing the public flogging of family members

---

2. Nichols, *Many Thousand Gone: The Ex-Slaves' Account of Their Bondage and Freedom*, 15; Bibb, *Narrative of the Life and Adventures of Henry Bibb, an American Slave, Written by Himself*, 55.

and friends, and they underscore the impact these incidents had on the development of their personal and social consciousness. "I remember the first time I ever witnessed this horrible exhibition," wrote Douglass.

> I was quite a child, but I well remember it. I never shall forget it whilst I remember any thing. It was the first of a long series of such outrages, of which I was doomed to be a witness and a participant. It struck me with awful force. It was the blood-stained gate, the entrance to the hell of slavery, through which I was about to pass. It was a most terrible spectacle. I wish I could commit to paper the feelings with which I beheld it.[3]

This "terrible spectacle" that introduced Douglass to slavery was the beating of his Aunt Hester. Although just a young child, Douglass was made painfully aware of his station as a slave through this violent act.

In a similar manner, Mary Prince, a West Indian slave, was made aware of her status as a slave in Brackish Pond, Devonshire Parish, Bermuda. Her 1831 narrative is a forerunner to Douglass's text, and with great clarity she records her own brutal account of the public flogging of a slave called old Daniel:

> Mr. D.—had a slave called old Daniel, whom he used to treat in the most cruel manner. Poor Daniel was lame in the hip, and could not keep up with the rest of the slaves; and our master would order him to be stripped and laid down on the ground, and have him beaten with a rod of rough briar till his skin was quite red and raw. He would then call for a bucket of salt, and fling [it] upon the raw flesh till the man writhed on the ground like a worm, and screamed aloud with agony. This poor man's wounds were never healed, and I have often seen them full of maggots, which increased his torments to an intolerable degree. He was an object of pity and terror to the whole gang of slaves, and in his wretched case we saw, each of us, our own lot, if we should live to be as old.

The egregious manner in which this slave was treated underscores the utility of the slave body/flesh as the vehicle by which and through which this slavemaster's power is publicly displayed. Daniel's wretched condition haunts the psyche of those who witness his suffering, and Prince herself is so moved by Daniel's plight that she writes, "Oh the

---

3. *Narrative in the Life of Frederick Douglass, an American Slave*, 5.

horrors of slavery!—How the thought of it pains my heart! But the truth ought to be told of it; and what my eyes have seen I think it is my duty to relate. . . . I have been a slave—I have felt what a slave feels, and I know what a slave knows." Prince's ability to tell the truth comes not only from that which she has witnessed—for these atrocities have certainly left their indelible mark on her psyche—but also from that which she has experienced. As she explains early in her narrative, her mistress, Mrs. Ingham, taught her more than just to wash, bake, and pick cotton and wool:

> [S]he taught me (how can I forget it!) . . . to know the exact dif-
> ference between the smart of the rope, the cart-whip, and the cow-
> skin, when applied to my naked body by her own cruel hand. And
> there was scarcely any punishment more dreadful than the blows I
> received on my face and head from her hard heavy fist. . . . My mis-
> tress was not contented with using the whip, but often pinched
> [my] neck and arms, exactly as they were. To strip me naked—to
> hang me up by the wrists and lay my flesh open with the cow-skin,
> was an ordinary punishment for even a slight offense.[4]

According to Saidiya Hartman, scenes such as these function as "an in-augural moment in the formation of the enslaved." They confirm, in short, "the origin of the subject and [demonstrate] that to be a slave is to be under the brutal power and authority of another." I would also ar-gue that these scenes establish a cultural and literary genealogy that counteracts the commonplace callousness to black suffering, as the recognition of personal pain becomes an acknowledgment of commu-nal pain. As Hartman concludes, necessary and tolerable violence, as a function of slavery, is a "designation of the absoluteness of power" and a form of "captive embodiment."[5]

Thus, for African Americans to reconstitute their humanity, they must return to the site of that violence—their own captive bodies. This primary attention to remembering the marks of the flesh is recognition of their cultural position at once as object and subject and as inanimate and animate being. As Lindon Barrett reiterates, "That African Amer-icans live within a culture where they are forced to deal first and fore-most with the spatiality-materiality of their existences (which finds its hyperbole in attention to their bodies) is recorded in the physical bru-talities described again and again in slave narratives."[6]

4. *The History of Mary Prince, a West Indian Slave, Related by Herself*, 74, 66.
5. *Scenes of Subjection*, 3.
6. "African-American Slave Narratives: Literacy, the Body, Authority," 421.

This merger of storytelling and the corporeal body established an inextricable tie between physical pain and voice that shaped the political and social texture of slavery. As Douglass explains in the passage quoted as an epigraph to this chapter, to understand the perils of chattel bondage, to fully identify with the bonded American slave, one must "be placed in the most trying situation"; one must inhabit, so to speak, the body of the "toil-worn and whip-scarred fugitive slave." This rhetorical move placed the disfigured slave body at the center of the representational practices of both the proslavery and the antislavery movements as such a strategy emphasized the differences between the bonded and the free and created a language for expressing black suffering. As Sanchez-Eppler reminds us, the slaves' ability to speak was predicated upon "the reinterpretation of their flesh," that is, each slave's ability to transform his or her flesh into a rhetorical force for political gain.[7]

Thus the alliance between abolition and political action rested not only on *seeing* the body in pain but also on *being* the body in pain because it is this rhetorical use of pain that marks the slave body and makes it visible. This refashioning of embodied political and personal discourses provided ample evidence of the mind's ability to extend itself beyond the physical limitations and conditions of the body. Moreover, by writing and controlling the versions of self, what James Olney terms "metaphors of self," Douglass and other slave narrators reclaimed the essence of their personhood by making the marks on their flesh visible, thus laying before the nation the material evidence of a people's wounded psyche. In calling into existence the scarred black subject, these writers made the slave's suffering "legible."

Body of Evidence

Although the slave's body bore the inextricable proof of the brutalities of slavery, there were thousands, even hundreds of thousands, of ex-slaves who left oral testimonials of their experiences in slavery. These narratives discuss in detail the horrific conditions and disturbing disfigurements imposed on people of African descent. When coupled with the written recordings of slavery by individuals such as Moses Roper, William Grimes, James Pennington, and Harriet Jacobs, these accounts create a haunting tapestry of the struggle for human equality unmatched at any time in current or previous history.

7. Douglass, *Narrative*, 107; Sanchez-Eppler, "Bodily Bonds: The Intersecting Rhetorics of Feminism and Abolition," 94.

Yet there were skeptics in the North and the South who did not be-lieve the charges leveled against Southern slaveowners. Ex-slaves who escaped to the North for sanctuary prior to the legislative passage of the Fugitive Slave Law of 1793 and the Fugitive Slave Act of 1850 found that they had to produce scars somewhere on their persons in order to validate their experience as survivors of this horrid system. Houston Baker notes in *Workings of the Spirit*, "A standard feature of abolitionist meetings . . . was what one commentator calls the 'Negro exhibit.'" During this portion of the meeting, the fugitive slave silently exposed his naked back to the audience displaying the wounds and scars evident there. This unveiling proved to be a powerful moral suasion in the cause against slavery as Northern sympathizers got to see, firsthand, the in-justices perpetrated upon the bodies of African American people. But this unveiling served a twofold purpose. It also set a framework for for-mulating a recognizable African American voice situated around the body and its scars. As Baker contends, African Americans such as Fred-erick Douglass were well aware of the discursive potential of the black body in the fight against slavery. These individuals were "quick to real-ize that it was not by display, essentialist play, or bodily exhibition for private, indoor use that [one] could flesh out a tale of slavery"; rather it was the use of this body in the symbolic order of things that allowed these individuals to make statements on behalf of their enslaved brethren. "By making themselves brilliantly ironic orators—self-reflexive masters of metaphor," Baker concludes, "Douglass and his fellow travelers were able to change the very definitions of both 'social' and 'public' in Amer-ican life,"[8] and, I would argue, change the very concept of speech in the oral and written traditions of North American culture.

But as is clear in Douglass's narratives, his mastery of language and metaphor did not come without consequence. Certain members of the Abolitionist Society, as well as his white employers, wanted him to re-tain the mannerisms and dialects of "plantation speech": "Better have a *little* of the plantation manner of speech than not; 'tis not best that you seem too learned . . . [or] people won't believe you ever was a slave, Frederick."[9] This belief, grounded not only in determining *how* the black body is read but also in determining the very manner in which this body *speaks*, suggests attempts to bind the speech of "the slave" to the social predicament of his body.

8. *Workings of the Spirit: The Poetics of Afro-American Women's Writing*, 13–14.
9. Douglass, *My Bondage and My Freedom*, 362.

Douglass and other blacks sought to invert this symbolic order by col-
lapsing the boundaries between the public and the private spaces. History bears witness to the very public manner in which the slave body
was handled. Women were stripped before an audience of prospective
buyers on the auction block; men had their genitalia frisked like cattle
in an effort to determine their market worth; men and women were
herded together irrespective of the mates they themselves had chosen
in order to "breed" more slave property—all these acts created a social
decorum that prohibited the enslaved African American from obtaining any sort of privacy at its basic level. Yet slaveowners were given the
privilege of privacy, of keeping certain "indiscretions" that occurred
within the community of their plantations confidential.

As early as the 1600s social attitudes and case law encouraged the restructuring of the dynamics of these public and private spaces. Thus, the
unjustified murders of "insubordinate" slaves, the rapes of slave women,
and the selling of the babies that resulted from these encounters were
all done under the cloak of privacy and sanctioned by the judiciary systems on both the local and the regional levels. For these and other reasons, black activists such as Douglass and Sojourner Truth sought to
make the private trafficking in the souls and bodies of African American men, women, and children public. As Douglass states in an open
letter to his old master Thomas Auld, "I intend to make use of you as a
weapon with which to assail the system of slavery—as a means of concentrating public attention on the system."[10] Through his reinvention
of the public "stage" upon which slave and master communicate, Douglass stakes claim to the black body as he inverts the social "script" that
binds this body to the system of slavery.

Critics have often pointed out the unusual platform Douglass employs to make his points. William L. Andrews notes, "It is not often that
chattels address their owners. Th[is] . . . letter is unique; and probably
the only specimen of the kind extant." Andrews also determines that
certain parts of Douglass's letter are not factually accurate, particularly
those passages that recount the relationship between Auld and Douglass's grandmother, Betsy Bailey, in the last moments of her life. Possi-
bly for rhetorical or political purposes, Douglass chose to reinterpret this
relationship within the scope of his letter. As Andrews concludes, "the
anti-slavery author chose the propagandistic advantage—and no doubt
savored the personal ironies—of finally putting the slaveholder Auld to

10. William L. Andrews, ed., *The Oxford Frederick Douglass Reader*, 108.

his service." This leads me to believe that Douglass was very well aware
of the power of the written word and of his ability to frame his arguments against slavery using the image of the slave body to underscore
his point. Douglass's letter is full of images of scarred bodies and laden
with his need to make public the wrongs visited upon his family and
upon the families of his fellow bondsmen still brutalized under the
hypocrisy and guise of Christian love and brotherhood. He states at one
point in his letter, "Your wickedness and cruelty, committed in this respect on your fellow creatures, are greater than all the stripes you have
laid upon my back or theirs. It is an outrage upon the soul, a war upon
the immortal spirit, and one for which you must give account at the bar
of our common Father and Creator."[11]

This public declaration of sure damnation for all who, like Auld, continued to enslave African Americans against their will, was a bold testament on Douglass's part. It put before the nation's conscience the sins
of its citizens—and, in part, indicted those not directly involved as co-
conspirators to these crimes. But Douglass's public declarations also accomplished another feat: rhetorical interplay. In citing his own disfigured body as an example, Douglass wrote, "My feet have been so cracked
with the frost, that the pen with which I am writing might be laid in
the gashes."[12] Here, Douglass draws attention to the semiotics of the
black body both as a social and as an embodied text as he uses the gashes in his feet to testify to the atrocities inflicted on his fellow bondsmen.
In speaking of his body's pain, in re-penning the scarification of his
body, Douglass refigures the wounds on his own body as the master's discourse becomes Douglass's own discursive instrument.

Published in 1845, *Narrative of the Life of Frederick Douglass, an American Slave* incorporates numerous incidents that focus on the process of
scarification and its lingering aftermath. In the opening paragraph, for
example, Douglass charts his painstaking realization of the nature of
slavery and demonstrates the psychological damage visited, at an early
age, upon a slave child as he realizes the unsettling context of his own
origins. Douglass states, "I have no accurate knowledge of my age, never having seen any authentic record containing it." Here, Douglass
shapes the dynamics of identity formation around the concept of
"knowing"—of knowing one's age and, as we learn in the subsequent
pages of his narrative, of knowing one's parentage: "The opinion was

11. Ibid., 102, 107.
12. Douglass, *Narrative*, 29.

also whispered that my master was my father; but the correctness of this opinion, I know nothing; the means of knowing was withheld from me."[13] By denying the slave child those posts that frame the identities of most young individuals, this institution, in effect, framed a context that left the adult slave functioning under the same ambiguous pretext.

Similarly, Douglass details the various ways the black body is marred and marked under the pretense of preventing subversive behavior and "the enslavement of the whites." The death of the slave Demby at the hands of overseer Mr. Gore, the brutal murder of two slaves by Mr. Lanman, and the untimely demise of Douglass's wife's cousin at the hands of her mistress, Mrs. Giles Hicks, demonstrate slavery's need to "mangle the person" and "preserve the dehumanizing effects of slavery." In each instance, the flesh is used to play out the notions of power and submission. Douglass states in his narrative that Mr. Gore was "ambitious enough to be contented with nothing short of the highest rank of the overseers. . . . He spoke but to command, and commanded but to be obeyed; he dealt sparingly with his words, and bountifully with his whip, never using the former where the latter would answer as well."[14] Here, the whip becomes a "speech act," an articulate extension of Gore himself. In this coded conversation between the whip and the body, Gore writes his identity as masterful overseer using the whip as pen and the flesh of the slave as his text.

Historian Charles H. Nichols observes that "the driver's lash was . . . an indispensable aid to the system's functioning." With it the master class was able to enforce its caste etiquette. He also relates an interesting story in which ex-slave Solomon Northrup was able to use the whip with such dexterity that he could throw a lash "within a hair's breadth of the back, the ear, the nose [of the slave] without . . . touching them." To prevent detection by the master, Northrup and his fellow bondsmen had an arrangement wherein upon the appearance of the overseer, the slave would "squirm and screech as if in agony" as Northrup whipped vigorously upon the intended victim's back.[15]

Although Northrup's ingenuous use of the whip stands as an astonishing moment of creative subversion, Gore's behavior typifies, to one degree or another, the various ways the master used "the whip" to enforce submissive behavior. Douglass, in focusing on this mode of "com-

13. Ibid., 1–2.
14. Ibid., 23.
15. Nichols, *Many Thousand Gone,* 62, 63.

munication," draws attention to the ways in which masters, using the whip as agent, attempt to, to a greater degree, mute the embodied "speech act" of the slave. In a passage worth quoting at length, Douglass explains:

> It would astonish one, unaccustomed to a slaveholding life, to see with what wonderful ease a slaveholder can find things, of which to make occasion to whip a slave. A mere look, word, or motion,— a mistake, accident, or want of power,—are all matters for which a slave may be whipped at any time. Does a slave look dissatisfied? It is said, he has the devil in him, and it must be whipped out. Does he speak loudly when spoken to by his master? Then he is getting high-minded, and should be taken down a button-hole lower. Does he forget to pull off his hat at the approach of a white person? Then he is wanting in reverence, and should be whipped for it. . . . Does he ever venture to suggest a different mode of doing things from that pointed out by his master? He is indeed presumptuous, and getting above himself; and nothing less than a flogging will do for him.[16]

In each instance cited, social behavioral patterns are reinforced and the rhetoric of the system of chattel bondage is instilled in those who fall under the jurisdiction of the whip. Notice Douglass's focus on the body. "Look," "word," and "motion" all refer to means of expression; each can be read as a "want of power," a seedling of independence, or a sign of resistance. The whip, then, becomes a way to respond to these utterances and, to a larger degree, to the language of the body. It *is* the language understood, the language spoken, and it is the device used to strip the slave of his or her humanity and reinforce a sense of superiority in those that wield its power.

Disfigured Images of Black Womanhood

Douglass was not the only national spokesperson to focus on the effects of enslavement on the African American body and soul. Others such as Harriet Jacobs, Sojourner Truth, and Ida B. Wells directly or indirectly questioned this system's cruel treatment of the African American family and emphasized its debasement of the African American

---

16. *Narrative*, 80.

woman. Each of these women was familiar with the ways slavery sought to physically mark the slave woman and reorder the social reading of her body. Tubman, who, like Truth, was classified as a female slave who was a match for any man, took a stunning blow to the head at the age of sixteen in her effort to help a fugitive slave escape. As one writer puts it, "With this, the seal of bondage was literally stamped upon her head, as though life must give this prisoner a number in the way that men brand cattle." But Tubman's mark became her "revolutionary badge of faith. . . . The region still rang with the story of her daring intervention in behalf of a fellow Negro, for although slaves were injured daily, not all bore the scars of a bold self-defense; and such a brand as Harriet had, that of taking another's blow, was almost unknown."[17] The ability to take that which was bad and make it good is at the heart of the African American's struggle. Tubman embodied that perseverance, as her scar became a legend in and of itself. The legacy she left behind, of freeing more than three hundred people from slavery, despite the sleeping spells that resulted from the near-fatal wound to her body, became part of the fabric of African America's oral and literary revolutionary history.

In a similar vein, Sojourner Truth is another figure who chose to make the invisible marking of the body—the desexualization of woman— visible as a testament to the cruelty of slavery. In order to define her role as a social activist and layperson for the bidding of the "Holy Spirit," Truth had to work against prevailing social attitudes that saw her body as exotic and overdetermined her identity in the written materials on her personal life and political activities. Many of these accounts, considered to be authorial collaborations, firmly established the separation between author and ethnographic subject and created contradictory and often unresolved impulses in the public and private life of Sojourner Truth. On the one hand, Truth's inability to read and write made her vulnerable to white reformers who sought to exert control over her public image. These individuals "packaged" Truth's persona, marking her in ways that fed into the racist assumptions of the day, casting her as a "Libyan Sibyl" in one instance, who "seemed to impersonate the fervor of Ethiopia, wild, savage, hunted of all nations, but burning after God in her tropic heart, and stretching her scarred hands toward the glory to be revealed." On the other hand, Truth sought public attention from the very audience in question—those white reformers and those who held the prevailing social attitudes—in order to feed herself and her

17. Earl Conrad, *Harriet Tubman*, 14, 17.

family. "I sell the shadow to support the substance" reads the caption that accompanies the picture distributed on Truth's behalf—the shadow constituting the photographic image itself, the substance Truth's actual bodily self. Truth's willingness to be photographed may appear to support the very system from which she attempted to divorce herself. But, according to Carla Peterson, "Truth . . . was aware of both the power of written language to authorize and interpret experience and her exclusion from this arena of power."[18] Thus, Truth's desire to offer a countertext in a representational image can be read as a form of resistance to commodification and, I believe, as a way to refigure the disfigurement of her body in the written chronicles of her life.

Truth's desire to separate her person into a "shadow" and a "substance" demonstrates the extent to which she sought to maintain some power over her life and public image. Truth's resolve would be tested again, however, in 1851 at the Akron Women's Rights Convention. In one of her famous speeches supporting the rights of black women, Truth is said to have asked the rhetorical question, "Ar'n't I a Woman?" Her alleged use of this phrase has been the subject of much speculation. Because Truth was bilingual—she spoke Dutch until the age of ten and learned the English language as it was spoken in the Northeast where she grew up—several critics believe that Frances Dana Gage, in publishing Truth's speech among other "reminiscences" of the convention, may have taken liberties with Truth's language, adding elements such as a crude southern dialect and inserting the clause for which Truth's famous speech is most commonly known. Carleton Mabee and Jeffrey C. Stewart both speak of the questionable way Truth's persona is recreated for public consumption. As Stewart notes, "Perhaps Gage believed that her reading audience in 1878 would find Sojourner Truth's words more authentic if they were rendered in Southern dialect. . . . Still, that a participant in the women's rights movement, who honored this black woman by lauding her contribution to the Akron convention, would make such a drastic alteration in the voice of her sister is puzzling. Perhaps this was how Gage *heard* Sojourner's voice." Perhaps. But just as important is the way Gage *perceived* Truth and the way she read her body. This is evident in Gage's recollection of the events that occurred during Truth's speech:

18. *Narrative of Sojourner Truth, a Bondswoman of Olden Time: With a History of Her Labors and Correspondences Drawn from Her "Book of Life,"* 161; Peterson, *"Doers of The Word": African-American Women Speakers and Writers in the North (1830–1880)*, 33.

'Nobody eber helps me into carriages, or ober mud-puddles, or give me any best place'; and raising herself to her full height, and her voice to a pitch like rolling thunder, she asked, 'And ar'n't I a woman? Look at me. Look at my arm,' and she bared her right arm to the shoulder, showing its tremendous muscular power. 'I have plowed and planted and gathered into barns, and no man could head me—and Ar'n't I a woman? I could work as much and eat as much as a man . . . , and bear de lash as well—and Ar'n't' I a woman? I have borne thirteen chillen, and seen 'em mos' all sold off into slavery, and when I cried out with a mother's grief, none but Jesus heard—Ar'n't I a woman?'[19]

What becomes very evident in this recounting of Truth's speech is the manner in which Gage stages Truth's body as text, allowing the audience that wasn't present—Gage's reading audience—to witness the marking of slavery on Truth's person, or to imagine, as Jean Fagan Yellin has argued elsewhere, the mutilated image of Stowe's "Libyan Sibyl."[20] But to consider only this image of Truth would diminish her legacy and minimize her impact on the women's movement. Her presence at the convention changed the very way in which we now *read* the black female body, so the credit must go to Truth. Her savvy display of her muscular arm—so antithetical to the feminine gentility of that day—became a sign for the ways in which the physical labor of slavery "rewrote" the language of her woman's body. Yet Truth returns again and again to those realms of social decorum that classify her as woman: motherhood and spiritual frailty. Truth's attempt to invert those social orders that bind her body to the margins of the cult of true womanhood, a cult that by its very nature places her body on the margins of the cultural femininity of the time, represents one of the earliest examples of black womanist thought.

Truth's sexuality was often questioned by members of the audience who came to hear her speak (these individuals traditionally belonged to the proslavery faction, but some were part of the antislavery movement as well). Historian Nell Irvin Painter writes of one 1858 group meeting in Indiana where Truth bared her breasts to silence her critics. Citing the October 15 issue of the Boston *Liberator,* Painter reports:

19. *Narrative of Sojourner Truth,* xxxiv–v; Mabee, *Sojourner Truth: Slave, Prophet, Legend,* 76.
20. Yellin, *Women and Sisters: The Antislavery Feminists in American Culture,* 81–82.

Sojourner told them that her breasts had suckled many a white babe, to the exclusion of her own offspring; that some of those white babies had grown to man's estate; that, although they had suckled her colored breasts, they were, in her estimation, far more manly than they (her persecutors) appeared to be; and she quietly asked them, as she disrobed her bosom, if they, too, wished to suck! In vindication of her truthfulness, she told them that she would show her breast to the whole congregation; that it was not to her shame that she uncovered her breast before them, but to their shame.

In making her "colored breasts" the foundation upon which many a white baby had "grown to man's estate," Truth indelibly inscribes the black female body with certain attributes that connect her explicitly to the patriarchal lineage of the United States. She turns the milk of black mothers into the substance that allegorically makes men "far more man-ly than they (her persecutors) appeared to be." She also reestablishes herself as mother—a role taken from her with respect to her own chil-dren while she was enslaved. These public speech acts, which use the body as their driving force, allow Truth to substantiate her claims of womanhood as they simultaneously make evident the forms of racial and gender prejudice that enslave Truth and other black women so-cially. "What had been intended as degradation became a triumph of embodied rhetoric," argues Painter. "Denying the womanliness of women speaking in public was a familiar ploy. . . . The challenge was to the woman's authenticity. A similar challenge, to his authenticity as a former slave, prompted well-spoken Frederick Douglass to write his first autobiography." Truth chose to rewrite her identity as woman using the very venue through which the black body was violated: public display. Although categorized by Douglass as "a genuine specimen of the un-cultured negro," who "cared very little for elegance of speech or refine-ment of manners," Truth was a force to be reckoned with as she brought to the forefront of the abolition and women's rights movements the un-told sorrows of the African American slave woman.[21]

Truth's public attempts to recoup the black female body should be se-riously considered in any study that scrutinizes the development of a womanist ideology built around the body and its scars. In particular, Truth's racial and sexual politics highlight the special concerns of African American women of that era regarding their continued associ-

21. Painter, *Sojourner Truth: A Life, a Symbol*, 139.

ation with overt and illicit sexuality, and Truth's judicious undertakings align themselves philosophically with the literary efforts of writers including Harriet Jacobs, Harriet E. Wilson, and Elizabeth Keckley. Jacobs especially is noted for her interrogation in her 1861 slave narrative, *Incidents in the Life of a Slave Girl,* of the principles that govern the conventions of true womanhood. According to Hazel Carby:

> Jacobs knew that to gain her own public voice, as a writer, implicated her very existence as a mother and a woman; the three could not be separated. She also knew from experience, as did [Mary] Prince and [Harriet] Wilson, that the white people of the North were not completely free from the power of the slaveholders, or from their racism. To be bound to the conventions of true womanhood was to be bound to a racist, ideological system.

Thus Jacobs created a pseudonymous narrator, Linda Brent, "as a mechanism of self-protection." This fictional narrator allows Jacobs some flexibility in the telling of her story, and Brent allows Jacobs to manipulate "a series of conventions that were not only literary in their effects but which also threatened the meaning of Jacobs's social existence."[22]

Incidents records the numerous acts of physical and mental abuse that shaped Jacobs's experiences as a slave in the household of Dr. and Mrs. Flint. Jacobs's sexual exploitation at the hands of Dr. Flint has been well documented by such literary critics as Carby and Sanchez-Eppler. What has not been given adequate attention is Jacobs's critical focus on the disfigured slave body. Her own physical impairment, as a result of her seven-year stint in her grandmother's attic crawl space, serves as a touchstone in the development of her own social and political ethos built around the slave body. Jacobs is crippled because she chose to run away. This fact is evident in her text. But less obvious are those wounds unseen, unmanifested on the surface of her body. Jacobs's physical debilitation directs critical attention to her internal conflict, and the physical manifestation of her disfigured body becomes the material reality of her wounded spirit. Jacobs *is* psychologically scarred because of her experiences in the Flint household. Her impassioned plea, detailing the multiple ways the slave girl's moral and spiritual character is maligned by those individuals who have authority over her life, stands as a written testament of the many "incidents" in the life of a young slave girl.

22. Carby, *Reconstructing Womanhood: The Emergence of the Afro-American Woman Novelist,* 50.

> Every where the years bring to all enough of sin and sorrow; but in slavery the very dawn of life is darkened by these shadows. Even the little child, who is accustomed to wait on her mistress and her children, will learn, before she is twelve years old, why it is that her mistress hates such and such among the slaves. Perhaps the child's own mother is among those hated ones. She listens to the violent outbreaks of jealous passion, and cannot help understanding what is the cause. She will become prematurely knowing in evil things. Soon she will learn to tremble when she hears her master's footfall. She will be compelled to realize that she is no longer a child. If God has bestowed beauty upon her, it will prove her greatest curse. That which commands admiration in the white woman only hastens the degradation of the famale [*sic*] slave . . . I cannot tell how much I suffered in the presence of these wrongs, nor how I am still pained by the retrospect.[23]

Jacobs's lament crystallizes, in vivid fashion, the depths of her despair. Her mental disposition, the very essence of her inner being, is transformed by her contact with Flint. These wounds, when placed next to Jacobs's physical scars, demonstrate to what extent Jacobs was willing to sacrifice her body to escape her vile situation.

Jacobs's eyewitness testimony to the travails of the slave woman foregrounds the "delicate" politics of sexuality and race in the nineteenth century—a politics that found the black slave woman inextricably tied to the rhetorical intersection of feminism and abolition. This "merger" of the literal flesh and the figurative body left the female slave vulnerable to the cultural exchange of literary figures. That is, the female slave became the unwilling participant in the culture's apprehension of what constitutes blackness and sexuality within the ideological confines of American society. Thus, as Sanchez-Eppler notes, the writings of antislavery women frequently project the sexual anxieties of white women onto the sexualized bodies of black slave women.[24] To tell their stories, women like Jacobs had to negotiate these cultural land mines by reinventing the space from which they spoke. Specifically, Jacobs rewrote the plot that, by design, objectifies black female sexuality under the pretense of white male desire by "romanticizing" the sexuality of the tragic mulatta. This literary convention renders the black female subject mute, unable to express her unwillingness to participate in these private

---

23. Brent, *Incidents*, 27.
24. "Bodily Bonds," 33.

acts of "seduction," or even perhaps rape. Jacobs's rejection of the traditions of this convention allows her to manipulate the novelistic genre of the sentimental narrative by exposing the fallacy of public-private separation for the female slave. Just as Douglass made the private activities of his master public in his open letter to his master, Jacobs makes known the "private" dangers in the life of a slave girl.

> Reader, be assured this narrative is no fiction. I am aware that some of my adventures may seem incredible; but they are, nevertheless, strictly true. I have not exaggerated the wrongs inflicted by Slavery; on the contrary, my descriptions fall far short of the facts . . . I have not written my experiences in order to attract attention to myself . . . Neither do I care to excite sympathy for my own sufferings. But I do earnestly desire to arouse the women of the North to a realizing sense of the condition of two millions of women at the South, still in bondage, suffering what I suffered, and most of them far worse.[25]

Jacobs's public conversations about the reality of slave life for black women, although coded so as not to offend her middle-class constituents, offer a larger space for the discursive meditation on the wounded body. Jacobs peoples her narrative with the stories of those who suffered more heinous and brutal abuse at the hands of their masters. In chronicling their stories, Jacobs pays homage to their spirit of resistance. One such slave was named James. He was the son of Charity, an acquaintance of Jacobs and her grandmother. Charity was taken to Louisiana when her young mistress married, and Charity's son James was sold away from her. Jacobs describes James as having the "manliness and intelligence" of his father, "qualities that made it so hard for him to be a plantation slave." James was sold to a number of masters during his childhood, but he grew into manhood under the ownership of a wealthy slaveholder known for his cruelty. After a severe flogging, James escaped into the woods to avoid another beating. Some weeks later, he was captured and returned to his master. James received hundreds of lashes. He then was washed with brine and put into the cotton gin, "which was screwed down, only allowing him room to turn on his side when he could not lie on his back." Every morning one of the other slaves placed a piece of bread and a bowl of water within James's reach. On the second morning, the slave noticed the bread was gone but the water was

25. Brent, *Incidents*, xiii.

untouched. On the fourth morning, he detected a horrible stench emanating from the gin house. When the press was unscrewed, James's dead body was found partly eaten by rats and vermin. "Perhaps," suggests Jacobs, "the rats that devoured his bread had gnawed him before life was extinct." The egregious fashion in which James died is mirrored by the conspicuous manner in which he was buried. "They put him into a rough box, and buried him with less feeling than would have been manifested for an old housedog. Nobody asked any questions. He was a slave; and the feeling was that the master had a right to do what he pleased with his own property. And what did *he* care for the value of a slave? He had hundreds of them."[26]

Other slaves met similar fates at the hands of this master. He shot one woman through the head after she was returned to him following an attempted escape. Another slave, who resisted being whipped, was fed to the bloodhounds, which literally tore his flesh from his bones. These represent but a few of the examples Jacobs gives ample space to in her narrative. In addition to their shock value, these stories underscore the ways in which the body bears witness to the brutality of slavery, and Jacobs's written narrative serves as a memory trace of these individuals' tenuous existence.

The Narrative of Lynching

The abolishment of slavery brought a change in the way African American writers depicted the wounded black body. Whereas previously these authors had focused on the social fabric of slavery—on the day-to-day workings of slavery that enabled the systematic abuse of African American people on the plantation and in its surrounding communities—the postslavery era found African American writers concentrating on more immediate political and economic issues that threatened to undermine those minimal social gains achieved during Reconstruction.

One such issue that jeopardized the very lives of African American men and women, particularly in the South, was that of ritualized mob violence, or lynching as it is commonly known. Lynching is a horrendous crime that often leaves its victims sadistically dismembered, tortured, burned, shot, and hanged or bound. It is the ultimate vision of

26. Ibid., 49.

bodily scarring as ideological presumptions of race and gender become permanently transfixed upon the flesh of the black man. Moreover, the psychological wounds visited upon the families and communities of these victims exist long after the body has been viciously violated and abused. Many of these acts were (and are) carried out with such vengeance as to warrant a discussion in this study. Consider, for example, the following passage from Sutton Elbert Griggs's *The Hindered Hand*:

> The mob decided to torture their victims before killing them and began on Foresta first. A man with a pair of scissors stepped up and cut off her hair and threw it into the crowd. There was a great scramble for bits of hair for souvenirs of the occasion. One by one her fingers were cut off and tossed into the crowd to be scrambled for. A man with a cork screw came forward, ripped Foresta's clothing to her waist, bored into her breast with the corkscrew and pulled forth the live quivering flesh. Poor Bud her helpless husband closed his eyes and turned away his head to avoid the terrible sight. Men gathered about him and forced his eyelids open so that he could see all.
>
> When it was thought that Foresta had been tortured sufficiently, attention was turned to Bud. His fingers were cut off one by one and the corkscrew was bored into his legs and arms. A man with a club struck him over the head, crushing his skull and forcing an eyeball to hang down from the socket by a thread. A rush was made toward Bud and a man who was a little ahead of his competitors snatched the eyeball as a souvenir.
>
> After three full hours had been spent in torturing the two, the spokesman announced that they were now ready for the final act. The brother of Sidney Fletcher was called for and was given a match. He stood near his mutilated victims until the photographer present could take a picture of the scene. This being over, the match was applied and the flames leaped up eagerly and encircled the writhing forms of Bud and Foresta.
>
> When the flames had done their work and had subsided, a mad rush was made for the trees which were soon denuded of bark, each member of the mob being desirous, it seemed, of carrying away something that might testify to his proximity to so great a happening.
>
> Little Melville Brant found a piece of the charred flesh in the ashes and bore it home.[27]

27. *The Hindered Hand: or The Reign of the Repressionist*, 133–34.

This graphic depiction makes explicit the ritualistic undercurrents that support the act of lynching: the burning, the mutilation, the gathering of trophies, and the initiation of children. Those familiar with Griggs's novel will recall that Bud and Foresta Harper are killed because they defended their home against a white intruder, Sidney Fletcher, who had come to kill Bud. Griggs's need to vividly portray the brutal murders of these characters speaks to the issue of power—or the lack thereof—over one's own life and one's own property. Because African Americans have been systematically denied the ability to act in their own behalf—whether economically or politically—these portraits become a way to lay before the nation the wounds of a people. "Black writers begin with the realistic depictions of violence in their history," notes Trudier Harris, so that they can "then move to a political level where such depictions become statements of the oppression of a people."[28]

What becomes evident from these depictions, and the various case studies Ida B. Wells-Barnett presents in the editorials and pamphlets she published during the height of the lynching activity, are the underlying issues of race, class, and gender. In her analysis of the socially sanctioned "lynch law," the origin of which dates back to 1780 when Col. William Lynch drafted legislation for "the purpose of suppressing a trained band of horse-thieves and counterfeiters whose well concocted schemes had bidden defiance to the ordinary laws of the land,"[29] Wells found that the lynch law was implemented to give private citizens the written authority to take matters into their own hands. However, the law was manipulated by white citizens who sought to protect interests not implied under its original doctrine. In an incident that would form the basis for Wells's crusade against lynching, three young black businessmen—considered too prosperous by their white counterparts—were carried about a mile north of the city limits of Memphis, Tennessee, and summarily shot to pieces in a field "by unknown hands." Thomas Moss, Calvin McDowell, and Lee Stewart had owned and operated the People's Grocery Store in an area of Memphis known as the Curve. This area, a thickly populated suburb, had a large constituency of African American citizens. Moss's white competitor had had a monopoly on the trade in this area and did not welcome the new store. A few days before the lynching, Moss, Stewart, and McDowell had gotten word that their store might be vandalized, and they sought legal help. A lawyer told them

28. *Exorcising Blackness: Historical and Literary Lynching and Burning Rituals*, x.
29. *Selected Works of Ida B. Wells-Barnett*, 74.

they were justified in protecting themselves and their property since this district lay outside the city limits and beyond the boundaries of police protection. Thus, when a late-night altercation, instigated by the white storeowner, resulted in three white men being wounded in the act of a felony (they were attempting to steal merchandise through the rear door of the People's Grocery Store), Moss, Stewart, and McDowell assumed they would be vindicated because they were acting in self-defense. However, they were arrested for the shootings. Despite the circumstances surrounding the altercation, despite the fact that, by law, the wounding of a white man was not punishable by death, these black men were taken from their jail cells and executed by a mob.

Wells, who was godmother to the child of one of the victims and a close friend of the other two, was outraged. She had received word of the incident while on a business trip in Natchez, Mississippi. So moved was she by this incident that she devoted three chapters to it in her autobiography, *Crusade for Justice*, in which she charts her conscious development from observer to active participant in the fight against lynching. As she states forthrightly, "Like many another person who had read of lynching in the South, I had accepted the idea meant to be conveyed—that although lynching was irregular and contrary to law and order, unreasoning anger over the terrible crime of rape led to the lynching; that perhaps the brute deserved death anyhow and the mob was justified in taking his life." But it was the Moss-McDowell-Stewart incident that opened her eyes to the insidious nature of lynching, that this was indeed a crime that sought to maintain power and control over a race of people through ritualized acts of violence and intimidation. She recalls:

> Thomas Moss, Calvin McDowell, and Lee Stewart had been lynched in Memphis, one of the leading cities of the South, in which no lynching had taken place before, with just as much brutality as other victims of the mob; and they had committed no crime against white women. This is what opened my eyes to what lynching really was. An excuse to get rid of Negroes who were acquiring wealth and property and thus keep the race terrorized and "keep the nigger down."[30]

Wells's analysis here is key to understanding the link between the materiality of the American Dream and the disfigured black body. As

30. *Crusade for Justice: The Autobiography of Ida B. Wells-Barnett*, 64.

Trudier Harris and Sandra Gunning have pointed out, the antagonistic relationship between blacks and whites has routinely inspired ritualized violence—particularly when the "accused" has encroached upon social or political space deemed "reserved" for white America. These acts of terrorism were more prevalent after Reconstruction because white Americans were coming to terms with post–Civil War anxieties over national unity, black emancipation, growing labor unrest, and the "continued evolution of the United States into an increasing multiethnic nation."[31] This struggle for material resources and markets erupted in 1892. It is estimated that during this single year, 241 men, women, and children were lynched in twenty-six states across America. Although Native Americans, Chicanos, Asians, and African American sympathizers comprise a portion of those individuals lynched, 160 of the victims were African American, an increase of 200 percent over the total for the previous ten years combined. Additionally, most of these lynchings occurred on southern soil, causing many to speculate about the connection between race and region and reconsider a history that had based its supremacy upon disfiguring the black male image.

In "The Case Stated," the first chapter to her *Southern Horrors*, Wells wrote:

> Beginning with the emancipation of the Negro, the inevitable result of unbridled power exercised for two and a half centuries, by the white man over the Negro, began to show itself in acts of conscienceless outlawry. During the slave regime, the Southern white man owned the Negro body and soul. It was to his interest to dwarf the soul and preserve the body. Vested with unlimited power over his slave, . . . the white man was . . . restrained from [certain forms of] punishment [that] tended to injure the slave by abating his physical powers and thereby reducing his financial worth. . . . The slave was rarely killed, he was too valuable. . . . But Emancipation came and the vested interests of the white man in the Negro's body were lost.

Southern whites, according to Wells, had been educated in a long tradition that drew "strict lines of action in dealing with the Negro." This tradition, grounded in seizing control of the black body and soul by whatever means necessary, framed the context for race relations decades after the institution of slavery. In reiterating the foundation upon which

31. Harris, *Exorcising Blackness*, ix–xiii; Gunning, *Race, Rape, and Lynching*, 6.

the acts of lynching are based, Wells unveils the ideology behind the commission of these acts against the black body, as again the flesh becomes a contested space—an entity to be marred and marked with the vestiges of racism and fear. In exploring why some Southerners felt the need to "protect their interests," Wells offers the following reflections:

> [For] the first fifteen years of [the Negro's] freedom he was murdered by masked mobs for trying to vote. Public opinion having made lynching for that cause unpopular, a new reason is given to justify the murders of the past 15 years. The Negro was first charged with attempting to rule white people, and hundreds were murdered on that pretended supposition. He is now charged with assaulting or attempting to assault white women. This charge, as false as it is foul, robs us of the sympathy of the world and is blasting the race's good name.[32]

Wells's comments bring into focus two important issues at the heart of lynching: fear of miscegenation and a displacement of power. History bears witness to the fact that black men were summarily lynched for alleged indiscretions against white women. Accusations such as these were routinely equated with guilt, and frequently black men found themselves at the other end of a rope. This (dis)figuration of black male identity—displaced as the myth of the black male rapist—not only created an atmosphere that exposed society's barely repressed fears of black male sexuality and masculinity; it also created a context for understanding the relationship between power and sexuality as American society and civilization became increasingly figured in terms of the white female body. According to Gunning, "sexual and political agency became increasingly linked in the figure of the black rapist precisely because of the dependent definition of citizenship on definitions of (white) manhood."[33] This subtext underwrites the cultural narrative of lynching as notions of manhood become inextricably tied to the "preservation" of nation, honor, and white womanhood. By extension, violence itself became a way for white men to "police" the state, protect it if you will, from the social encroachment of black men who were considered citizens and social equals after emancipation. This "social rape," as Gunning terms it, was the ultimate threat against everything

32. *Southern Horrors and Other Writings: The Anti-Lynching Campaign of Ida B. Wells, 1892–1900*, 75.
33. *Race, Rape, and Lynching*, 7.

sacred to the Anglo-Saxon citizenry as voting power and economic supremacy eroded under the weight of a changing political and social climate. Wells, in attacking the stereotyping of black men as rapists, creates a national platform wherein she exposes the nation's fears of miscegenation—as both a physical and an economic entity.

More than recounting the endless atrocities perpetrated upon the black community, Wells's writings provide a cultural template upon which to build a theoretical framework shaped around the body and its wounds. Her keen observations on the social, political, and communal paradigms that "justify" these actions present other examples of the ways in which the black body was used to make very public statements about race relations—in a language unmistakably vile, unmistakably visible.

In surveying the wide spectrum of works by African American writers and social activists from Douglass to Wells, I hope to have cultivated a space from which to begin my examination of the contemporary cultural uses of the scar in selected works by African American writers. Those persons mentioned in "The Call" have set a precedent that allows us to see the unique ways African Americans manipulate and re-envision the sites of abuse to their bodies and make them signs of empowerment and self-ownership. In examining the contemporary responses to these "calls," I hope to demonstrate the importance of literature as a bridge that allows respondents an opportunity to "converse" with their predecessors. As Valerie Smith points out, "Afro-American writers traditionally have attached great significance to the acts of reading and writing."[34] In this way, writing becomes an antidote to pain, a way to reinterpret the language of the body and heal the wounds of the psyche. Douglass, Wells, and Truth employ both written and oral forms of communication in their efforts to free their fellow countrymen. In the process they focus attention on the black body and the traumas visited upon it. In this way, they undeniably make their discussions "personal" by framing their rhetoric around the very thing that makes us all equal and human, and they challenge future respondents—both critics and creative writers alike—to do the same.

34. *Self-Discovery and Authority in Afro-American Narrative*, 2–3.

The Response

[R]eclaiming that from which one has been disinherited is a good thing. Self-possession, in the full sense of that expression, is the companion to self-knowledge. Yet, claiming for myself, a heritage the weft of whose genesis is my own disinheritance is a profoundly troubling paradox.

—Patricia J. Williams, *The Alchemy of Race and Rights*

All of African American literature may be seen as one vast genealogical poem that attempts to restore continuity to the ruptures or discontinuities imposed by the history of black presence in America.

—Kimberly W. Benston, "I yam what I am . . ."

The system of slavery and segregation caused many Negroes to feel that perhaps they were inferior. This is the ultimate tragedy of segregation. It not only harms one physically, but it injures one spiritually. It scars the soul and distorts the personality. . . . But through the forces of history something happened to the Negro. He came to feel that he was somebody.

—Martin Luther King Jr., "The Current Crisis in Race Relations"

Three

Bodies of Texts

Literal and Figurative Visions of History in Sherley Anne Williams's *Dessa Rose*

> When I first began to work on the manuscript that would become the historical novel *Dessa Rose* . . . [some people] asked me . . . Why slavery? . . . why would I want to probe that old scar. Slavery, however, is more scab than scar on the nation's body. It's a wound that has not healed and, until the scab is removed, the festered flesh cut away, it cannot heal cleanly and completely.
>
> —Sherley Anne Williams, "The Lion's History: The Ghetto Writes B[l]ack"

Sherley Anne Williams was motivated to write *Dessa Rose* in part as a healing ritual and in part as a meditation on history. As the opening epigraph suggests, the very act of writing about slavery, the very exploration of a subject one critic calls "the American heart of darkness,"[1] requires the excavation of an old national wound and the removal of a scab that masks the festering flesh just below its surface. In many ways, Williams's novel becomes an exercise in identifying the "agents" that continue to infect the nation's bodily wound.

On another level, Williams wrote out of the experience of her own wounded spirit. As she states in the author's note to *Dessa Rose:* "I loved

---

1. Deborah E. McDowell and Arnold Rampersad, eds., *Slavery and the Literary Imagination*, vii–viii.

history as a child, until some clear-eyed young Negro pointed out, quite rightly, that there was no place in the American past I could go and be free. I now know that slavery eliminated neither heroism nor love; it provided occasions for their expressions . . . [and] maybe it is only a metaphor, but I now own a summer in the 19th century." Williams's desire to "own a summer in the 19th century" can be traced to her "being outraged by a certain, critically acclaimed novel of the early seventies that travestied the as-told-to memoir of slave revolt leader Nat Turner." As she goes on to say, "Afro-Americans, having survived by word of mouth—and made of that process a high art—remain at the mercy of literature and writing; often these have betrayed us." This betrayal, which Williams identifies in William Styron's controversial novel *The Confessions of Nat Turner*, she attributes to the hypocrisy of a literary tradition that has continued to deny African Americans agency. Similarly, Williams asserts that Styron's novel "dismissed the brutal social and political conditions that led to Turner's revolt," and it neglected to detail the strengths of black culture evident during this time.[2]

Williams was not the only African American writer to respond to Styron's depiction of Nat Turner. In 1968, shortly after the appearance of Styron's *Confessions*, a collection of essays was published entitled *William Styron's Nat Turner: Ten Black Writers Respond*. The contributors included noted social historian Lerone Bennett Jr., novelist John O. Killens, history professor Vincent Harding, and professor of psychiatry Alvin F. Poussaint. Of particular concern to these writers was Styron's fantastical portrait of Turner as a weak and indecisive leader, a leader fanatically religious and sexually obsessed with white women. As civil rights activist Mike Thelwell explains, Styron's Nat "becomes an inverted, frustrated, onanistic, emotionally short-circuited lecher after white women. Presumably, if he had given way to his secret lust and raped the white girl he is later to murder, the rebellion would never have occurred." Analogously, Styron's inclusion of a homosexual encounter between Turner and one of his followers, Willis—an encounter unsubstantiated by any historical records available—and his omission of the role Turner's family and wife played in his life led many in the volume to accuse Styron of intentionally and maliciously maligning the character of Nat Turner. As Lerone Bennett Jr. puts it, "We are not quib-

---

2. Williams, *Dessa Rose*, author's note; subsequent references to this novel will appear in the text. Williams in Shirley M. Jordan, ed., *Broken Silences: Interviews with Black and White Women Writers*, 286.

bling here over footnotes in scholarly journals. . . . We are objecting to something more insidious, more dangerous. *We are objecting to a deliberate attempt to steal the meaning of a man's life.*"[3]

It was in this cultural climate that Williams began her work on a novella she called "Meditations on History," which would eventually serve as the introductory section to *Dessa Rose*. In these texts Williams in part parodies Styron's (and many critics have argued Thomas R. Gray's) methodological approach to writing *his* version of Nat Turner's confession. She frames her narrative around the life of Dessa Rose, a sixteen-year-old female slave who is about to be hanged for her part in leading a slave coffle insurrection that left five white men dead and another badly maimed. The narrative underscores the motivation behind the uprising as it details the mental and physical abuse slaves like Dessa suffered while in chattel bondage. As Williams states in a 1992 interview with literary critic Shirley Jordan, "Meditations on History" was begun during a time when

> many, many black intellectuals were still incensed about Styron's portrayal of Nat Turner. . . . [My] short story is told through the journal entries of Nehemiah, and I took great delight in finding ways for Dessa's true story to come through to the reader without Nehemiah, in fact, being aware of what was going on and being truly ignorant of what was being said . . . the idea of setting up [this] situation was my way of saying to Styron "See what you missed. You went for the easy thing—the stereotyped thing. This is the real story that you missed."

Williams's efforts to reveal to Styron "the real story" he missed speak to a larger issue that positions *Dessa Rose* as not only responding to *Confessions* but, as Mary Helen Washington has argued in her analysis of this text, as "also representing the relationship of the black female speaker to a white (male) literary world and challenging the racist and sexist practices of white history and white literature."[4]

To understand Williams's "questioning" of the narrative practices of nineteenth-century (and, I would argue, some twentieth-century) white writers, to understand the narrative strategies she employs to in-

---

3. Thelwell, "Back with the Wind: Mr. Styron and the Reverend Turner," 85; Bennett, "Nat's Last White Man," 5.

4. Williams in Jordan, ed., *Broken Silences*, 288–89; Washington, ed., *Black-Eyed Susans / Midnight Birds*, 227.

terrogate and at once subject these texts to critical scrutiny, one must examine closely the intertextual weaving of the multiple perspectives of the novel's fictive narrator(s) as well as the interconnectedness of the narrative's various sections. The novel is composed of three central parts, each distinct in presenting the various ways the slave body is read and named. The epithets of the first two parts, "The Darky" and "The Wench," denote the ways the slave body is classified, each term signifying on the racial and sexual stereotypes that bind the slave body, in this case the female slave body, to the discourse of slavery. Interestingly, Williams couples these "titles" with key passages from the narratives of Frederick Douglass and Sojourner Truth. This gesture posits simultaneous readings of the black body—one grounded in racist ideology, the other framed in what Henry Louis Gates Jr. terms the "double-voicedness" of black texts—a narrative strategy that allows an author to "signify" on history and tradition through a process of repetition and representation.[5] I would also add that this rhetorical voice becomes refigured, for the purposes of my discussion, through the site of the body, as the body, too, becomes a signifier of the black voice in writing. On the title page of part I, for example, Williams records the following oft-quoted passage from Douglass: "you have seen how a man was made a slave." This passage has particular resonance when we consider the fact that slaves *were* made—legally and socially created by a society that sanctioned the abuse of another based on the arbitrary sign of skin color. In Williams's novel, we are made aware of the dynamics of this "creative" process through the interaction of Nehemiah and Dessa, and we are equally made aware of Dessa's efforts to thwart this process.

In part II, Williams couples the title "The Wench" with a passage from Sojourner Truth's well-known speech "Ar'n't I a Woman." As we have seen, black slave women often had their sexuality challenged and their identities refigured within the dictates of chattel bondage. In this part of the novel, Williams comments on the different standards of womanhood and motherhood afforded black and white women, highlighting in particular the strained relationships that existed between these two groups of individuals. Part III, "The Negress," changes the perspective of the novel as Williams makes Dessa the primary narrator. (In part I, the story is told from the perspective of a white male southern writer, Adam Nehemiah. In part II, a white slave mistress, Miss

5. Gates, *The Signifying Monkey: A Theory of African-American Literary Criticism*, xxv.

Ruth Elizabeth Sutton—Miss Rufel as she is called by the slave characters in the novel—is the primary narrator.) This shift, when coupled with the prologue and the epilogue (which are also told from Dessa's perspective) "lays bare," as Marta E. Sanchez determines, "the elements of [the novel's] artifice—its reporting modes, its narrative impersonations . . . its implicit critique of social perceptions and prejudices." Attention to these particulars sheds light on Williams's ability to (re)present a contemporary fictionalized version of a slave narrative that exposes the semiotic relationship certain subjects share with the written text(s) of history. In doing so, as Sanchez argues, Williams "instructs readers about the specificities of white and African-American histories," revealing to the reader the cultural matrices that inform the cultural productions of historical and literary texts. These "narrative strategies" allow Williams to "appropriate representations of dominant culture [in an effort] to throw them into question and turn them against themselves."[6] In the process, Williams marks her territory as an African American female writer, making her text the vehicle through which she asserts her subjectivity as author as she simultaneously realigns the gendered and cultural frames of reference associated with slave resistance.

As early as 1971, black activist Angela Davis determined that "no extensive and systematic study of the role of black women in resisting slavery had come to [her] attention. . . . With the sole exceptions of Harriet Tubman and Sojourner Truth," black women's counterinsurgency during the slave era remained more or less "shrouded in unrevealed history." Academic interest in this area remains stagnant even today. Except for a few well-known studies, such as Herbert Aptheker's *American Negro Slave Revolts,* or David Barry Gaspar and Darlene Clark Hine's *More than Chattel,* this history remains "unrevealed." This fact is striking given the vast number of academic studies that consider the cultural and historical significance of slavery, but they fail to acknowledge the multitudinous manner in which Africans and their American progeny rejected chattel bondage. "The magnitude and effects of black people's defiant rejection of slavery has not yet been fully documented and illuminated," argues Davis. "There is more than ample evidence that [black people] consistently refused to succumb to the all-encompassing dehumanization objectively demanded by the slave system."[7]

Indeed, the historical references to Nat Turner's insurrection or to

---

6. "The Estrangement Effect in Sherley Anne Williams' *Dessa Rose,*" 21, 22.
7. "Reflections on the Black Woman's Role in the Community of Slaves," 9, 6.

Cinque's staged revolt aboard the slave ship *Amistad* attempt to isolate these incidents as rare acts of insolence. But as Davis points out, these acts were far from isolated. They were, in fact, part of a larger structure of resistance embedded in the slave community. "The reality, we know now, was that these open rebellions erupted with such a frequency that they were as much a part of the texture of slavery as the conditions of servitude themselves," contends Davis. "And these revolts were only the tip of the iceberg: resistance expressed itself in other grand modes and also in the seemingly trivial forms of feigned illness and studied indolence."[8]

Davis's attention to the wider spectrum of resistive acts performed daily by African and African American people allows us to consider, side by side, those feats accomplished by Harriet Jacobs and Denmark Vesey, or Harriet Tubman and Gabriel Prosser. And, as Earl Conrad points out, even Harriet Tubman's role in the fight against slavery has been grossly minimized. Tubman is traditionally credited with making up to nineteen trips into the South to free more than three hundred slaves. But her accomplishments far exceed this limited characterization. In addition to freeing slaves, Tubman was also head of the Intelligence Service throughout the Civil War in the Department of the South, and she is the only American woman to lead black and white troops on the field of battle.[9] Her work with other leaders in the antislavery movement (Martin Delany and Frederick Douglass, for example) has been continually overlooked.

Similarly omitted from historical discussions are the less visible day-to-day occurrences of other forms of subtle resistance performed by black slave women. Those black women who, for example, poisoned their masters' food or set fire to their houses are seldom mentioned.[10] Harriet Jacobs's own courageous attempts to elude the sexual exploitations of her master point directly to her grandmother's limited but successful efforts to evade the dehumanizing effects of chattel bondage by challenging its economic supremacy; she is seldom acknowledged for these efforts. Critical omissions such as these led writers like Williams to speculate about the interior lives of fugitive slaves and to consider, artistically, the role of black slave women in the fight against slavery.

---

8. Ibid., 6.
9. Conrad, "I Bring You General Tubman," 4.
10. See Aptheker's *American Negro Slave Revolts* for incidents of two slave women convicted and executed in 1740 and 1776 for acts of arson. See the same study for the 1803 case of Margaret Bradley, a slave woman convicted of poisoning two white people.

Williams's novel is influenced by the actual case of a pregnant black woman from Kentucky who was sentenced to die in 1829 for her help in leading an uprising on a slave coffle but was kept alive because of the impending birth of her baby. Williams's narrative begins where the historical story ends as she has her protagonist escape from prison and seek refuge on the plantation of a slave mistress who provides sanctuary for runaway slaves.[11] What makes Williams's literary journey of interest to this critic is her focus on the intimate details of Dessa's life prior to her incarceration: her familial and communal ties are introduced to the reader, as is the relationship she shares with her lover, Kaine, whose baby she is carrying. By making this relationship the primary motivation behind Dessa's desire to stay alive, Williams shifts the focus away from the larger political and social concerns associated with the discussions of slavery as these issues become embedded in Dessa's quest for self-fulfillment and human recognition. Williams invites us to consider how a woman like Dessa might have assessed her world and her situation. The result is a novel that posits the slave's narrative as a contested site as various "interests" compete for the right to articulate *the* story of the bonded individual by claiming ownership of the slave body.

Williams's novel keenly portrays these tensions. Its opening, a vivid reminder of the paradox inherent in being an African American female slave, frames a struggle of wills between Nehemiah, an "ethnographic sociologist" who wants to write a book entitled "The Roots of Rebellion in the Slave Population" utilizing "the darky's story," and Dessa, a fugitive slave who seeks to articulate her own narrative through a poignant recounting of her personal life. Dessa's insistence in telling who she is, how she lived, and who she loved is an attempt by her to construct a persona different from the one that classifies her as a "rebellious" slave under the gaze of Nehemiah and his pen.

Dessa's discursive battle with Nehemiah reveals, to a larger degree, the struggles inherent in articulating the claims of ownership over the bodily text of the slave. In his efforts to "textualize" the various areas of Dessa's body—mapping her psyche in terms of the slave revolt leader "profile," designating the scars on her person as bodily evidence of that profile—within the space of his personal journal, within the discourse(s) of "traditional History," and within regional southern history specifically, Nehemiah finds that the slave body "disturbs what was pre-

---

11. The character Rufel was based on a white woman in North Carolina who was said to have provided sanctuary for runaway slaves in 1830 (Aptheker, *American Negro Slave Revolts*).

viously considered immobile; it fragments what was thought unified."[12] As the person empowered to rewrite and "formally" name the qualities of the slave's identity, as someone empowered to "decipher" and "reconstruct" the text of the slave story through "scientific" and literary means, Nehemiah invests as much energy in trying to garner "the facts" about the insurrection as he does in studying the eyes, skin, and reproductive practices of Dessa. Nehemiah is frustrated that his "attempts to get the darky to talk had not been particularly fruitful" in getting her to reveal the "facts" about the revolt. Instead, Dessa tells her story of love and conveys to Nehemiah the anguish she experiences when she loses that love. Nehemiah, puzzled, comments, "there had been nothing in the darky's halting speech and hesitant manner to suggest the slave revolt leader she was convicted of being" (23). These apparent contradictions in what Nehemiah *observes* about Dessa and what he *believes* to be true about her character create an interesting dynamic in the narrative that allows Dessa to use her personal story as a site of resistance.

Williams's staging of Dessa's personal story as the countertext to Nehemiah's historically based narrative allows her to construct, for all intents and purposes, an authentic "speakerly" slave text within the framework of the novel, one that is centered around Dessa's body and voice. In this respect, Dessa not only becomes a literary granddaughter to figures like Douglass, Truth, and Tubman, who sought to author their own texts using the body as voice; she also becomes the literary embodiment of those attempts by other African American "authors," past and present, to legitimize oral history as a process of archival recovery. Williams's use of folk culture and folk history, her use of black dialect and what Mike Thelwell terms *para-language*—language based on "gesture, physical expression, and modulation of cadences and intonation"—creates a cultural/historical metanarrative which, as Mary Helen Washington has determined, "represents black dialect as having an integrity and power that standard English does not provide . . . it signifies a character's inner autonomy and ability to remain connected to sustaining black traditions" and also functions as a site of resistance for those who wish to counter the characterization of folk/oral history as inferior to the history of the written text.[13]

Critics including Henry L. Gates Jr. have commented on what they see as the "curious tension" that exists between the black vernacular

12. Michel Foucault, "Nietzsche, Genealogy, History," 82.
13. Thelwell, "Back with the Wind," 80; Washington, ed., *Black-Eyed Susans*, 228.

and the literate white text. As Gates writes in *The Signifying Monkey*, "This tension has been represented and thematized in black letters at least since slaves and ex-slaves met the challenge . . . to their humanity by literally writing themselves into being through carefully crafted representations in language of the black self." In designing a language that structures representations of the "self" under the rubric of slavery, the body becomes a formidable ally in the process of creating alternative avenues of self-expression. As Dolan Hubbard reiterates, "black expression begins and ends with the body. . . . [When] stripped of all else, the African American's own body became his prime artistic instrument." Thus the move from verbalized voice to the body as a "carefully crafted" representation of language seems to me a logical progression.[14]

But why is this move necessary? What is gained by crafting a language built on the artistic merits of the body? According to bell hooks, claiming the right to speak is essential to claiming the right to one's self, one's identity. It is the movement from silence to speech—from object to subject—that is "for the oppressed, the colonized, the exploited . . . a gesture of defiance that heals, that makes new life and growth possible." In a similar vein, African Americans claim their right to speak through a reclaiming of the black body—literarily and socially. In these ways, they "affirm and legitimize their psychological autonomy by telling the stories of their own lives." Not only do these actions grant them significant and figurative power over those individuals who wish to manipulate their stories for personal gain (as is the case with Dessa and Nehemiah), but in detailing "the processes of plot construction, characterization, and designation of beginnings and endings—in short the process of authorship"—these "authors" also provide for themselves "a measure of authority unknown to them in either real or fictional life."[15]

In noting how Williams addresses these issues in her novel, the concept of "voice" becomes framed in a context in which the struggle to define one's self centers on the act of figuratively (in Dessa's case) and literally (in Williams's case) writing a self in spite of other attempts to represent that self in competing social discourses. In Williams's novel, Dessa is seen as acting on her own behalf despite the fact that the root cellar has become her prison and the battleground in which the impending birth of her love child with Kaine vies with the impending

14. Gates, *Signifying Monkey*, 131; Dolan Hubbard, *The Sermon and the African American Literary Imagination*, 2.
15. Hooks, *Talking Back*, 9; Smith, *Self-Discovery and Authority*, 2.

"birth" of Nehemiah's text: "'Kaine—' She didn't know she had spoken aloud until she became aware of a voice in the stillness and knew it in the next instance as her own. How hoarse and raspy it sounded. She had not spoken above a whisper, except in muttered response to some white man's questions, in weeks. Caught in her own flow, she listened and continued, seeing as she spoke the power of Master" (54–55). Dessa speaks "the power of Master," allowing her to move from object to subject, allowing her to liberate her voice so that she can reaffirm her dignity as a human being.

Because Nehemiah views Dessa as property, as a text to be written on and written for within the discourse of slavery, Dessa *must* speak so that she can image herself differently from the persona Nehemiah ascribes to her in his journal. This dynamic can be more readily seen in the encounter between Nehemiah and Dessa as he tries to find out *why* Dessa rebelled. During this interrogation, Dessa recalls for Nehemiah the painful events that led up to Kaine's death:

> [W]hen Emmalina meet me that day, tell me Kaine done took a hoe at Masa and Masa done laid into him wid a shovel, bout bus in his head, I jes run . . . Kaine jes layin there on us's pallet, head seeping blood, one eye closed, one bout gone. Mamma Hattie sittin side him wipin at the blood. 'He be dead o' sold. Dead o' sold.' . . . Kaine jes groan when I call his name. I say all the names I know bout, thought bout, Lawd, Legba, Jesus, Conquerooo—anybody. Jes so's Kaine could speak. (12)

Nehemiah's callous question, "And what has that to do with you and the other slaves rising up against the trader and trying to kill white men?" and Dessa's retort—"'I kill white mens,' her voice overrode [Nehemiah's], as though she had not heard [him] speak. 'I kill white mens cause the same reason Masa kill Kaine. Cause I can'" (12)—underscores Nehemiah's ineptness at viewing Dessa as a complete person, as one who feels and expresses anger or pain, as one who feels and expresses the emotion of love. Dessa's ability to articulate her feelings—to speak into existence those wounds that *cannot* be seen—creates a dialogue of wills as the meaning of the term *violence* becomes reconstituted within the two separate texts, Nehemiah's and Dessa's. As Ann E. Trapasso so acutely determines in her analysis of this encounter, "Nehemiah's attempts to locate violence within those who are enslaved are undermined by the textual distinctions between anger as violence and anger as resistance. Nehemiah's anger . . . springs from a desire to dominate, whereas Dessa's anger propels her toward actions that eventually lead to her escape from slavery."[16] Nehemiah's text has us view Dessa as a "fiend," a "devil woman," one who belongs to a "species" whose females are as deadly as its males. Dessa grounds her definition of violence in that which is perpetrated upon her person and upon those whom she loves. It is her willingness to use her body and that of her unborn child as testimony of the horrors of slavery that amplifies her presence within her slave community and vilifies her image among the masters who seek to break her will. These concerns presuppose a dilemma in the novel that positions Dessa's body as the framework around which "Roots of Slave Rebellion" will be written and that stages, for Williams, the framework around which the text of resistance will be penned.

Unveiling the Story "Writ about Her Privates"

Williams is clever in that she stages the slave's *story* as the site of contested ownership in her novel. In doing so, she places the essence of the black slave community—its culture, its humanity, its very existence—at the core of the matter. It is also important to remember that the very language of slavery inscripted on the body of Dessa Rose—present in the form of those horrid scars she bears—is part of this storytelling process. As we are told in the novel, Dessa is lashed about her hips and legs (so as to not "impair her value") because she physically fought with her mistress. Dessa drew blood and had "bits of pink flesh beneath her fingernails" (57). After this incident, she is sold by her mistress to a slaveowner named Wilson who, knowing she was scarred, purchased her for four hundred dollars (remember that Dessa is with child).

It is on Wilson's slave coffle that the insurrection occurs. Partly it is due to the repeated rape of a mulatta slave named Linda, who "every night since Montgomery, one of the white men had taken into the bushes"; Dessa and the other slaves on the coffle "had been made wretched by her pleas and pitiful whimperings" (60). It is also partly due to the negligence of the coffle guard, who, "in his lust and alcoholic daze . . . had failed to secure the chain after he removed Linda from it" (60). It is in the ensuing battle, when the slaves chained to Linda realize they are unsecured and Linda, dress torn, appears in the clearing still clutching the rock she used to kill her rapist, that Wilson loses part of his arm.

16. "Returning to the Site of Violence: The Restructuring of Slavery's Legacy in Sherley Anne Williams's *Dessa Rose*," 224.

Blaming Dessa for his condition, he becomes "obsessed with seeing, and selling, the kid [Dessa] carried . . . [T]he court, fearing for Wilson's sanity, had delayed the darky's execution until she whelped" (15).

Wilson's "obsession" with Dessa's baby mirrors Nehemiah's pursuit of her as each man seeks to exploit Dessa for his own personal gain. This blatant will to disembody Dessa, to separate her person into two independent entities, marks the life of the female slave. In *Reconstructing Womanhood*, Carby explains, "As a slave, the black woman was in an entirely different relation to the plantation patriarch. Her reproductive destiny was bound to capital accumulation; black women gave birth to property and, directly, to capital itself in the form of slaves."[17] Thus, for the slave woman, not only is her identity formed within the confines of capitalism, but her slave body becomes the ground on which this monetary system of exchange is enacted. For Dessa, this means dying a social death not once but twice as her child's body becomes the weapon of choice to punish her for her desire to be free.

Similarly, when Dessa is sold to Wilson by her former mistress, Mary Terrell, who feared the child Dessa carried was her husband's, Dessa's body becomes the "text of indiscretion," that text read by Nehemiah and mistresses like Mary Terrell who consider the growing bellies of women like Dessa evidence that masters are sexually involved with their slave women. As Carby points out, "the effect of black female sexuality on the white male was represented in an entirely different form from that of the figurative power of white female sexuality. Confronted by the black woman, the white man behaved in a manner that was considered to be entirely untempered by any virtuous qualities; the white male, in fact was represented as being merely prey to the rampant sexuality of his female slaves."[18] These ideological assumptions left the black woman stigmatized as her body became the figurative border upon which this system gauged its own "moral" behavior. As is the case with Dessa, the female slave became the scapegoat for all the ills evident in the familial ranks of the slaveholding community as masters and mistresses alike exerted power over her person and over those whom she loved.

But Dessa is seen as challenging these structures of power within the context of her personal narrative as Williams creatively refigures Dessa's personal space—her mind, her womb, her body—as "building

17. *Reconstructing Womanhood*, 24–25.
18. Ibid., 27.

places,"[19] metaphoric chambers of transformation for the renewal of her spirit and her soul. Although Dessa's transformation is not actual because her body still bears the inscription of slavery and, literally, she is chained to the floor of the cellar (at least at the beginning of the novel), Dessa's mind—the incubus for her motive will—affords her the opportunity to reform the space that encloses her body, positioning her in a place that reaffirms her humanity. The reader is privy to Dessa's struggle to reclaim this part of herself, to re-vision herself within her own mind as she returns again and again to "the horror that scarred her inner thighs, snaking around her lower abdomen and hips in ropy keloids that gleamed with patent-leather smoothness" (56). These images hold Dessa captive in her own mind as she realizes the power and the permanency of their presence on her person. "I couldn't hide them no way," she states towards the end of the novel, "they told plain as day who I was" (246). It is in this moment that the narrative makes clear the explicit ways in which these scars affect/effect identity formation as Dessa is seen wrestling with the meaning of the marks inscripted on her person and encoded within the channels of her mind.

Yet, in the same motion, it is Dessa's return to these scars on her person that demonstrates her attempts to change her circumstance. "Impulsion from need," suggests John Dewey, "starts an experience that does not know where it is going." For Dessa, her impulse gives her the courage to live, to find that "loophole of retreat," that "ambiguity of meaning that extends to the literal loophole as well."[20] We see Dessa returning to those moments where her body is *un*marked, speaking to "the haunts that had crowded about her in the cellar" (51), providing her with the warmth of their presence. It is here that we see the *process* of self-definition and the refashioning of the meaning attached to the body as memory becomes the impetus for a reconnection with family, friends, and loved ones.

This struggle is most clearly depicted in the first section of the text (in the prologue in particular) but is evident throughout the novel. For example, Williams opens the narrative with a "wet dream" of sorts, an explicit lovemaking session Dessa imagines she is experiencing with Kaine. The "dry spasm" Dessa experiences in the dream's aftermath is directly linked to her imprisonment. In other words, Dessa is seen "recreating" her body by imagining herself loving her body and being

19. I borrow this term from Baker's *Workings of the Spirit*.
20. Dewey, "The Act of Expression," 486; Smith, *Self-Discovery and Authority*, 29.

loved. Williams notes this splitting of the self in the way she records Dessa's conscious efforts to return to her lover Kaine (her dream is italicized). These efforts to return to a "safe space" are important as they underscore Dessa's efforts to cultivate a spirit of resistance. Furthermore, Williams's need to return to the site of the body—to reinterpret the abstract and artificial dictates of cultural practices that reinforce the codes Carby speaks of in *Reconstructing Womanhood*—gives her the authority to reinterpret the realities of the African American slave woman by reinstituting another paradigm that emphasizes the communal and familial strengths of self-love. "In stressing the power dynamics underlying the very process of definition itself," notes black feminist critic Patricia Hill Collins, "black women question not only what has been said about African American women but the credibility and the intentions of those possessing the power to define."[21] In *Dessa Rose*, Williams's "questioning" of these paradigmatic structures leads her to craft a narrative that has Dessa "talking back" to those very structures that imposed sanctions on her right to be.

Framing the Historical Text

As the novel suggests, Nehemiah's efforts to understand and "historicize" the *story* of the insurrection are twofold. Initially, Nehemiah seeks to capitalize upon the "secret fears of non-slave holder and slave holder alike," who, like him, were afraid of "Negro rebellions" (19). The titles of his books, *The Masters' Complete Guide to Dealing with Slaves and Other Dependents* and *The Roots of Rebellion in the Slave Population and Some Means of Eradicating Them*, reveal the need to control this fear by controlling the source of this fear—black bodies. Similarly, the play on words and phrases like "some means of eradicating *them*" and "dealing with slaves and *other dependents*" (emphasis mine) points to a more sinister need to dominate, eliminate, and control persons of African descent. The term *other dependents* not only underscores the paternalistic nature of slavery but also sheds light on the twisted familial ties that had some slaveowners sleeping with their black daughters and selling their own children.

Nehemiah's desire to infiltrate this circle by developing an illustra-

---

21. *Black Feminist Thought: Knowledge, Consciousness, and the Politics of Empowerment*, 106.

tive example of the typical slave revolt leader is rooted in his need to overcome his humble beginnings, for "[h]e freely acknowledged that his own father had been a mechanic, owner of a small wheelworks in Louisville, . . . [but] Nehemiah was drawn to the wealthy planters because they possessed many of the objects of his taste, the clothing and jewelry that delighted the eye, the foods that enchanted the tongue, the houses and furnishings that charmed and gratified some inner sense of continuity and style" (18). Thus the class structure of the South was inextricably tied to the trafficking of human beings, and, as author, Nehemiah could enter this class by *writing* about the handling of slaves without having owned slaves himself.

But in *writing* the story of slave rebellion, Nehemiah discovers that the system of slavery has encoded within its ranks its own method of recording the history of the rebellious slave. Nehemiah notes, "though the darky had no scars or marks of punishment except on her rump and the inside of her flanks—places only the most careful buyer was likely to inspect—these bespoke of a history of misconduct" (13). The etching of this history upon the body of the subject for which it speaks contests, in Dessa's case, the outward manifestations, or the "lack of" scars Nehemiah initially observes on her body. As he explains, "Neither the attack nor the scars were mentioned in her description in the coffle manifest"—a written chronicle of each slave's ownership in bondage. This conflict between what is seen—the scars between her thighs and around her hips—and what is not seen—that information missing from the coffle manifest—is masked in the very fabric of this system's bartering codes and leads Nehemiah to speculate "how many others on Wilson's ill-fated slave coffle had . . . similar histor[ies] writ about their privates?" (13). His desire to expose these private writings inscripted on her body, those writings Mae Henderson calls the "master's code," causes him to question "the obvious complicity between slave trader and slave owner in the resale of a dangerous slave" (14). For Nehemiah, the omission "of a darky's mean streak went beyond sharp dealing and bordered on outright fraud" (14).

But here again we find a play on words, and here again the reader must return to the site of the scar. As we learn through Nehemiah, the scars "on [Dessa's] rump and the inside of her flanks . . . bespoke of a history of misconduct" (13). This evidence of malfeasance—bound in the language of the scar—not only functions as a signifier of Dessa's desire to resist bondage but also speaks directly to the issue of writing the presence of her body *in* the language of slavery. This language articulates that which cannot be seen, the *motive* will of the slave. Because intangible emotions like "anger" cannot be qualified in physical terms but instead are *manifested* in physical terms, Dessa's scars become a testament of her will. Similarly, I would argue that Nehemiah's need to *know* the language inscribed on her body, his need to *transcribe* this language of slavery into a form known by himself and his reading public, establishes the slave body and its scars as a viable text.

As is demonstrated in Williams's novel, the process of "othering" continually positions the black body as text—as symbolic of everything non-American. Coupled with this fact is the concern that certain cultural narratives were/are programmatically refused. Hayden White, in commenting on the value of narrativity and its representation of reality, observes,

> To raise the question of the nature of narrative is to invite reflection on the very nature of culture and possibly, even on the nature of humanity itself. So natural is the impulse to narrate, so inevitable is the form of narrative for any report of the way things *really* happened, that narrativity could appear problematical only in a culture in which it was absent—absent or, as in some domains of contemporary Western intellectual and artistic culture, programmatically refused.[22]

This sentiment is particularly telling when you consider that Dessa's efforts to humanize her story—to connect it to family and loved ones— are summarily rejected by Nehemiah in his pursuit of the "real" story behind the slave insurrection. At one point in the narrative Nehemiah wonders, "were darkies the subject of romance, . . . smiling at his own whimsy" (35), as if to question the fact that black slaves loved and were loved. It is at this point in the narrative that Dessa's body also serves as a rhetorical tool for translating what Hayden White calls "*knowing* into *telling*." As White observes, "We may not be able to fully comprehend specific thought patterns of another culture, but we have relatively less difficulty *understanding* a story coming from another culture." There is power in telling. And in fashioning a "human experience into a form assimilable to structures of meaning that are generally *human* rather than *culture*-specific,"[23] Williams humanizes the plight of the fugitive slave as she carves out a tale of resistance based on what White allows

22. "The Value of Narrativity in the Representation of Reality," 5.
23. Ibid., 3.

us to see as the universal language of humanity. Focusing on Dessa's body makes her discussion intimate as the flesh becomes symbolic of what makes her "human." It is through her body (and that of her unborn child) that she "speaks" the universal languages of pain, of fear, of love, and of anger. The resulting tension created in the narrative between Nehemiah's vision of history and Dessa's version of (her)story hinges on the fact that in order for Nehemiah to write *his* story of the fugitive slave, he must acknowledge, read, and understand the scars on Dessa's body, for here is where *the* story lies—sealed in the delicacy of her femininity, cloaked in "that part of the past [that] lay sealed in the scars between her thighs" (58).

The Public and Private of the Matter

The location of the marks on Dessa's body is important as they bespeak of a more sinister effort to "relegate," in Mae Henderson's estimation, "the black woman to the status of discursive object, or spoken subject."[24] Williams describes Dessa's disfigurement in terms of "deep scars plowed through her pubic region so no hair would ever grow there again" (154). In another instance, Dessa's scars are said to "look like a mutilated cat face" (166). This active sculpting of the body typifies an attempt by the master to permanently control Dessa's ability to "reproduce"; in this instance it happens to be hair in her pubic region. Secondarily, I would argue that this marking of the body also presents another instance of violent efforts being made to control the "speech" the slave body utters by actively writing on the surface of the body itself.

In *Dessa Rose*, not only is this "response" to Dessa's desire to change her slave condition directly manifested in the scars she bears, these scars also signal, according to Henderson, "an attempt to inscribe the sign *slave* in an area that marks her as *woman*."[25] These discursive attempts to culturally reorder the parameters of the *meaning* of Dessa's body by literally etching the public discourse of slavery onto the private area "that marks her as woman" underscore the multiple ways slavery sought to recharacterize the image of the black slave woman through a violent muting of her embodied voice. When you consider the fact that slave women were invisible in the eyes of the law (they could not cry "rape,"

24. "Speaking in Tongues: Dialogics, Dialectics, and the Black Woman Writer's Literary Tradition," 26.
25. Ibid.

for such pleas went unheard) and were considered unworthy to be called "women" based on the philosophical tenets of the cult of true woman-hood (for surely *they* could not be considered virtuous by any stretch of the imagination), scarring *this* area only magnifies these wounds "writ about her privates."

Yet here is where we see a collapse of the discursive fields of private and the public, of past and present, as they relate to the interpretative reading of Dessa's physical scars within the slave community. In view-ing the narrative Williams frames around the bodily presence of Dessa Rose, binary constructs such as voice and silence, presence and absence, public and private become part of the discourse that defines who she is and how her body and its inscriptions function dialogically in the sys-tem of slavery. For example, as Dessa's "private" scar is read in the pub-lic sphere by other slaves in the area, it becomes part of the communal discourse that surrounds the oral history of the slave rebellion in which she participates. The scar is the material evidence of Dessa's motive will. At one point in the novel, another runaway slave, Harker, relays to Rufel the circumstances surrounding Dessa's imprisonment: "They'd just about whipped that dress off her and what hadn't been cut off her— dress, drawers, shift—was hanging round her in tatters or else stuck in them wounds" (143). When the authenticity of this narrative is ques-tioned (Rufel asks him, "How do you know? . . . How you come to *see* all this?"), Harker validates his claims based on his *eyewitness* accounts of Dessa's torture: "I was there," he declares. "I *seen* her when she come out the box" (143, emphasis mine). This testimony, when juxtaposed against Rufel's initial reading of Dessa's body, "That wench don't have a scar on her back" (142), and Harker's intuitive reading of Rufel's in-terest in Dessa's story, "The mistress have to see the welts in the darky's hide, eh?" (147), underscores the overall tenor of Williams's narra-tive: that some stories aren't believed unless one *sees* the "body of evi-dence"—the actual scars on the body.

Similarly, Nehemiah's complicity in exploiting this "private" history for personal gain—turning what is essentially a private conversation between two individuals into a material substance (a book) ready for public consumption—only serves to highlight the manner in which the inscriptions of the pen, like the inscriptions of the whip, sought to re-produce the meaning of black female subjection. Dessa's ability to keep Nehemiah at bay by denying him access to her story is an effort on her part to recoup that which has been violated in the public sphere. This inversion of public and private space renders Nehemiah impotent at several moments in the novel as Dessa continually leads him "back to the same point as the previous session [where] he had taken notes on nothing save the names she called in her first burst of speech" (34). These moments occur during Dessa's initial interrogation at the beginning of the narrative when Nehemiah has trouble "translating" into "language" certain "unfamiliar" idiomatic phrases Dessa speaks, and at the end of the narrative when Nehemiah's "literate" male text is made "illegible" by another black woman, Aunt Chloe, as he tries to reimprison Dessa based on the information he has "reconstructed" in his journal.

Nehemiah's attempts, however, to claim ownership of Dessa's body based on the discursive and material power he holds in the notations in his journal—"I know this darky, I tell you; I know her very well . . . I got her down here in my book" (254)—turns on his (in)ability to place his written text next to Dessa's inscribed bodily text. In other words, Nehemiah is unable to publicly translate the "secret" writings of Dessa's body, nor is he able to *verify* his writings based on *her* text. Aunt Chloe's role in protecting Dessa's "secret" points to her unwillingness to acknowledge the signs of the master's script imprinted on the flesh of Dessa's body. Although Aunt Chloe is blind, she is able to see what Nehemiah can't see: Dessa's private text.

One could also say that Aunt Chloe's behavior was motivated by another factor: money. In a clever twist of the narrative, Nehemiah's failure to recapture Dessa comes at the hands of the very thing he sought to acquire based on the public production of her story. But these assumptions undermine Dessa's own prowess in keeping her story veiled. As Deborah McDowell so aptly concludes, "Dessa has avoided the public exposure [of her story] as fiercely as she has hidden her bodily scars. To expose them is to expose the horrors of victimization, to participate symbolically in a slave auction—to be publicly exhibited, displayed." For McDowell, Dessa's ability to conceal her story is "a radical act of ownership" in that she stakes claim "over her own body/text in a system that successfully stripped slaves' control over this, their most intimate property, . . . [in this way] Dessa's body is *her* text and, owning it, she holds the rights to it."[26]

Ironically, McDowell's reflections on Dessa's desire to control that most intimate part of herself—her body—can also be applied to

26. "Negotiating between Tenses: Witnessing Slavery after Freedom—*Dessa Rose*," 154.

Williams in that she, too, stakes claim to the text of the slave body. As she writes in her author's note, "I now own a summer in the 19th century," and in owning this summer she, too, commits "a radical act of ownership" in a literary tradition that has, more often than not, continued to violate the humanity of African Americans by obscuring the horrors of slavery and neglecting to demonstrate their agency within its ranks. Williams's "meditation on history" allows us not only to apprehend that other history but to consider, as well, "how many others . . . have similar histor[ies] 'writ about their privates'?"

Four

Dis-Membered to Re-Member

Bodies, Scars, and Ritual in Toni Morrison's *Beloved*

> And the purpose of making her [Beloved] real is making history possible, making memory real—somebody walks in the door and sits down at the table so you have to think about it.
>
> —Toni Morrison, "In the Realm of Responsibility"

If *Dessa Rose* represents, for Williams, a "meditation on history," then Toni Morrison's fifth novel, *Beloved*, represents, for Morrison, the very materialization of that history. Morrison weaves a haunting tale of past and present remembrances, of futures contemplated in the here and in the afterlife. Set in the post–Civil War era, the novel focuses on one community of ex-slaves who are drawn together by a common horror— their memories of slavery. Polyrhythmic in its narrative dimensions, the novel revolves around the life of one particular ex-slave, Sethe, who, as a fugitive, cut the throat of her infant daughter in order to prevent her from being sold back into slavery. Haunted by the guilt of this act, and the violent recollections of her former life in slavery, Sethe is literally consumed by these memories. The fleshly manifestation of her dead daughter some fifteen years later makes *Beloved* a unique literary venture; it is as much a story about history as it is a tale of ghosts and haunted houses. But Morrison's ghost appears in the flesh, and this specter proves that Sethe's memories are not her own; they have taken on their own life. The resulting literary interplay is powerful. It is as disheartening as it is hopeful; it is likewise as judgmental as it is understanding. In the end, Morrison not only creates a novel that questions our conceptions of what is "real" and what is known about the *human* conditions of the enslaved; she also gives voice to the "disremembered and unaccounted for,"[1] those overlooked and underseen in the recorded histories of slavery.

Like Williams, Morrison responds to a literary call that seeks to restore some continuity to a cultural history fragmented and undertold at best. Both writers articulate, to some degree, the daily struggles to be free both mentally and physically once the body has been marked. Their focus on the interior lives of enslaved African Americans makes their portraits of these individuals three-dimensional. That is, their narratives provide a countertext for generic depictions of *slaves*, a term that by its very nature signifies *sameness*. But Morrison takes Williams's literary exploration a step further: she makes her protagonist's story the center of a communal healing that must acknowledge its *shared* historical legacy. Sethe's private pain, amplified in the flesh of Beloved, begins a process of recovery that acknowledges the "Negro grief packed to the rafters" of every "house in the country" (5). In the process, Sethe's struggle to restructure her life and that of her daughter Denver, under the burden of these memories, forms a communal bond that is both transformative and transcendent in its ability to aid this community in forming new relationships in the shadow of these legacies.

Morrison has said that the idea for her novel came from "two or three little fragments of stories" that she had "heard from different places."[2] One such "fragment" involved a newspaper clipping about a fugitive slave named Margaret Garner who in January 1856 escaped from Kentucky with her four children, her husband, and two other individuals, across the Ohio River and into Cincinnati, where they sought refuge at the residence of her mother-in-law. Shortly thereafter they were missed and subsequently tracked to Cincinnati by their masters, Archibald K. Gaines and John Marshall. According to Samuel J. May, Gaines procured the necessary warrants from U.S. Commissioner John L. Pendery and proceeded to the residence where the fugitives were concealed. Upon arriving at the residence, he asked the fugitives to surrender. When they did not, the deputy and his officers broke open the door and were met with gunfire. Conflicting reports state that Garner's husband wounded one of the officers before being overpowered himself. Seeing

---

1. Morrison, *Beloved*, 274; subsequent references to this novel will appear in the text.
2. Gloria Naylor, "A Conversation: Gloria Naylor and Toni Morrison," 586.

the futility of attempting to escape, Margaret tried to kill her four children and herself. She succeeded in killing one; the other children were injured, and before she could take her own life, the officers overpowered her. Margaret was subsequently tried and convicted and returned to her master.[3]

What struck Morrison about this case became clearer when she read another story in Camille Billops's *The Harlem Book of the Dead*, which featured photographs of Harlem funerals taken by James Van Der Zee. In examining Van Der Zee's phototexts, Morrison was moved by the story of an eighteen-year-old girl who was killed while dancing at a party. Apparently, she was shot (with a silencer) by her ex-boyfriend or someone who was jealous. When questioned about who had shot her, this young lady repeatedly stated, "I'll tell you tomorrow," more than likely so that the assailant could get away. The young lady died shortly thereafter without divulging the name of her assailant. In the foreword to Billops's book, Morrison wrote: "The narrative quality, the intimacy, the humanity of his photographs are stunning . . . one can only say 'How living are his portraits of the dead.' So living, so 'undead.'"[4]

Morrison's fascination with the "undead" would find its way into many of her writings, including her 1973 novel *Sula* (where Sula speaks after her death) and her critical essay on the "rootedness" of African ancestors, whom she argues speak from their forgotten place in history. But it is in *Beloved* that she masters this subject, weaving two strands of historical material—the Garner case and the Van Der Zee phototext—into one complex and haunting tale. Sethe's story becomes *their* story as the "undead" become articulate in Morrison's novel. Specifically, the dead daughter in the Garner case is imagined to have come back in adult form (as the character Beloved) to question her mother's motives for killing her. Morrison believes this daughter is the only one who can question her mother and demand of her the answers she sought. In the interim, Beloved becomes the filter through which the internal suffering of the slave is made plain, and the novel itself becomes the vehicle through which a nation "sees" itself.

3. The ending to the Garner story is at best vague. Some critics believe she tried to kill herself again with her other daughter on a boat ride back to her former master's plantation. Others believe that she died of typhoid fever. For an interesting glimpse into the Garner case, see Steven Weisenburger's *Modern Medea: A Family Story of Slavery and Child-Murder from the Old South*.
4. Toni Morrison, foreword to Camille Billops, *The Harlem Book of the Dead*.

Unspeakable Things Spoken

Morrison's writing of *Beloved* stemmed from multiple impulses. On one level, she wanted to explore, as an artist, the dynamic of human relationships, particularly the bond between mother and child, in an effort to uncover those things that would make "a woman love something other than herself so much . . . she would rather kill them, have them die" than to "see them hurt [or] see them sullied." Morrison's literary journey echoes the sentiments of nineteenth-century writers such as Harriet Jacobs who felt "death was better than slavery" for their children.[5] To understand this posture, one must revisit the horrible conditions of slavery, and it is on this level that *Beloved* functions as a written testament, a literary invocation of the ways in which slavery irrevocably changed these maternal bonds.

Those things repressed in Jacobs's own narrative become expressly pronounced in Morrison's fictional account. Morrison's insistence on remembering these women through an unveiling of the true *horrors* of slavery provides not only a context for understanding a slave mother's motives for death but also a forum for understanding the national and cultural implications of her own novel. As Morrison states in a 1989 interview:

> There is no place you or I can go, to think about or not think about, to summon the presences of, or recollect the absences of slaves; nothing that reminds us of the ones who made the journey and of those who did not make it. There is no suitable memorial or plaque or wreath or wall or park or skyscraper lobby. There is no 300 foot tower. There's no small bench by the road. There is not even a tree scored, an initial that I can visit or you can visit in Charleston or Savannah or New York or Providence or, better still, on the banks of the Mississippi. And because such a place does not exist (that I know of), the book had to.[6]

Morrison's desire to concretize the experiences "of the ones who made the journey and of those who did not," to make palpable those incidents in the life of a slave that were "things past telling," signals her response to a complex literary and historical tradition framed around absences. As Nellie McKay suggests, Morrison's publication was "a con-

5. Naylor, "A Conversation: Naylor and Morrison," 587; Brent, *Incidents*, 63.
6. Robert Richardson and Toni Morrison, "A Bench by the Road."

scious act toward healing a painful wound: a studied memorial to the great social wrong of the enslavement of Africans. Her powerful words, on behalf of millions, give voice to a profound lament: the absence of a historical marker to remind us never to let this atrocity happen again. For its absence has neither erased nor diminished its pain; rather, it reminds us only of itself: of what is missing."[7]

What is missing is that which has been buried and repressed or consciously exorcised from the public recantations of slavery. "In some ways," critic Mae Henderson reminds us, "the texts of the slave narratives can be regarded as classic examples of the 'return of the repressed,' primarily because the events relating to violence and violation (which are self-censored or edited out) return in 'veiled allusions.'"[8] These "veiled allusions" are unmasked in Morrison's novel through a series of repetitive accountings of the dead and the forgotten. Much of the narrative centers around naming the wounds and renaming the wounded. The roll call is impressive: Stamp Paid, formally known as Joshua, whose obsession with "a red ribbon knotted around a curl of wet woolly hair, clinging still to its bit of scalp" (180), reveals more about "the gift" he gave his master's son than it does about the nameless little girl it belonged to; Baby Suggs, whose slave name, Jenny Whitlow, signifies not only the loss of her body, with its "busted legs, back, head, eyes, hands, kidneys, womb, and tongue" (87), but also the loss of her husband and seven of her children (the eighth child, Halle, having worked all of his Sundays to free her, is left to smear butter on his face after witnessing the violation of his wife, Sethe); and finally "crawling already?" who is renamed Beloved *after* her death by a mother who thought her only option was murder. The stories behind the wounds on the psyches of many of these characters are as important as the scars evident on the flesh itself. Freedom for these individuals rests on tracing the multiple figurations of the scar—from its fleshly denotation to its cerebral connotation.

The tree on Sethe's back is endemic of this process as her body functions as a template for viewing the rootedness of mental sufferings. As the narrator concludes, "In all of Baby's life, as well as Sethe's own, men and women were moved around like checkers. Anybody Baby Suggs knew, let alone loved, who hadn't run off or been hanged, got rented out, loaned out, bought up, brought back, stored up, mortgaged, won,

7. McKay, introduction to *Toni Morrison's* Beloved: *A Casebook*, 3.
8. "Toni Morrison's *Beloved:* Re-membering the Body as Historical Text," 63.

stolen or seized." But more disturbing, what she considered "the nasti-ness of life was the shock she received upon learning that nobody stopped playing checkers just because the pieces included her children" (23). Baby Suggs's sentiments are echoed in a powerful passage that finds Sethe explaining to her surviving daughter, Denver, why she killed her sister, Beloved. For Sethe, what was far worse than death was the realization that "anybody white could take your whole self for anything that came to mind. Not just work, kill, or maim you, but dirty you. Dirty you so bad you couldn't like yourself anymore. Dirty you so bad you for-got who you were and couldn't think it up." This realization terrifies Sethe because "[t]he best thing she was, was her children [and] she could never let it happen to her own . . . her beautiful, magical best thing— the part of her that was clean." Although Sethe has seen and experi-enced horrible things, has often wondered "whether the headless, feet-less torso hanging in the tree with a sign on it was her husband or Paul A" (251), she has never quite relinquished the hope envisaged in her children. That is, until her memories appear in the flesh. Sethe's lament is therefore Baby Suggs's lament, and Paul D's bewitchment, and Ella's anger at having spent her puberty in a house "where she was shared by father and son, whom she called 'the lowest yet'" (256). The horror of these situations lies in the *telling*, or in what Barbara Solomon calls the "elliptical, ambiguous, and repeated descriptions of events."[9] It is here that these symphonies of voices speak the unspeakable, with power, with passion, with conviction.

Morrison's meticulous attention to detail—to revealing, at the most basic level, the irony of life and death for African Americans at the close of the nineteenth century—makes *Beloved* more than just a slave's nar-rative. In many ways, I regard Morrison's novel as revisionist in its ap-proach to the era of Reconstruction, an era that has been creatively and critically neglected because of its proximity to slavery. Morrison's cre-ative achievements echo the efforts of predecessors such as W. E. B. Du Bois, whose *Black Reconstruction* anticipated the findings of modern scholarship. As Eric Foner states, Du Bois's 1935 study closed with "an indictment of a profession whose writings had ignored the testimony of the principal actor in the drama of Reconstruction—the emancipated slave—and sacrificed scholarly objectivity on the altar of racial bias."[10] Morrison's novel answers Du Bois's call, bridging the gap between slav-

9. *Critical Essays on Toni Morrison's* Beloved, 5.
10. *Reconstruction: America's Unfinished Revolution, 1863–1877*, xxi.

ery and Reconstruction as she presents them as joint spheres of existence, not dissimilar states of being. This blurring of the boundaries allows Morrison to present a more complex view of the sociopsychological and sociocultural experiences of African Americans. As black culture specialist James Newton reiterates, Morrison's novel provides a small opening into an era almost forgotten in current and past discussions of the African American experience. Of particular interest to Newton is Morrison's focus on the wandering black man, a man displaced by his social, economic, and political disfranchisement. Newton feels Morrison's novel may provide a glimpse into the legacy of this man's journey to find himself and his place among women-centered African American communities. Likewise, McKay asserts that Morrison "takes large steps beyond the genre of the slave narrative tradition to excavate, then to reclaim and re-create, the hitherto hidden lives of those who survived the ravages of the inhuman institution."[11]

These social critiques allow Morrison the opportunity to interrogate particular notions of pedagogy and epistemology; that is, she questions the very history of knowledge and the universal manner in which this knowledge becomes a *known* national history. Those "unspeakable things unspoken" then become the nationalist tendencies reified in the very way we look at and record history, in the very way we read and acknowledge one's humanity in that history. In order to disentangle the deeply encoded rejection of certain histories in our culture, Morrison must embark on a literary journey that restores to the forefront of American cultural studies that which has been *dis*remembered. As she explains:

> The gap between Africa and Afro-America and the gap between the living and the dead and the gap between the past and the present does not exist. It's bridged for us by our assuming responsibility for people no one's ever assumed responsibility for. They are those that died en route. Nobody knows their names, and nobody thinks about them. In addition to that, they never survived in the lore; there are no songs or dances or tales of these people. The people who arrived—there is lore about them. But nothing survives about . . . that.[12]

11. Introduction to Beloved: *A Casebook*, 10.
12. Marsha Darling, "In the Realm of Responsibility: A Conversation with Toni Morrison," 5.

This social (and Morrison would argue cultural) *dis*recognition stems from an inability to fully recognize the *horror* of slavery. This horror, found in the fragmented recollections of daily life, haunts the individual and collective memory to the extent that any formation of a new identity in the *aftermath* of slavery becomes predicated upon remembering and *dis*remembering these moments. "There is a necessity for remembering the horror," Morrison explains, "in a manner in which it can be digested, in a manner in which the memory is not destructive." But herein lies the paradox of *remembering* itself. "I thought this has got to be the least read of all the books I'd written," Morrison told reporter Bonnie Angelo, "because it is about something the characters don't want to remember, I don't want to remember, black people don't want to remember, white people won't want to remember."[13] Morrison expresses this tension within the very pages of her novel as she takes the reader back and forth in time, through fragmented recollections of the personal and communal histories of her characters, reenacting what Bernard Bell calls the *socialized ambivalence* of double consciousness.[14] To say the least, *Beloved* is about reconciling these warring sides, the freed body and the enslaved soul/psyche, as all of these individuals attempt to restructure their lives, their communities, their familial relationships in the aftermath of chattel bondage. To her credit, Morrison is able to articulate such nontangible concerns in a literary form that makes the wounds of the mind and spirit visually accessible not only to the reader but to her characters as well. This latter confrontation provides the framework for understanding the sheer energy of Morrison's narrative as the past and present collide in the embodied form of Beloved.

Memory as Flesh

Morrison has said that she wanted Beloved to be a filter, "another kind of dead which is not spiritual but flesh, which is, a survivor from the true, factual slave ship."[15] Beloved's introduction into the novel as a "fully dressed woman" who "walks out of the water" and her soliloquy

13. Ibid., 5; Angelo, "The Pain of Being Black: An Interview with Toni Morrison," 121–22.
14. "*Beloved:* A Womanist Neo-Slave Narrative; or 'Multivocal Remembrances of Things Past,'" 7.
15. Darling, "In the Realm of Responsibility," 5.

in the later chapters of the book are attempts to relive this experience via literature. In making Beloved *flesh*, Morrison makes this historical moment *tangible* as Beloved's physical frame becomes a material symbol of those bodies unaccounted for—those sixty million or more lost on various sea voyages between Africa and America. She is the conduit through which these disembodied victims of the Middle Passage gain a literate voice. Moreover, in making this memory "real," Morrison also "calls forth" other silenced narratives—those of the people of "broken necks, of fire-cooked blood and black girls who had lost their ribbons" (181). It is Beloved's ability to serve as a host for these "other" spirits that makes her a complex entity within the narrative itself.

In her disembodied state, Beloved is the ghost that haunts 124 Bluestone Road, the "spiteful, baby venom" that wreaks havoc in the lives of those who reside there. Each of Beloved's family members "had put up with the spite in his own way, but by 1873 Sethe and her daughter Denver were its only victims." Sethe's sons, Howard and Buglar, had run away "the moment the house committed what was for him the one insult not to be borne or witnessed a second time" (3). For Buglar, it was a shattered mirror; for Howard, it was two tiny handprints that appeared in a cake. Baby Suggs dies shortly thereafter, a death (the narrative intimates) brought on by her disinterest in living a life whose "past had been like her present—intolerable" (4). When Paul D reappears in Sethe's life some years later and forces the "spirit" of Beloved out of the house, Beloved—as if responding to Paul D's command "you want to fight, come on!"[16]—reemerges in the flesh to resume her battle with the occupants in 124.

In her embodied state, Beloved is much more deadly, a material source to be reckoned with as she seeks solace from the woman who cut her throat some fifteen years earlier. But her battle with her mother comes only after she has driven Paul D from the house through a series of spiritual and sexual "negotiations." Once this is accomplished, Beloved sets her sights on Sethe as she reenacts Sethe's "too thick" love.

---

16. Many critics argue that Paul D performs the first "exorcism" in the novel. Trudier Harris, for example, argues, "Paul D *wills* Beloved's spirit away. His vocal masculine will is stronger than her silent, though sometimes noisy, desire. The power of his voice to command behavior, even that of spirits, is ultimately stronger than the spirit's desire to resist" ("*Beloved*: Woman, Thy Name Is Demon," 131). I agree with Harris's assessment of this scene, particularly since it provides a nice complement to the climactic scene of the thirty women praying outside Sethe's house. In short, the novel begins and ends with this ritualistic "clearing."

The parasitic relationship Beloved develops with her mother is chilling:

> Then it seemed to Denver the thing was done: Beloved bending over Sethe looked the mother, Sethe the teething child, for other than those times when Beloved needed her, Sethe confined herself to a corner chair. The bigger Beloved got, the smaller Sethe became; the brighter Beloved's eyes, the more those eyes that used never to look away became slits of sleeplessness. Sethe no longer combed her hair or splashed her face with water. She sat in the chair licking her lips like a chastised child while Beloved ate up her life, took it, swelled up with it, grew taller on it. And the older woman yielded it up without a murmur. (250)

Sethe's decline into a state of being that has Beloved assume the role of mother, and Sethe the role of child, underscores the manner in which the "*un*dead" differ from the "dead"; the "*un*dead" are roaming spirits, "unburied" entities who are called forth, as Margaret Atwood suggests, and kept alive by the passions of the living.[17] In Sethe's near mute stage, the novel suggests that painful memories themselves can superimpose their own overwhelming demands on the individual, rendering this person "silent" or "mute": the unspeakable *cannot* be spoken in this instance, not because the subject does not wish to speak but because there is no viable communicative system that affords this individual the opportunity to *fully* articulate the body's pain or, in this instance, the mind's pain. According to Elaine Scarry, the imprisoned body, "in its physical strengths, in its sensory powers, in its needs and wants . . . is made a weapon against [itself], made to betray [itself] on behalf of the enemy, made to be the enemy." This exploration of the body/soul split emphasizes the symbolic order of torture itself; the body and mind are made bipolar opposites: on one hand, the "goal of the torturer is to make the one, the body, emphatically and crushingly *present* by destroying it, and to make the other, the voice, *absent* by destroying it."[18] Moreover, the physical and verbal acts against the abused, formed in this elusive dialogue of body and voice, are "consciously and unconsciously acknowledged in the language of the torturers themselves." Screams then become answers to questions posed in a system that has the torturer "speak" for the empowered and the disempowered. But Scarry's assess-

17. "Haunted by Their Nightmares," 42.
18. *The Body in Pain: The Making and Unmaking of the World*, 48, 49.

ment applies primarily in those instances where the tortured and the torturer "communicate" in an act of wounding, an act "consciously or unconsciously acknowledged in the language of the torturers themselves."[19] The paradoxical nature of Beloved suggests the inadequacy of language, the inconsistency of desire, the fallibility of sustained passion of this magnitude. If Beloved indeed reminds certain characters of "something . . . look like [they] supposed to remember" (234)—that is, if she functions as memory itself—then Beloved's fear of disintegration represents the simultaneous experience of wanting to remember *and* wanting to forget:

> Beloved looked at the tooth and thought, This is it. Next would be her arm, her hand, a toe. Pieces of her would drop maybe one at a time, maybe all at once. Or on one of those mornings before Denver woke and after Sethe left she would fly apart. It is difficult keeping her head on her neck, her legs attached to her hips when she is by herself. Among the things she could not remember was when she first knew that she could wake up any day and find herself in pieces. She had two dreams: exploding, and being swallowed. (133)[20]

Here, Beloved seems to sense that her ability to stay "whole" rests on the insatiable appetites of others who want to see her remain before them as if to remind them of their own physical existence. Or, one may argue that Beloved's presence within the novel suggests a need to confront personal and communal memory, reimagining it, reordering it in an effort to claim ownership of that freed self once the physical body has been emancipated. To this end, Morrison's novel posits the concept of *re-memory* as a plausible avenue for the materialization of that freed self, and I would argue that Beloved's bodily appearance is a manifestation of this process. Her physical presence affords previously enslaved individuals a visual representation of that damaged slave psyche. In this regard, I view Beloved as a walking wound whose "healing" only comes from devouring the pain of others or, in some instances, inflicting pain

19. Ibid., 46.

20. Langston Hughes's poem "Harlem" seems particularly helpful in assessing Morrison's use of dreams—in this case a "dream" that has reappeared in the flesh. If Beloved represents the dreams of those who want to be remembered, if she represents the dreams of those still alive who want to forget a painful past too horrible to disremember, then she represents all those things mentioned in Hughes's poem: she is that dream that "festers like a sore . . . and sags like a heavy load."

so that those who receive it recognize their own. Hence, Beloved's existence represents the essence of *being;* she is the precipitation of the process "to be" and the epitome of the desire to exist in some form of wholeness as those who read her attempt to define themselves by *seeing* her and acknowledging their connection to her.

The novel traces the process of this journey in vivid fashion as Morrison establishes a link between public and private memories. Sethe remarks in an exchange with her daughter Denver, "Some things go. Pass on. Some things just stay. I used to think it was my rememory. You know. Some things you forget. Other things you never do. But it's not . . . even if I die, the picture of what I did, or knew, or saw is still out there," living, breathing, eating. When Denver asks her mother whether other people can see it, Sethe replies: "Oh yes. Oh, yes, yes, yes. Someday you be walking down the road and you hear something or see something going on. So clear. And you think it's you thinking it up. A thought picture. But no. It's a rememory that belongs to somebody else" (36).

In acknowledging this shared history, this shared pain, Sethe lays the groundwork for Beloved's appearance in the novel. Sethe's struggle to live with her painful memories gets "projected out" into the community as her personal experience creates an atmosphere of shared communal experiences. Sethe's external manifestations, embodied in the presence of Beloved, highlight the internal conflicts of many of the characters in the novel. Ella's connection to Sethe, for example, surfaces as Ella remembers her own jaded experience with motherhood. For others, Beloved's presence may well be read as the spiritual supplication of an ancestral past or a blending of two forms of spiritual expression—African and "Americanized" African—wherein Beloved's entry into this spirit world calls forth not only the river spirits but also those other restless spirits, "the people of the broken necks, of fire-cooked blood and black girls who had lost their ribbons" (181). This is the roaring Stamp Paid cannot decipher when he tries to knock at the door of 124. Thus I see Beloved not only as a function of Sethe's guilt, or a byproduct of selfish personal memories gone awry; she is also the bridge that joins the individual to the community or, in a larger sense, the bridge that joins personal history to communal history. The two are intricately linked in her fleshly form as she makes it possible to confront these remembrances in a manner that allows for the healing of some wounds.

This blending is nowhere more evident than when Ella and twenty-nine other women from the African American community return to

Sethe's house to extricate Beloved from its premises. Because these spirits have gathered over time, inhabiting various linguistic and cultural spaces, language itself becomes problematic to the extent that the women who perform the final exorcism must engage in a "call and response" dialogue with these restless spirits that does not privilege Western or African religions—it acknowledges an origin in the beginning when "there were no words. In the beginning was the sound, and they all knew what that sound sounded like." This sound allows these women to blend the essence of their painful experiences with that of their ancestors, forming, in effect, one united chorus of voices that builds one upon the other "until they found it" (259), the key that would allow them to recover and lay to rest the disembodied spirits of 124. The blending of the geographical spaces of water and land—of Africa and America through sound—serves to link the experiences of the past and the present communities in word and deed.

But Beloved's fleshly appearance also allows these women to visualize—to actually *see*—the pain Sethe is experiencing: "the singing women recognized Sethe at once and surprised themselves by their absence of fear when they saw what stood next to her. The devil-child" (261). In their ability to access Sethe's "rememory" they differ starkly from other members of that community who question whether Beloved actually exists. This clearing scene also lends itself to a more complex interaction between the past and the present—the very definition of rememory, I would argue—as these women confront not only Sethe's past but their own past as well: "when they caught up with each other, all thirty, and arrived at 124, the first thing they saw was not Denver sitting on the steps, but themselves. Younger, stronger, even as little girls lying in the grass asleep" (258). Thus their Edenlike visions of a younger self—triggered by the presence of Beloved—allow them to acknowledge a spirituality unencumbered by the experiences of slavery. In this way, their shared energy can reconnect body to soul in a manner that calls forth another being that counters the dismembered self created in chattel bondage.

Whether real or imagined, Beloved's presence directs critical attention to the remarkable process of creation, of developing agency where before there had been none. To *will* into existence that which cannot be seen—primarily the pain, the burden of a relinquished and splintered selfhood—Sethe, and likewise Morrison, becomes the midwife to a startling modality that shows "the movement of the mind both in recognizing its own *shape* and in maintaining that shape in the face of attack or change."[21] Morrison figures both the interiority and the exteriority of consciousness in ways that allow her to *texturize* the relationship between image and meaning. That is, narrativity becomes transformed into a configured, embodied image solidified through its association with "a thought picture." Re-memory is the still image moved through the power of *will*, much as a still photograph becomes an image in a slide show.

Morrison's fictive process can be usefully compared with Scarry's description of the transfiguration of pain into an objectified medium that allows others to see the interiority of that pain. "Though we may say," Scarry suggests,

> 'The ghost she speaks of exists only in her own mind,' the very fact that she has gotten us to speak that sentence means that the object, though unreal, is externalizable and sharable: she has made visible to those *outside* her own physical boundaries the therefore no longer wholly private and invisible content of her mind. What is remarkable is not that one person should enable another person to see a ghost (for this seldom happens), but that one person should routinely enable another person to *see the inside of his or her consciousness*.

In making this consciousness "visible," Morrison makes her characters speaking subjects as Beloved becomes the interior language of pain, externalized. According to Scarry, "the imagination's object is not simply to alter the external world, or to alter the human being in his or her full array of capacities and needs, but also and more specifically, to alter the power of alteration itself, to act on and continually revise the nature of creating."[22] In other words, Morrison's creation of Beloved offers another way to read the language of the scar itself as Beloved's inability to speak can be viewed as a manifestation not only of her young age at the time of her death but also of the inadequacy of language to fully articulate pain.

According to Morrison, there was a "complete erasure of all language that the victim or the oppressed had" during slavery. Instruments like "the bit" were created "to shut you up, so that you could not say, you could not talk back, you could not articulate a contrary position or do

---

21. Richard Ellmann, *The Consciousness of Joyce*, front jacket. Words in italics in this quote represent my own emphasis.

22. *Body in Pain*, 327 n. 4, 324.

any violence with your tongue or your words." For these reasons, I would argue, Morrison frequently ties her discussions of language to the body, or she centers them in the realm of sound (the "unspeakable unspoken") or the lack thereof (silence) in an effort to lay bare the complex systems of communication inherent in her text. Silence is its own language in *Beloved* as body becomes voice and voice becomes the signification of consciousness and of African Americans as speaking subjects. As Michael Silverblatt reminds us, there are several "witnessings" that occur in *Beloved* without voicings.[23] Denver's behavior and Halle's reaction to Sethe's violation underscore the complex nature of bearing witness, which is calling into existence that which cannot be spoken. His reaction, "the smearing of butter and its clabber all over his face because the milk they took is still on his mind" (71), leads one to speculate about the visual presentation of voice/language and the potency of "quiet noise."[24]

As Michael Awkward suggests elsewhere, the process of *reading* voice in literature should hinge not on *hearing* voice in its customary state but on viewing voice uniquely as the author or literary character in question presents it. In placing Halle's response within the context of Awkward's proposal, I do not wish to suggest that Halle *consciously* framed his answer. However, his role as protector and provider for his family was horribly distorted under the system of slavery. Surely the knowledge of this reality had to have had a detrimental effect on Halle's psyche. As Sethe concedes, "If he was that broken then, then he is also and certainly dead now" (70), this death being both literal (physical/spiritual) and figurative (social/political) as Halle's whereabouts after this incident are unknown. Halle's "witnessing" underscores that body language is a viable form of communication, a viable form of bearing witness to things beyond imagining.

For Ella, these imaginings take the form of a "hairy white thing [that] lived five days never making a sound" (258). As an inaudible scar, this child's bodily presence stands as a powerful reminder of the inarticulate nature of rape. Within the system of slavery, these atrocities are often muted by legal and social sanctions; the African American slave woman was not recognized as a human being under the law—she did not even

23. Silverblatt and Morrison, "The Writing Life: A Conversation between Michael Silverblatt and Toni Morrison."
24. I'm signifying here upon Mary Helen Washington's use of the term *quiet anger* in her analysis of Gwendolyn Brooks's *Maud Martha*. See "Taming All That Anger Down: Rage and Silence in Gwendolyn Brooks's *Maud Martha*."

have control over her own body. Ella's soundless child directs attention to this social edict as it simultaneously foregrounds a more haunting dialectic that places Ella's pain on the edge of language. As the narrative states, "Ella had been beaten every way but down. She remembered the bottom teeth she had lost to the brake and the scars from the bell were thick as rope around her waist" (258). These physical scars amplify the psychological wounds Ella bears as her child's inability to make a sound represents that "indeterminate space of imaginative experience" in her life.[25] Having spent her puberty being "shared by father and son, whom she called 'the lowest yet,'" Ella's journey has been one filled with comparisons between those acts of savagery directed at all African Americans and those of her own very personal experience. "A killing, a kidnap, a rape—whatever, she listened and nodded. Nothing compared to the 'lowest yet.'" Ella's connection to Sethe centers on this shared experience of hoping to keep the past at bay. As Ella states, "Sethe's crime was staggering and her pride outstripped even that; but she could not countenance the possibility of sin moving on in the house, unleashed and sassy . . . nobody needed a grown-up evil sitting at the table with a grudge" (256–57).

Although Ella refused to love the "hairy white thing" born of her repeated rapes, her narrative, coupled with Sethe's story of "too thick love," returns the reader to the structural current of Morrison's novel as the "dis-membered" is "re-membered" through the complex pragmatisms of external and inner speech. As Scarry concludes, "the human being who creates on behalf of the pain in her own body may remake herself to be one who creates on behalf of the pain originating in another's body; so, too, the human beings who create out of pain (whether their own or others') may remake themselves to be those who create."[26] In essence, we see what is meant by consciousness—or, in this case, the remaking of a consciousness—and Beloved, to some degree, functions as the literal formation of that process.

By placing the unseen wounds alongside the physical ones, Morrison suggests other ways to read the literal and figurative signs of the embodied slave narrative. The tree on Sethe's back represents but one

25. Silverblatt uses these words to define the place Morrison's fiction takes the reader—that space that cannot be defined, that space where words are inadequate clothing for the experiences of the heart ("The Writing Life," 3). I borrow from Silverblatt's comments when formulating my own thoughts on the expressiveness of the inaudible scar.

26. *Body in Pain*, 324.

manifestation; Beloved, I would argue, represents the other. In focusing on the marked bodies of African Americans, Morrison draws attention to the systematic use of language in slavery as the scar becomes an obvious signifier of the maliciousness of hatred, a fleshly reminder of the material inscription of violence. As Rafael Perez-Torres argues, "the language of slavery within *Beloved* is comprised of signs written with whips, fires, and ropes." These signs not only determine the production and meaning of language; they also reveal the relationship between the defined and the definer: "Morrison's narrative 'plays' not just with language but with the traces of ideology that leave their mark in language. . . . Language, never innocent of power, becomes in Morrison's text a central means by which power disperses itself." If, in Morrison's narrative, language is "never innocent of power," then it would follow that there is power in using language and power in refiguring a space from which the spoken for speak for themselves. I agree with Perez-Torres that the "defined do not entirely lack power. Those who live with the absence of power reserve to themselves the persistent practice of decoding and recoding signs."[27] In retelling the stories of slavery, in "decoding and recoding" the signs on the body, Morrison allows her characters to redefine themselves and thus reclaim their agency. This rhetorical move shapes the very way we read and write about the experiences of African American people as the master's script becomes the subject of, rather than the giver of, meaning.

Hauntingly enough, the passages in the novel where silence is reinvented as that space that responds to the violence of language, these quiet meditations, represent the most fascinating instances of voice recreation. It is at these times that "actions speak louder than words" as the participants use their bodies, often employing tactile motions in responding to what they witness. Three of these moments are connected with the viewing of Sethe's scar. Upon seeing the wounds upon Sethe's back, her mother-in-law, Baby Suggs, "hid her mouth with her hand . . . wordlessly, the older woman greased the flowering back and pinned a double thickness of cloth to the inside of the newly stitched dress" (93). Paul D "could think but not say, 'Aw, Lord, girl,'" once he saw what "the sculpture [on] her back had become" (17). Amy Denver is also "struck dumb" by this display on Sethe's back: "Amy unfastened the back of her dress and said, 'Come here, Jesus,' when she saw. Sethe guessed it must

27. "Knitting and Knotting the Narrative Thread: *Beloved* as Postmodern Novel," 696, 697.

be bad because after that call to Jesus Amy didn't speak for a while. In the silence of an Amy struck dumb for a change, Sethe felt the fingers of those good hands lightly touch her back. She could hear her breathing but still the whitegirl said nothing" (79). At each moment, language in its traditional sense seems unable to fully articulate a response for these acts visited upon the body. Silence, then, becomes an alternative site of human expression as these individuals attempt to heal Sethe's wounds with their hands. According to Henderson, "Significantly, Baby Suggs does *not* speak of the wounds on Sethe's back,"[28] as if to muffle, I would argue, the intensity and meaning of that language directed at Sethe. This is the silence that will not speak, that will not repeat that violence uttered with the whip.

The Inaudible Scar

Sethe's scar offers intriguing ways to view not only the *process* of scarring but also the aftermath of that process, the scar itself. If, in Awkward's estimation, the "inaudible voice" is a function of *action* rather than of *sound*,[29] then Morrison's use of silence within the novel invites another way to view the scar itself. Beloved's body, for example, serves as an embodied wound, an "inaudible" trauma whose function belies the narrative system that supports her very existence. She is movement itself, the expression that precipitates the oppressed's journey from object to subject(ivity). Conversely, when assessing the earlier analyses of Sethe's scar, for example, those who saw it were rendered speechless, or they used silence to refigure the meanings branding and/or whip-scars implied for their subjects. These interactions point up the dilemma of articulating a meaning, of finding a language for a scar that is "inaudible" or so painful that it exists beyond the realm of traditional linguistic systems. Paul D uses his mouth to touch every ridge and leaf on Sethe's back as if to "translate" the message inscribed there. Thus, touch becomes Paul D's way of communicating with Sethe, void of the weight of words as he attempts to reclaim Sethe's back for herself. Amy Den-

---

28. "Toni Morrison's *Beloved*," 69.

29. I borrow this term from Awkward's *Inspiriting Influences: Tradition, Revision, and Afro-American Women's Novels,* wherein he signifies upon Zora Neale Hurston's use of the term in her novel *Their Eyes Were Watching God.* I build upon Hurston and Awkward's use of the term in my reading of the presence of scars in *Beloved.*

ver not only uses her hands to heal but also alters the master's script by recoding the mark on Sethe's back: "It's a tree, Lu. A chokecherry tree. See, here's the trunk—it's red and split wide open, full of sap, and this here's the parting for the branches. You got a mighty lot of branches. Leaves, too, look like, and dern if these ain't blossoms. Tiny little cherry blossoms, just as white. Your back got a whole tree on it. In bloom" (79). In renaming this mark, Amy Denver signifies the possibility of imagining the scars of slavery as something other than what the master had in mind. Perez-Torres emphasizes, "The power to rename represents a reclamation of agency when many other venues are closed that would help the characters establish a sense of subjectivity."[30] This agency extends to Sethe when she names her daughter Denver, after the woman who saved her life and named her scar. These "genealogical revisions"[31] represent Sethe's attempts to construct alternative sites of identity outside the formal boundaries of slavery. Given the fact that masters name their property, and that even in the aftermath of slavery these names speak of that slave past, Denver's name represents the power language has to relocate and reidentify Sethe's familial genealogy.

But Sethe is unable to forget her past despite her efforts to move forward in freedom. Denver, as a young woman, is able to witness her mother's struggle to redefine herself against the scars of slavery as Sethe's body illustrates what her mind will not do—go beyond that point of the uncanny, the unspeakable. There was "the single slow blink of her eyes; the bottom lip sliding up slowly to cover the top; and then a nostril sigh, like the snuff of a candle flame—signs that Sethe had reached the point beyond which she would not go" (37). Denver's ability to read her mother's body textually allows her to witness the paradoxical nature of remembering. But it is Denver's fragmented history that Sethe wishes to piece together, providing for her a context from which to carve out her own unique identity. Although Denver bears no physical marks or scars directly attributable to slavery—she was born in a "middle passage" of sorts, born when Sethe was on the run—her connection to slavery is immediate because of her mother, her father, her sister Beloved, and her grandmother Baby Suggs. These narratives sketch her genealogy as they form the essence of who she is and who she will become. Baby Suggs tells Denver in a passage that represents her last words to her: "'You mean I never told you nothing about Carolina? About your

30. "Knitting and Knotting," 697.
31. I borrow this term from Kimberly Benston's "I yam what I am."

daddy? You don't remember nothing about how come I walk the way I do and about your mother's feet, not to speak of her back? I never told you all that? Is that why you can't walk down the steps?' . . . But you said there was no defense. 'There ain't.' Then what do I do? '*Know it*, and go on out the yard. Go on'" (244).

Baby Suggs's insistence on naming the marks of slavery inflicted upon the bodies of her family members is crucial. Like the charge given to the character Ursa in Gayl Jones's *Corregidora*, Denver is told to "bear witness. That scar that's left to bear witness. We got to keep it as visible as our blood."[32] This charge, embodied in Baby Suggs's command to "Know it, and go on out the yard," suggests that knowledge is power, and the power comes in knowing when to move on with the rest of your life. This change is not easy for Denver. In viewing the relationships she has with her mother and her sister, relationships that in no way infer an intentional need to harm or destroy, silence becomes the communicative measure that "witnesses," that reformulates *internalized* torture— that punishment self-inflicted by the victims themselves. For Sethe, it is the moment when telling Denver of her past causes her body to signify she has reached her limit. For Denver, it is her inability to hear following Nelson Lord's question about the murder of her sister at the hands of her mother, a question she cannot bear to hear the answer to that directs critical attention to the ideological function of silence in Morrison's novel. As Jean Wyatt points out, Denver's period of silence follows her period of verbal exchange, an exchange that found her delighting in the "pleasures of the mouth as the conflation of learning with eating implies: 'sentences roll[ed] out like pie dough'; Lady Jones 'watched her eat up a page, a rule, a figure.'" Her refusal to speak after this experience complements her mother's silence as Denver's unresponsiveness challenges the self-consuming mother-child cycle evident between Sethe and Beloved. Denver's paralysis, in Wyatt's estimation, allows Denver to retreat "into her mother's world, making the rejection of speech and the obsession with the unnamed" her reproduction of corporeal language; the repressed returns in silence as Denver's "own primal hunger . . . for words [becomes] her mother's wish that the story remain unspoken, the act unnamed, the memory repressed."[33]

But it is language that feeds this hunger. As Denver realizes, "Some-

32. *Corregidora*, 72.
33. "Giving Body to the Word: The Maternal Symbolic in Toni Morrison's *Beloved*," 482.

body had to be saved, but unless [she] got work, there would be no one to save, no one to come home to, and no Denver either" (252). Thus, Denver's ability to move out of the yard that confines her to the stigma of 124 Bluestone Road and chains her to the horror of her mother's former life as a slave occurs with her ability to hear the kind words of a friend. In this instance, Morrison demonstrates the power language has to heal. Denver's encounter with Nelson Lord stresses a need for her to find *her* self in lieu of her mother's painful past. This realization is an important first step in the process of healing. As Paule Marshall notes in *Daughters*, the scar can function "like the keloid of an old wound that keeps compulsively piling on scar tissue long after it's healed,"[34] if the individual does not make a concerted effort to change her circumstance. Denver seems to sense this challenge. However, the road to acquiring a self to look out for and preserve is not an easy one. As we observe Sethe's repeated attempts at redefining herself, we see that her efforts center on lashing out at a system whose intent was to violate the very core of African and African American humanity.

Sethe's response to this assault is twofold. Indicatively, Sethe's identity revolves around the signs of her body, primarily the tree sculpted on her back. This mark, written while she was in captivity on the Sweet Home plantation, shapes the legacy Sethe is able to construct inside and outside the formal boundaries of enslavement. Communally, Sethe is known for the marks she bears on her body, as she is also simultaneously recognized as a bodily inscriptor herself. Her marking of her sons Buglar and Howard, as well as her marking of her daughter Beloved, provides a complicated example of competing social discourses that posit the constitution of slavery against the conventions of motherhood. Because the social contract of slavery mandates the taking of a child from its parents, the intent being the destruction of black families and the severing of familial bonds, Sethe's rebuttal to this affront on her personal space is to write back in a language as brutal and as violent as that spoken to her. After Denver says of the baby whose throat Sethe cut, "For a baby she throws a powerful spell," Sethe replies, "No more powerful than the way I loved her" (4). This suggests that Sethe's demonstration of love is an effort to transform the language of slavery written upon the black bodies of her family through a forceful reclaiming of the bodies of her children.

Although the narrative is careful to detail the bodily marks Sethe in-

34. *Daughters*, 38.

flicts on her infant child Beloved, it is in the borderland of re-memory—
that space of shared experiences and altered images—that Beloved ac-
quires a revised bodily appearance: "She had new skin, lineless and
smooth, including the knuckles of her hands. . . . Her skin was flawless
except for three vertical scratches on her forehead so fine and thin they
seemed at first like hair, baby hair before it bloomed" (50). The narrative's focus on Beloved's lack of scars—the "new skin," the "smooth"
knuckles—presents in an ironic way, and reaffirms in another way,
Sethe's wish to protect her children from the harshness of slavery.
Beloved bears none of the scars attributable to picking cotton or doing
other hard labor, whether domestic or agricultural—her hands are void
of calluses. Her skin has not hardened from working long hours in the
hot sun, nor has her skin aged before its time from the stress associated
with existing in subhuman conditions. When juxtaposed against the
marks of slavery Sethe bears, Beloved's body expresses a form of renewal that can only be achieved in re-memory's imaginary space. It is in this
space that one can *imagine* the body without its wounds, but as the narrative intimates this process has its drawbacks. For Sethe, the paradox
of this imagining is the realization that *she* has become the marker and
the marked; the scars that she sees on Beloved's body are the ones inflicted by her, and this knowledge proves too much for Sethe. It is only
through the help of others that Sethe is able to reemerge from this space
and reclaim a portion of her personhood. Her chilling final words spoken at the end of the narrative suggest that Sethe wonders if there is a
"me" to be found, unmarked and unburdened by the past. In the end,
Sethe must become her own "best thing" and love herself despite the
tree on her back and the haunting that threatens to consume her very
being.

Refiguring the Scar: The Tobacco Tin Heart

Sethe's attempts to reorder her past in a palpable form she can mentally digest mirror the struggles of other characters in the novel to rebuild their lives outside the formal boundaries of slavery. Sethe's personal conflicts are crucial to understanding the overall function of scars
in the novel: her tree not only represents the master's script; it is narrative itself as a tracing of its intricate branches reveals much about the
interconnectedness of many of the personal histories in the novel. According to Deborah Ayer Sitter, the intertexual meanings of the scar on

Sethe's back can be best understood within the context of discussions of manhood and heterosexual love.[35] Sitter's observations prove useful when examining the relationship Paul D has with Sethe. As the narrative suggests, Paul D and Sethe's relationship is built upon desire—a desire unfulfilled eighteen years earlier when Sethe chose Halle as her partner on the Sweet Home plantation. Paul D's desire for Sethe has not diminished in all those years; upon their reencounter some years later, Paul D finds himself drawn to Sethe—and she to him. "There was something blessed in his manner," the narrative discloses. "Women saw him and wanted to weep—to tell him things they only told each other . . . therefore . . . he was not surprised when Denver dripped tears into the stovefire. Nor, fifteen minutes later, after telling him about her stolen milk, her mother wept as well" (17).

Paul D's ability to "touch" Sethe, to relate to her on some instinctual level, stems in part from his willingness to share her pain and in part from his need to understand his own. Paul D's prior experiences with women have left him wandering and searching for something, some key or secret remedy that would help him unlock the rusty lid to "the tobacco tin lodged in his chest" (113). His encounters with women have been essential in helping him achieve some sense of himself as a human being. Like Milkman's in Morrison's *Song of Solomon*, Paul D's journey is placed within a larger social and communal history. Both characters' quests for true identity center around their association with the women in their lives. For Milkman, it is his association with Pilate that finally teaches him how to fly. For Paul D, it is his relationships with Beloved and Sethe that cause him to pry open the lid to his tobacco-tin heart. As for the other women in Paul D's life—particularly the weaver lady of Wilmington, Delaware—each represents an important "stop" on his journey to selfhood. Morrison is deliberate in her efforts to make Paul D a *man*, not a user of women as some stereotypically depicted black men can be.

Paul D's efforts to understand the complexity of his wound are renewed with his reading of the scar on Sethe's back. Like a man learning to read Braille, Paul D explores "the wrought-iron maze," determined to piece together the fragments of his own past. Although Sethe is unable to feel Paul D's touch, for "her back skin had been dead for years" (18), it is the act of reading the scar itself that allows Paul D to reclaim his body (and Sethe's to some extent) in ways unimaginable in

35. "The Making of a Man: Dialogic Meaning in *Beloved*," 17–29.

their former capacity as slaves on the Sweet Home plantation or, as is the case for Paul D, as a member of the chain gang in Georgia. For Sethe, Paul D's exploration of her inscripted past allows her the opportunity to give the responsibility of her breasts to someone else, someone empowered to take the burden of the theft of her milk. But more important, this process connects Paul D to Sweet Home, where he first learned the ideals of manhood and the delimiting prospects of heterosexual love under the system of slavery. This complicated history forms the critical subtext of Paul D's journey to claim ownership of his freed self as his reencounter with Sethe forces him to confront the demons of the past and to search for the true meaning of manhood from both its African and American roots.

Paul D's tenure at Sweet Home unfolds as one of competing definitions of black male identity. Mr. Garner, as master and paternalistic father, readily asserts to other farmers that his "niggers is men every one of em. Bought em thataway, raised em thataway. Men every one" (10). The irony of this statement presents itself in the fact that Mr. Garner sees himself as a "maker" of men; he "raises" them, as one would chickens or cattle; he buys "em thataway," even though he tests the limitations of their resolve as men and as human beings. As Paul D recalls, the Sweet Home men were forced to engage in bestiality because of the absence of female companionship. Garner's inability or unwillingness to allow "his" men the opportunity to express themselves heterosexually demonstrates that his actions are not above those of Schoolteacher, who taught the Sweet Home men they were anything but men. These constructions of black male identity, coupled with Paul D's stint on the Georgia chain gang, have led him to question his own sense of manhood by the time he finds his way to Sethe's house.

During his stint on the chain gang, Paul D and the other chain gang members are forced to perform fellatio on the guards: "'Breakfast? Want some breakfast, nigger?' 'Yes, sir.' 'Hungry, nigger?' 'Yes, sir.' 'Here you go'" (108). It is safe to say that the guards in this instance chose to challenge African American male identity in the context of power. That is, the construction of black male identity becomes predicated upon one's willingness to take a bullet to the head or acquiesce to the guards' demands. Although sexuality is the means by which this dynamic is played out, the guards force these men into a life-and-death struggle. What is telling in this encounter, however, is the way Paul D works around these demands: "Convinced he was next, Paul D retched—vomiting up nothing at all" (108). This speech act not only removes him from participating in the orgy but also spares the other men, as the "engaged one decided to skip the new man for the time being lest his pants and shoes got soiled by nigger puke" (108). Paul D's subtle "answer" to the guard's demands does not go unpunished—he is smashed in the shoulder with a rifle, proving once again that the body as voice is a powerful ally in overt and subtle acts of resistance.

Paul D's actions are similar but not equal to those acts of resistance performed by Sixo during their botched escape attempt. Sixo—whose presence at Sweet Home reminds Paul D not only of Africa but also of manhood itself—begins to sing when the bounty hunters corner him. Fighting them with bound hands, Sixo is finally hit in the head with a rifle after he cracks the ribs of one of the men. Schoolteacher, who had wanted him alive, decides to burn Sixo at the stake. "The song must have convinced" (226) Schoolteacher that Sixo would not be suitable for slave life. As he hangs there, Sixo begins to laugh because he knows what the white men can't "see"—his lover, Thirty-Mile Woman, is pregnant with their child, Seven-O. Sixo's laugh has the same effect on the bounty hunters that Medusa's stare has on men who dare to look upon her— it castrates them, and in the case of Sixo, the bounty hunters' sense of authority is undermined by Sixo's laughter, so "they shoot him to shut him up. Have to" (226), because what is at stake is not only male pride but power itself. Sixo's willingness to accept the consequences of his actions leads Paul D to question the integrity of his own manhood. As Sitter concludes, "What Paul D perceives as innate manliness may be attributable to Sixo's African upbringing."[36] I would also add that Sixo's refusal to speak English, and his refusal to give up certain African customs, frames for Paul D a standard of black male identity that he cannot obtain for himself. His ideals of manhood were shaped on American soil and fermented in the relationships he had with Mr. Garner, Schoolteacher, and the guards of the Georgia chain gang.

Resistance, for the most part, has been overlooked in the critical examinations of *Beloved*. The ingenuity and resistance of African American slaves, however, were what attracted Morrison. "The book was not about the institution—Slavery with a capital S," she explains. "It was about these anonymous people called slaves. What they do to keep on, how they make a life, what they're willing to risk, however long it lasts in order to relate to one another—that was incredible to me."[37] Mor-

36. Ibid., 23.
37. Angelo, "The Pain of Being Black," 121.

rison's comments are particularly helpful when viewing the relationships African American men formed among themselves during slavery. As is demonstrated in the novel, these bonds were important not only in establishing black male communal ties but in forming pockets of resistance as well. Sixo's song, his laugh, Paul D's act of vomiting—all point to instances in the novel where authority is wrestled away from the oppressor and the body is reclaimed by the individual oppressed. In the case of Sixo, his death meant that he would no longer be written about in the pages of Schoolteacher's journal. For Paul D, his humanity would remain intact as *he* chose to avoid the form of sexual abuse enacted by the guards. Other examples in the novel suggest that the reformation of language itself becomes a means of resistance. One such example presents itself during Paul D's stint with the chain gang. Within the world of those confined to this system (the bonded men themselves), "the look" becomes an alternative system of communication and another site for subtle resistance: "each man stood in the other's place, the line of men turned around, facing the boxes they had come out of. Not one spoke to the other. At least not with words. The eyes had to tell what there was to tell: 'Help me this mornin; 's bad'; 'I'm a make it'; 'New man'; 'Steady now, steady'" (107).

The ability of these men to recode their messages to one another—in essence, reclaiming their right to speak—functions as a means of empowerment and defiance against the insanity that could result from such brutal conditions. In an apparent reliving of the Middle Passage, the men are forced to sleep underground in boxes, chained to each other by a coffle. The sanctity of mother earth reconstructs for these men a womblike atmosphere that allows them to regain the power to live despite being buried under five feet of earth in three-sided cages that serve as living graves. At one point, the men are put in boxes that begin to flood after a torrential downpour. The earth above their heads begins to cave in and the boxes fill with mud and water. It is at this time that the men talk "through that chain like Sam Morse" (110). One by one they dive under the mud, groping for the surface above. Those that lose direction are snatched around and redirected. By yanking on the chain, each man is able to communicate with the others, finding a lifeline that keeps him from drowning in the mud. This ability to understand that if one perishes they all do suggests the importance of community and its role in freeing those who are held captive. For the men on the chain gang, community is formed in the moment of crisis. Through nonverbal communication, these men are able to create an alternative system of speech that allows them to transfer messages from site (the body) to site—in essence, reclaiming their body as voice.

It is in instances such as these that Paul D learns the "dollar value of his weight, his strength, his heart, his brain, his penis, and his future" (226). This value, affirmed through his relationship with others, affects how Paul D views himself as a man and as a person. In her interview with Michael Silverblatt, Morrison points to a scene in the novel in which Paul D, silenced by a bit in his mouth, compares his self-worth to that of Mister, the rooster he helped raise. According to Morrison, she wanted Paul D to compare himself to a creature so beneath him that one could sense his lack of authority over himself and that "little three or four pounds of nothin' [in the yard]. To have him feel less than that and, more important, to have him know that rooster's name," allows one to see "a man who will never be called Mister walking out of that yard, looking at a rooster that is already called Mister."[38] This defining moment of black male identity frames a critical dialogue in the novel in which Paul D's personal narrative becomes emblematic of the interpersonal relationships he develops with other people.

As he critically assesses his relationship with Sethe, Paul D's definition of manhood becomes predicated upon his definition of trees, trees like the ones at Sweet Home, "inviting; things you could trust and be near; talk to if you wanted" (21), eat under if you chose to. It is also under these trees that Paul D experiences male bonding—with Halle, the other Pauls, and more important, Sixo. The stark contrast between these encounters and the ones he experiences, literally, "under" Sethe's tree returns the narrative's focus to the scar itself and the meanings attached to it. As Deborah Sitter aptly observes, "On the chain gang in Alfred, Georgia, . . . Paul D can no longer imagine a tree, 'old, wide and beckoning,' like Brother," the tree that formed the essence of his manhood on the Sweet Home plantation. Instead Paul D imagines himself "an aspen, 'too young to call a sapling.'" This diminished self-image forms the basis for his relationship with Sethe. For Paul D, the tree on Sethe's back functions in much the same way as the aspen because he is unable to satisfy his desire or Sethe's. These moments of inadequacy return the reader repeatedly to those instances in the novel where Paul D's manhood is brutalized, fragmented under the weight of slavery. But it is Paul D's witnessing of the death of Sixo that reduces him to a shadow of himself. "After watching Sixo burn, after the neck collar, after the

38. Silverblatt and Morrison, "The Writing Life," 9.

humiliation of Rooster's gaze, Paul D is changed into something else,"
suggests Sitter, "and that 'something was less than a chicken sitting in
the sun on a tub.'"[39]

In viewing Paul D's relationship with Beloved, one could speculate
that it is her position as automaton that forces him to acknowledge his
vulnerability. Through her, Paul D is able to melt away that rusty tobacco tin he equates with his heart so that *he* can love himself and Sethe.
The fear Paul D experiences when he is sexually aroused by the "light"
Beloved emanates when he sees her in Sethe's kitchen mirrors the fear
he feels when Beloved approaches him in the shed. This fear, expressed
in his wish not to "look" at her lest he be frozen or relegated to a state of
nothingness under her gaze, implies that Paul D is afraid to face his own
"reflection." It is interesting to note the reference to Lot's wife at this
point in Paul D's narrative. I tend to believe that Paul D was afraid that
if he succumbed to the power of Beloved's gaze he would be situated in
a "permanent" position in his history, unlike those temporary positions
he was confined to in the chain gang and on the plantation. With this
possibility in mind, the reasons Lot's wife is turned into salt become intriguing. As the story is told in Exodus, she is turned into a pillar of salt
either because she "looked" back at the city of Sodom and Gomorrah
with her eyes (physically), which was contrary to what she had been told
to do by the angel that saved her and Lot from destruction in the city, or
she looked back with her heart, desiring to stay there, with all her world-
ly possessions and maintain the life she had become comfortable with.

Paul D's desire to sleep with Beloved can be viewed in a similar fashion. "As long as his eyes were locked on the silver of the lard can," the
narrative states, "he was safe. If he trembled like Lot's wife and felt some
womanish need to see the nature of the sin behind him; feel a sympathy,
perhaps, for the cursing cursed, or want to hold it in his arms out of respect for the connection between them, he too would be lost" (117).
Thus, desire itself becomes the tempting force. I also believe that Paul
D's expressions of fear at this particular moment in the narrative are com-
pounded by his previous constructions of manhood/personhood under
the system of slavery. This image, patched together through his exposure
to others reading him, and reading his sexual identity in particular, forces
him to shrink from the light Beloved sheds upon this fractured part of
himself. Beloved's ability to force Paul D to "see" himself and the complex way he is formed is suggested by the fact that his chain-gang narrative immediately precedes his lovemaking scene with Beloved.

39. "The Making of a Man," 24.

As Paul D's states, through the process of rememory, Beloved "moved him . . . and [he] didn't know how to stop it because it looked like he was moving *himself*" (114, emphasis mine). I believe that the force of his desire to copulate with Beloved alarms him, given that the ability to express one's self sexually has been thwarted by the dictates of all sorts of forums: Sweet Home, the chain gang, slavery itself. All these factors suggest that Paul D is startled by this newfound desire because now his desire is being forged in new territory—freedom—and Paul D's mind has not fully accepted his human worth. This fear may also explain Beloved's need to "hear" her name called, suggesting a need for Paul D to "speak" into existence a beloved self free from the restraints of psychological bondage, free to love himself and others. In this scene of consummation between that self Beloved forces Paul D to remember and that newly, badly built self he has tried to develop over the years with women (he often speaks of his inability to remain anywhere for a long period of time), Paul D succeeds in "touching Beloved on the inside part" (116). When he arrives there, *he* touches *his* inside part, not realizing that "the [old] lid" of his heart has given way, and a "new" heart, produced through his coupling with Beloved, has joined his fragmented selves, re-creating for him a self that has the ability to feel.

This act of lovemaking is essential to Paul D's survival. It gives him the "air" to breathe, to live as a complete being. This intimacy also allows Paul D the freedom (if you can call it that) to express himself using the very body that had been abused and misused under the system of slavery. This exchange between the past, embodied in the form of Beloved, and Paul D's "brainless urge" to move forward to some place in himself in the present that will allow him to become intimate with those selves dismantled under the gaze of slavery suggests an attempt on his part to revisualize, that is "rememory," his genealogical and cultural histories. The references to "ocean-deep place[s]," places Morrison constructs as historical and cultural by their very nature, presuppose that Paul D must reconcile his memories with those of the ancestors long gone but not forgotten. It is within the framework of this cultural strength that healing can occur. For Paul D, that healing comes when he places his story next to Sethe's, for she is the only woman who "gather[s] the pieces and give[s] them back to [him] all in the right order" (273). She left his manhood intact. She was his very best thing.

Linda Krumholz argues that, in *Beloved*, Morrison not only challenges the assertion that ritual processes imply homogeneous ways of collective and spiritual being; in addition, ritual, as a model, serves to transform "the cultural specificity of knowledge [that] springs from the methods of categorizing and judging, of understanding and distributing knowledge."[40] Indeed, Morrison uses the ritual of storytelling itself to paint "flesh-and-blood" portraits of people traumatized by their conditions in slavery. Scars have a life of their own in Morrison's novel. They breathe, eat, and sleep; they grow on the back of their possessor. But more important, these wounds can be healed if the body is re-membered.

40. "The Ghost of Slavery: Historical Recovery in Toni Morrison's *Beloved*," 398.

Five

"Walking Wounded"

The Urban Experience in Ann Petry's *The Street*

> We might well ask if this phenomenon of marking and branding actually "transfers" from one generation to another, finding its various symbolic substitutions in the efficacy of meanings that repeat the initiating moments?
>
> —Hortense Spillers, "Mama's Baby, Papa's Maybe: An American Grammar Book"

> White supremacist ideology is based first and foremost on the degradation of black bodies in order to control them. . . . Two hundred and forty-four years of slavery and nearly a century of institutionalized terrorism in the form of segregation, lynchings, and second-class citizenship in America were aimed at precisely this devaluation of black people. . . . [T]his white dehumanizing endeavor has left its toll in the psychic scars and personal wounds now inscribed in the souls of black folk.
>
> —Cornel West, *Race Matters*

As *Dessa Rose* and *Beloved* show, slavery provides a context for assessing the cultural markings of the African American body. These signs, figuratively and literally transfigured onto the bodies of African American people, are evident not only in the psychic scars and personal wounds so indelibly "inscribed in the souls of black folk" but also in the

111

social institutions that continue to devalue black people and rerupture these wounds through a persistent reworking of the social and political discourses that shape the racial imaginings of the black body. It is in these instances that the scar functions both as a literal extension of these imaginings (a fleshly representative, a demarcator of the sign/language of difference) and as a cultural repository for other forms of bodily marking not readily manifested on the surface of the body.

As the previous chapters illustrate, the presence of tears or lesions on the body often leads to the speculation of (and "fleshly" evidence of, as was the case in *Beloved*) trauma and/or injury to other aspects of the person, namely the mind and soul. Again, the physical evidence of a scar (usually a sign of the body's attempt to heal itself) does not necessarily mean that the *wound* has healed. As Paul Laurence Dunbar reminds us in "Sympathy," "a pain still throbs in the old, old scars / And they pulse again with a keener sting— / I know why [the caged bird] beats his wing!" Both Sherley Anne Williams and Toni Morrison explore the dimensions of Dunbar's claims, advocating alternative ways to envision African American subjectivity despite the somatic markings of the slave body. In reflecting on these and other questions explored thus far, it becomes quite evident that scars are an integral part of one's identity—they help shape the essence of one's being.

In *The Wounded Body*, Slattery argues that on some sacred level the wounded body is a gift, "a body specialized and formed by experience." In this specialized state of being, the body possesses something it had not possessed before, both rhetorically and mimetically. As a metaphor, this body forces us to "imagine it in relation to violence, to the sacred, to language, and to the city," thereby bestowing "incarnational meaning" to everything to which it relates. As Slattery concludes, perhaps there is a "significant mythic sensibility surrounding the body in its markings that ritualizes in a communal way our own unique incarnations. A deep mimesis is explicit in the markings of the words on the page and the lines in the flesh."[1]

Approaching this issue from a different perspective, I'd like to engage in a sustained reading of Ann Petry's novel *The Street*. It is a narrative that, for me, examines identity formation in the urban setting using the disfigured black body as its critical subtext. If, as Slattery states, the wounded body is a "rich poetic metaphor that offers its own ontology," its own knowledge "that helps us to understand the poetic work's

---

1. *Wounded Body*, 135.

entire meaning," Petry's use of the wounded body invites us to view scars simultaneously as signs of wounding and as signs of healing. Petry's novel allows us to move the discussion of the disfigurement of black bodies to a rhetorical level, demonstrating that unmarked bodies can be marked in interesting ways, sometimes more insidious than those visible on the flesh. Considered by some to be a poor imitation of Richard Wright's *Native Son*, Petry's novel has been critically eclipsed by what Bernard Bell calls the misrepresentation of her talent. "Whether valid or not," Bell concludes, "these . . . views do not adequately express the complexity and distinctiveness of Ann Petry's aesthetic vision and achievement."[2] This "aesthetic vision" includes, in my estimation, a substantive focus on the body as text.

Like Wright, Petry presents an array of characters that have, to some degree or another, been traumatized and/or "tattooed" by their experience in the city. Critics have lauded the intensity of Wright's characterization of Bigger Thomas and his unflinching depiction of the challenges of urban living, particularly for African American men. Few critics have examined, however, the ways in which Petry's novel responds to and reinvents what Andrew Delbanco terms Wright's daring presentation of "the imperatives of the body," those compulsory acts committed out of a "sense of exile from the world of satisfactions." This consciousness, induced by a socially generated self-hatred, a loathing of one's own "color and physiognomy and dialect and all the features of . . . [an] irreparable social ugliness,"[3] is constituted in the simultaneous gesture of being made aware of one's own blackness, one's own internal conflict and pain.

Petry herself is quoted as saying her characters are the walking wounded—marked, I would argue, by the prejudices of race, class, and gender and bruised by the many systems of oppression that relegate them to poverty, obscurity, and even death. Petry's characters are the grandchildren and great-grandchildren of the generation Toni Morrison explores in *Beloved*—those of Sethe's generation who left the rural areas and life on the land with dreams of a better life in the city. Their migratory experiences, and the resulting aftereffects, make plain the sociological underpinnings that enable the subjugation of African American people. Just as slavery institutionalized the marking of the black

2. Ibid., 52; Bell, "Ann Petry's Demythologizing of American Culture and Afro-American Character," 105.
3. Delbanco, "An American Hunger," 139, 141.

body as chattel, poverty—the new neo-slavery condition—becomes the vehicle by which millions of urban dwellers are made cognizant of their black skin, and subsequently their disenfranchisement.

Many, including Barbara Christian, have argued that ghettos are "the concrete plantations of the North. These areas are an extension of the slave/plantation/master system wherein the master changes faces and 'space.'" Thus the extension of this system invites us to reconsider the subjugation of people of color in terms that reveal the sociological and textual dimensions of the ritualistic marking of the black subject in the urban setting. In exploring the ways postmodern texts signify on their antecedents, revising those discursive tropes to more adequately assay their urban truths, one can envisage the uncanny ways the past is kept alive in the present. As William L. Andrews concludes, "the function of consciousness mediated through language" allows us to preserve "Afro-American realism as a literary tradition, a bridge between the antebellum and modern eras." This bridge "makes Tuskegee available for the Invisible Man to reinvent and enables the transposing of the 'apparently incoherent' slave songs of Douglass's *Narrative* into the *Song of Solomon*."[4]

To this end, I propose that Petry's novel reaffirms and recapitulates the call of her nineteenth-century predecessors, in that her narrative bears witness to the dehumanizing conditions of African American life with the urban center as her institutional model. Material possessions are the key to understanding and naming the open and closed wounds marking the psyche and flesh of these individuals. The suggestion has already been made that the figurations of wounds and scars can take various forms: decay or disease, mutilation or fragmentation, or textualization in the shared experiences of a community. In viewing the dehumanizing conditions of urban life, one is made acutely aware of the rhetorical link between the meanings inscribed on black bodies in the nineteenth century and those inscribed in the twentieth—meanings that through their very nature make clear the historical significance of the ritualized disfigurement of the black body. Petry's statements of authorial self-definition that name Harriet Wilson as her literary ancestor suggest such a connection: "Having been born black and female," notes Petry, "I regard myself as a survivor and a gambler, writing in a tradition

4. Christian, *Black Feminist Criticism: Perspectives on Black Women Writers*, 11; Andrews, "The Representation of Slavery and the Rise of Afro-American Literary Realism, 1865–1920," 76.

that dates back to 1859 when *Our Nig,* the first novel written by a black woman in this country, was published in Boston, Massachusetts."[5]

Petry's identification with Wilson is telling. It confirms the widely held notion that African American writers read each other's work and engage in a conscious process of evoking this literary tradition in order to revise it. This self-reflexive posture, inherent in African and African American artistry, forms the basis of African American interpretive and theorizing practices. And it is within this culture-specific context, as Toni Morrison intimates, that African American writers come to "tell other stories, fight secret wars, limn out all sorts of debates blanketed in their texts."[6] Petry exemplifies this mode of writing (as does Wilson) as she explores the nexus of race, class, and gender from her own unique perspective. Wilson's novel was the first to examine the stifling conditions of indentured servitude in the North from the perspective of the African American woman; likewise, Petry became the first woman novelist to depict a black mother's struggle to survive in the inner city.

Secondarily, Petry's allegiance to Wilson underscores their shared interest in speaking the body's pain. Wilson's narrative is replete with images of suffering, sorrow, and torture. *Our Nig* tells the story of Alfrado, a biracial six year old who, after the death of her black father, is abandoned by her white mother and black stepfather and suffers unimaginable hardships for twelve years as an indentured servant in the home of Mr. and Mrs. Bellmont. Alfrado's young life consists of severe mental and physical abuse as her day-to-day routine remains unchanging, "adding a little more work" to an already expansive repertoire of household duties "and spicing the toil 'with words that burn,' and frequent blows on her head."[7] Alfrado is repeatedly beaten, kicked, and whipped with a rawhide and is twice forced to endure a severe lashing with a piece of wood inserted in her mouth. Over the course of the narrative, Frado's once healthy body is maimed, tortured, and beaten.

These encounters are disturbing, to say the least, but they are essential to Wilson's overall objective. In *textualizing* the body's sufferings, Wilson is able to redefine the communicative aspects of body and voice within the space of her narrative. Rather than silencing her, it is precisely this pain that compels Wilson to speak. As Cynthia J. Davis aptly discerns, "the fact that a black woman like Wilson does manage to

5. Petry, "Ann Petry," 253.
6. *Playing in the Dark,* 4.
7. *Our Nig: or, Sketches from the Life of a Free Black,* 29–30.

speak of her own pain . . . means that she has quite literally mapped out uncharted territory, in which both pain and the black female body are redefined via powerful language as capable of both power and language. Language in *Our Nig* is no longer antithetical to pain; instead, language serves to make pain and even 'our nig' herself intelligible."[8]

Ironically, it is the *absence* of the physical evidence of pain (scars, tears, fissures in the skin) that joins Wilson's efforts with those of Petry. Whether by authorial design, or what P. Gabrielle Foreman terms "the undertell,"[9] Wilson was unable or unwilling to commit to paper the disfigured image of a black woman. This omission is striking given the severity of Frado's childhood abuse. To date, no reading of *Our Nig* has taken up the implication of such an omission. Perhaps it is because no real explanation can be given. Perhaps it is because Wilson's characterization of the wounded body underscores her claims that words can burn, leaving their own indelible mark. Nonetheless, Wilson's narrative is important in illuminating the correlation between textual silences and the reconfiguration of speech. Maybe that which is undertold in her narrative becomes her greatest source of power, for the reader surely knows that such brutal violations of the body must have left their somatic markings on the fragile frame of Alfrado.

Wilson's choice to forgo the literal presentation of a physically scarred body in her narrative raises a number of questions about the language of trauma and its literary representations in African American literature. In Wilson's case, her allegorical ties to slavery as well as her unique ability to depict the precarious labor conditions of marginalized women in the North complicate the cultural paradigm that underscores the delimiting circumstances of not only "speaking" the black body in pain but also politicizing that body's pain explicitly and implicitly in writings of the flesh not directly associated with slavery. Because Wilson's narrative deals with indentured servitude, she may not have wanted to offend her counterparts writing in the South by undermining their physical descriptions of the hardships of slavery (including the presentation of the branded or whip-scarred slave body). If the scarred slave body is the "rhetorical stead," as Foreman and others have argued, of campaigns against the ills of chattel bondage, then using that same body in her own cause may have been problematic for Wilson.

8. "Speaking the Body's Pain: Harriet Wilson's *Our Nig*," 399.
9. "Manifest in Signs: The Politics of Sex and Representation in *Incidents in the Life of a Slave Girl*," 77. I borrow the term *undertell* from Foreman and use it as the means to discuss the second story, the undercurrent that is unspoken in Wilson's narrative.

More to the point, Wilson's rethinking of the literal and/or metaphorical disfigurement of the black woman's body provides further evidence that African American women writers have continually used this frame referentially, if not for the explicit then for the implicit way it concretizes the embodied experiences of African American people, and more specifically African American women. As Marilyn Sanders Mobley concludes, "*The Street* . . . must be examined in the context of the black female literary tradition of which it is a part. Thus examined, the novel is both a cultural critique and a cultural response to the conditions Petry had observed during her years in Harlem."[10]

As a journalist for the *Amsterdam News* and *People's Voice*, Petry witnessed daily the challenges of urban living. As a New Yorker, she absorbed the smells, sounds, and despair of ghetto life. "You don't have to work on a Harlem newspaper," she wrote, "to get a picture of the violence and poverty there. . . . Just live in one of those houses for a week. Any night you're liable to wake up and hear somebody screaming his head off—because he's sick, or because he's being beaten. You'll hear rats scratching around in the walls, see garbage piled in the halls and strewn in the backyards."[11] This exposure, coupled with the overt and subtle racism she faced as a young child in the provincial New England town of Old Saybrook, Connecticut, no doubt helped shape the tenor of her novel.

"Carved and Tattooed": Marking the Urban Body

> my body is scarred
> by your dry december tongue
> i am word bitten.
>
> —Sonia Sanchez, "haiku 5"

The Street revolves around the life of Lutie Johnson, a single African American mother whose futile attempts to escape the poverty of New York's inner city provide one of the most startling examples we have of the corrosive effects of racism and poverty on the human psyche. Lutie's saga unfolds as one of competing forces—that of history and that of "the street." The novel opens with Lutie's search for an apartment,

10. "Ann Petry," 352.
11. Theodore L. Gross, "Ann Petry: The Novelist as Social Critic," 43.

and it is here that we witness the lawlessness of the street and its ability to literally and figuratively change the dynamic of the body.

To underscore the point, Petry personifies the wind as a shrewd and willing ally to the street in discouraging people from traveling along its walkways. It is the wind that finds the dirt and grime on the sidewalk and lifts it up into the noses and eyes of urban travelers, making it difficult to breathe or see. The rhetorical strategies Petry employs to point up the adverse conditions of the street foreshadow Lutie Johnson's adversarial relationship with the city. From the time Lutie embarks on her journey to find an apartment for herself and her young son, Bub, until the end of the narrative, which finds her a fugitive from the law, the reader is privy to Lutie's struggles against those elements that undermine her aspirations to leave the ghetto.

Petry's complex rendering of the physical assault Lutie endures in the street allows for a critical rereading of those cultural conventions that configure society's response to Lutie's body. Rosemarie Garland Thomson argues that Lutie is a version of the nineteenth-century domestic heroine, imprisoned in her body as "each one of Lutie's conventional feminine assets turns out to be a disastrous liability in the context of the street."[12] Indeed, much of the action surrounding Lutie's narrative involves her encounters with individuals who want to exploit her or use her body for their own material or personal gain. Mrs. Hedges, for example, who runs a bordello in the tenement in which Lutie lives, wishes to add Lutie to her "menu of offerings," thereby securing her own economic relationship with the white owner of the building, Junto (who wants Lutie for himself). As a bonus, Lutie's presence would, at the same time, enhance the caliber of Mrs. Hedges's business. Many critics, including Thomson, Christian, and Theodore Gross, have commented on Lutie's fight to maintain her ethical and moral integrity despite the overwhelming influence of poverty and sexual/racial discrimination in the street. Mrs. Hedges recognizes this quality in Lutie and knows that, if used materially, it could bring Mrs. Hedges much economic gain. In the meantime, Lutie's building superintendent, Jones, is horribly obsessed with her and wants to use her body for his own distorted pleasures.

On the surface, these encounters appear to be just two in a long series of conflicts that pit Lutie against her own body. According to Trudi-

---

12. "Ann Petry's Mrs. Hedges and the Evil, One-Eyed Girl: A Feminist Exploration of the Physically Disabled Female Subject," 610.

er Harris and Calvin C. Hernton, Lutie's struggle is constant, for the men and women who control her access to money "offer it to her only at the price of her body."[13] Thus Lutie's desire to escape poverty, to challenge the social patterns that deny her access to her "American Dream," is reflected in these disturbing embodied experiences. Lutie's awareness of the way her body is read and visually interrogated by others is revealed in her role as a maid in the home of Mr. and Mrs. Chandler. It is here that Lutie overhears the female acquaintances of Mrs. Chandler express their stereotypical notions about the virtues of African American women. Whenever she enters a room to serve them, their peculiar disposition and their inquisitive stares make Lutie uneasy. Moreover, these encounters find Lutie questioning the motives of these women who seem to be preoccupied with the sexual habits of black women and doubting their ability to see past "the veil" they themselves have constructed. Despite the fact that Lutie herself is married, Mrs. Chandler's acquaintances still feel that all black women are whores. The knowledge of this accusation makes Lutie feel as if "she was looking through a hole in a wall at some enchanted garden. She could see, she could hear, spoke the language of the people in the garden, but she couldn't get past the wall."[14] Lutie's apt description of her Du Boisian experience underscores the way some women feel trapped in their bodies, "walled in" from the rest of the world. If *double consciousness* is the "peculiar sensation" of "always looking at one's self through the eyes of others," then Lutie's ability to recognize her predicament sets her apart from other fictional female characters of this period. "Until Petry," claims Hernton, "there had been no such women as Lutie Johnson, Min, and Mrs. Hedges in the entire history of black fiction."[15]

Some critics may dispute Hernton's assertions, but they direct attention to Petry's complex rendering of inner city life: "Since the first wave of black migration out of the South shortly after the demise of Reconstruction, black women had been coming to the northern cities. But there had simply been no serious treatment of black underclass women, neither in the narratives and early novels, nor in the 'primitivist' and 'tragic mulatto' portrayals of Harlem Renaissance writers, such as

13. Harris, *From Mammies to Militants: Domestics in Black American Literature*, 96.
14. Petry, *The Street*, 41; subsequent references to this novel will appear in the text.
15. Du Bois, *Souls of Black Folk*, 3; Hernton, *The Sexual Mountain and Black Women Writers*, 60.

Claude McKay and Nella Larsen or Jessie Fauset." In this regard, Petry not only fashions anomalous characters, but she also revises, as Mobley points out, "the naturalistic rendering of black people, especially black women, as helpless, passive victims." These characterizations dominate the fiction of Richard Wright and of other black male writers of the 1940s and 1950s. Although most critics have maintained that Lutie Johnson is a female version of Bigger Thomas, only a few have acknowledged that Petry's *Street* is revisionary, not only in its attempts to redeem Bessie, the girlfriend Bigger Thomas silences in *Native Son*, but in its efforts to revise the character of Bigger as well.[16]

The Tie That Binds

Bigger Thomas's brutal murders of Mary Dalton and Bessie Mears undoubtedly make him a controversial character, yet for historical reasons Bigger is significant both in terms of his uniqueness to American letters and in terms of his impact on the development of an urban aesthetic insistent on revealing the dimensions and depths of its estrangement from America's social and economic realities. According to Arnold Rampersad, "no one quite like Bigger Thomas had ever been seen before the publication of *Native Son*," although he does concede that "American literature had witnessed cameo appearances by renegade blacks."[17] Wright's motivation for novelizing such a character stemmed, in part, from his exposure to rebellious young black men in the North and South who, in an effort to rid themselves of the *veil* that held them captive in their own bodies, violently projected out into the universe that which they were given by the confining dominant culture.

For Bigger Thomas, this dualism takes the form of violence directed at those individuals closest to him or in a position to affect his quality of life. In one instance, Bigger forces his friend Gus to lick Bigger's knife blade during a confrontation at Doc's pool hall, mainly out of a desire for power and recognition on Bigger's part, but also out of a sense of misplaced fear. As Bigger admits later in the narrative, "he had hoped the fight he had had with Gus covered up what he was trying to hide. At least the fight made him feel the equal of them."[18]

16. Hernton, *Sexual Mountain*, 60; Mobley, "Ann Petry," 353.
17. Introduction to *Native Son*, xi.
18. Wright, *Native Son*, 41.

Bigger's helplessness, epitomized in this social rape of his friend Gus (Gus's manhood and stature in the gang are certain to be compromised by his "submission" to Bigger), echoes Bigger's own failed attempts at "inserting" himself into America's economic, racial, and social mainstream. Bigger's willingness to use illicit methods of obtaining access to this wealth masks his own feelings of material impotency: "Like a man staring regretfully but hopelessly at the stump of a cut off arm or leg," Bigger recalls, "he knew that the fear of robbing a white man had had hold of him when he started that fight with Gus." To overcompensate for his sense of loss, Bigger utilizes other "prosthetic" means—namely a gun and a knife—to fill his void. "He was going among white people, so he would take his knife and his gun; it would make him feel that he was the equal of them, give him a sense of completeness."[19] Wright's decision to make Bigger Thomas a mutilated being in search of "completeness" speaks directly to the bitter and tragic consequences of his squalid life. But more important, Bigger's plight resonated with the moods and reactions of an entire people struggling to come to terms with their shadowy existence in the city.

Centuries of abuse and exploitation created ways of life for African Americans both foreboding and lethal. A whirling vortex of unbridled historical and social impulses brought about the societal conditions that would produce the many variations of Bigger Thomas. As Wright recalls, the Bigger Thomases of his childhood were conditioned organisms whose emotional and cultural hunger made them intense and hateful, angry and self-destructive. Yet these individuals "were the only Negroes . . . who consistently violated the Jim Crow laws of the South and got away with it, at least for a sweet brief spell. Eventually, the whites that restricted their lives made them pay a terrible price. They were shot, hanged, maimed, lynched, and generally hounded until they were either dead or their spirits broken."[20] Wright's fascination with these tragic heroes is a key not only to understanding his tortured feelings about the political and legal structures of the United States; it is also crucial to understanding his obsession with the literal and allegorical disfigurement of the black male psyche—a psyche whose emotions were predetermined by America's racial climate. Wright traces Bigger's historical and genealogical lineage to the period of slavery: he makes him a third-generation descendant and deconstruction of Harriet Beecher

19. Ibid., 42, 43.
20. Wright, "How 'Bigger' Was Born," 437.

Stowe's "Uncle Tom." Stowe's depiction of the emasculated and mild-tempered Uncle Tom proved to be the first in a long line of literary disfigurements of black male characters that would people the pages of American literature.

Wright's initial attempt at deconstructing the belletristic persona of "Uncle Tom" came in a collection of short stories entitled *Uncle Tom's Children*. In the epigraph to this volume, Wright proclaims, "The post Civil War household word among Negroes—'he's an Uncle Tom!'—which denoted reluctant toleration for the cringing type who knew his place before white folk, has been supplanted by a new word from another generation which says—'Uncle Tom is dead!'" In slaying his literary predecessor, Wright had hoped to augur another generation of literary men. But as he argues in "How 'Bigger' Was Born," this attempt was unsuccessful. "I found that I had written a book which even bankers' daughters could read and weep over and feel good about," Wright laments. "I swore to myself that if I ever wrote another book, no one would weep over it; that it would be so hard and deep that they would have to face it without the consolation of tears."[21]

Having affirmed his authorial purpose, Wright reimagines "Uncle Tom" some one hundred years later as Bigger Thomas—the antithesis of his earlier persona—angry and disillusioned at how little things had changed since antebellum times. In *Native Son*, the plantation has been replaced by a tenement building; Bigger's master has become violence itself—something he experiences in his own environment on a daily basis. From the opening scene of the novel, which finds Bigger at war with a black rat in a small one-room apartment he shares with his mother, brother, and sister, to the end of the novel, which finds Bigger in an even smaller space, his jail cell—an incarcerated shell of a man who has murdered to satisfy his yearning to be recognized as a human being, only to be killed *again* by the system that created him—Wright's "Frankenstein" is an American-grown product, a dispossessed and disinherited man in the land of plenty, looking, as Wright argues, for a way out. It is in watching Bigger come to terms with his own disfigurement, his own disenfranchisement, that we see the figurations of the "walking wounded."

Wright's dark tale of woe and horror makes vividly clear the bleakness of the opportunities available to young black men in America's urban centers. Petry addresses many of these same issues in *The Street* through the characterizations of her male figures, especially Boots and

21. *Uncle Tom's Children*, vi; "How 'Bigger' Was Born," 454.

the Super Jones, whose basement craziness makes him a shadow of
Wright's Bigger Thomas. Petry, though, anchors her social critique in
the portraits of her female characters. This gesture is, to a degree, Petry's
expansion of Wright's urban vision as well as her own feminist intervention. In her novel, Petry points up the historically grounded social
institutions that oppress African American women and focuses on the
efforts of black women to circumvent those institutions that mark them
as Other. Women are viewed as sovereign beings in Petry's novel, or at
the very least they are seen acting in their environments to improve the
quality of life for themselves and their families.

Petry's affirmation of the psychological autonomy of her female characters can be seen in the internal dialogues of her central character,
Lutie Johnson. Lutie is a strong woman who refuses to accept the prescribed gender limitations and conditions of her urban life. As she determines, "streets like 116th Street or being colored, or a combination
of the both with all it implied, had turned Pop into a sly old man who
drank too much; had killed Mom off when she was in her prime" (56).
These same streets were responsible for turning Min into "a drab drudge
so spineless and so limp she was like a soggy dishrag," and they pushed
Jones "into basements away from light and air until he was being eaten
up by some horrible obsession" (57). Lutie resolved that none of these
things would happen to her. "She would fight back and never stop fighting back" (57). As a symbolic representation of cultural attitudes and
societal marking, Petry suggests that, in the street, individual existence
is predetermined by mitigating factors that affect not only how people
live but also how their identities are constructed in the public and private spheres.

The Lyncher's Scar

The physical and psychological deterioration of other individuals in
the street points to the *figurations* of urban scarification evident in
everyday life experiences. In many instances, the decay of the environment mirrors the personal deterioration of most of its inhabitants. Lutie's cumulative efforts to envision her circumstances differently, to
"fight back and never stop fighting," unfold as part of a larger narrative
of white social control that ensnares black men and women in a cultural déjà vu—"Streets like the one she lived on were no accident," Lutie concludes. "They were the North's lynch mobs" (323). Petry's iden-

tification of the urban environment as a northern lynch mob is telling. According to You-Me Park and Gayle Wald, Petry's designation "renders in material form immaterial, invisible ideologies."[22] That is, the trope of lynching suggests a violation of black bodies materialized in the very method used to, as Lutie explains, "keep Negroes in their place" (323).

Petry's reference to the North's lynch-mob mentality echoes Harriet Wilson's claims some one hundred years earlier of similar measures being used to tighten the noose of oppression. As Wilson's narrator declares at one point, "Strange were some of her adventures. Watched by kidnappers, maltreated by professed abolitionists, who did n't want slaves at the South, nor niggers in their own houses . . . traps slyly laid by the vicious to ensnare her, she resolutely avoided." Petry's assertions similarly resonate with the experiences of her father, Peter Clark Lane Jr., who, when confronted by a white messenger in the small New England community in which they lived, exhibited great courage in the face of a physical threat to his family and his business. When told by this messenger, "they don't want no black druggist in this town. If you ain't gone by to-morrow night they're going to run you out of town," Petry's father grabbed the man and told him, "I come from Madagascar and we slit throats. We're stranglers. If I have to leave here, I'll be back. And I'm going to bring my great-grandfather, and my grandfather, and my father, and my ten brothers with me. And this damn town will never look the same again." Then he threw the man out the door.[23] Thus, Petry's tropological use of the term *lynching* contextualizes those historical wounds inflicted not only on the racial memory of African Americans but on the psyche of inner-city dwellers as well.

Although the lyncher's scar is not physically manifested on the bodies of the characters that inhabit Petry's *Street*, it is nonetheless very evident in the *material* conditions of the urban poor. Approaching lynching as a performative spectacle centered around the black male, but nevertheless effective in traumatizing the entire African American community, civil rights activists such as Ida B. Wells and Walter White make clear that lynching often revolved around the contested space of economic (in)security. Lutie's reference to her father's inability to get a job, and her comment that her ex-husband, Jim, slowly disintegrated

22. "Native Daughters in the Promised Land: Gender, Race, and the Question of Separate Spheres," 618.
23. Wilson, *Our Nig,* 129; Petry, "Ann Petry," 256.

because he also could not find employment, speaks to the personal fall-out of economic "lynching." Denying an African American man the opportunity to take care of his family cuts off, metaphorically, the blood supply not only to the African American family but to the entire African American community.

This same scenario plays itself out in single-parent households headed by mothers. Lutie's inability to find employment that would enable her to provide a secure environment for her son reflects the harsh reality of poverty. Moreover, this cycle repeats itself as young boys like Bub witness the deterioration of their families and their fathers. This observation is certainly true of Bigger's mother, Mrs. Thomas, who forces him into the role of surrogate father as he is made to fill the shoes of his absent father. Their lives are built around this wound, this absence, this pain. Bigger's downward spiral, and Bub's subsequent demise at the hands of the Super, who promises Bub that he can make enough money to help his mother, vividly illustrates this paradox. Taken in this context, Petry allows us to theorize not only about the traumatic experiences of her urban characters but also about African American people in general.

Petry's literary methodology clearly delineates the street's overwhelming impact on her characters. Her use of environment places her in a tradition of writers—including James Baldwin, Audre Lorde, and Gwendolyn Brooks—who have used landscape images to examine African American subjectivity from a multitude of perspectives. What I find telling about Petry's depictions is her ability to allegorize the scarred or wounded body using inanimate objects directly associated with her characters. For example, Lutie's failed marriage, a consequence of her employment situation, is metaphorized in the "scarred bedroom set" she owns. Lutie's marriage, a casualty of poverty and disillusionment with the American Dream, suffers greatly when she must live at the Chandlers' residence as a maid while her own family is left to fend for itself. Thus the bedroom set, like the rest of the items she owns, "the radio, the congoleum rug, [the] battered studio couch and easy chair" (54), comes to signify the remnants of a dream deferred. Similar illustrations occur throughout the novel as Petry describes in detail how, for those who live on the street, neglect and decay become emblematic of the "lyncher's rope": from the rusted metal of a street sign "where years of rain and snow had finally eaten the paint off down to the metal and the metal slowly rusted, making a dark red stain like blood," to the tenements whose old and discolored floors could not conceal "the scars and the old scraped places" (3). In tracing the patterns of urban life evident in the crevices of these marks, Petry not only represents the body in pain; she devises another way to conceptualize the very notion of agency in an environment that renders resistance ineffective if not impossible.

In a provocative and underutilized study, Gaston Bachelard suggests that "the essence of life is but a feeling of participation in a flowing onward necessarily expressed in terms of time and secondarily expressed in terms of space." One can extend this view to argue that the life Bachelard speaks of is the life of the literary text—the living, breathing words of expression inherent in the text. Enclosed in the perimeters of this sphere are space and its extension, imagination, which operate as tools of implementation to express the inexpressible. Bachelard goes on to say that "poetic space, because it is expressed, assumes values of expansion." That is, poetic space allows each character the opportunity to uniquely position himself or herself within the space of the novel. Broadening Bachelard's theory of textual expansion, Houston Baker argues that "where Afro-American women's expressivity is concerned, the particular construction and accountability of the critic must allow him or her to negotiate metalevels of space, place, and time in order to figure forth a new expressive world." Thus, Baker deems the critic responsible for proposing alternative ways of viewing African American female expression in the literary imagination. I would further suggest that this "new expressive world" Baker speaks of allows the observer to view phenomenologically the ways in which female characters express themselves through their interactions with their environment. "After all," as Baker continues, "phenomenology seeks to move transcendentally beyond indicative signs that govern 'ordinary communication.'" Thus, the possibility of movement affords the voiceless individual the opportunity to gain a voice affirmed by sight, vision, or touch.[24]

Baker's evaluation of African American female expressivity is intriguing in that it enables the reader to more clearly ascertain, in Petry's text, the ritualistic healing of urban wounds. Morrison's characters use spirituality, song, and dance to heal the body's wounds. Baby Suggs's decision to occupy a space in the woods "known only to deer and whoever cleared the land in the first place" signals, on her part, a need to reconnect body to soul in a place unpolluted by social order.[25] "The

24. Bachelard, *The Poetics of Space*, 201; Baker, *Workings of the Spirit*, 50, 53.
25. *Beloved*, 87.

Clearing" thus becomes, in Morrison's novel, a centralized site that allows disempowered individuals the opportunity to gain a renewed sense of self. In Petry's narrative, "self" becomes a product of interstitial possibilities as characters such as Min and Mrs. Hedges are seen creating their own loopholes of retreat. They redefine themselves in environments that do not acknowledge their existence as people, and in the process they circumvent the political and social systems that wound them mind, body, and spirit.

Shapeless Forms

At first glance, the character of Min appears to be of little importance. Critics have focused on the personal struggles of other characters in the novel, namely Mrs. Hedges or Junto, paying Min little or no attention as a character of any theoretical significance. She is overlooked, her presence veiled by the fact that she does not wish to pursue the "American Dream," nor does she embody the idealisms of her gendered counterparts, who strive for material gain at the expense of their social conscience. Min instead dreams of finding a place—a safe space—to exist free of harm or danger. These attributes make Min an unattractive character for some to analyze because on the surface she seems to embody the typical characteristics of the submissive woman. For my purposes, however, Min deserves a closer look because she shows that the body not only gives voice to the individual in pain but also determines whether one is recognized within the competing forces of the city.

When we are introduced to Min, we are told that she is a shapeless small dark woman whose shrinking manner causes her to blend into the chair in which she is sitting. Min's "shapelessness" is so pervasive that after bowing to her upon entry into the room, Lutie completely forgets she is there. Lutie's inability to "see" Min (and see past her shapeless form) has as much to do with Lutie's absorption of the elitist views encoded in the American Dream as it does with Lutie's inability to read certain bodies within the symbolic social order of the street.[26] Yet as

26. This is a very complicated notion stated simply. One would need more space than is appropriate here to fully explore the implications of black women reading each other within certain paradigmatic structures. I would like to point out, however, that for all of Lutie's fortitude, pride, and perseverance, she is naive when it comes to discerning the behavior and motives of others in the street. She does a better job of reading the stereotypes about women in the very different cultural

Lutie continues to survey the Super's apartment, one item "speaks" to her and causes her to return her attention to Min: "It was a very large table with intricately carved, claw feet and looking at it she thought that's the kind of big ugly furniture white women love to give their maids. She turned to look at the shapeless little woman because she was almost certain it was hers" (24). Min takes on ghostlike features as she is constantly referred to in these passages as "shapeless." Although Min wishes to remain invisible, her desire is circumvented by the relationship she shares with the table.

Min's connection to her table becomes more intriguing in the context of Baker's theory of the relation of material and medium when one examines how communication occurs between an object and a corresponding literary character. Bachelard, whose work informs Baker's ideas in *Workings of the Spirit,* theorizes that "to give an object poetic space is to give it more space than it has objectivity." Therefore, while the object retains its aesthetic boundaries, it figuratively transcends this space to become an extension or expansion of its owner's space. If a "medium" is "an agency, such as a person, object, or quality, by means of which something is conveyed, accomplished, or transferred,"[27] Min's table transfers the power of space and voice to her, accomplishing visibility for a woman who seeks invisibility. Min and the table seem to reverse their roles in this instance as Min becomes the object and the table the speaking subject. This relationship foreshadows the interaction of person and medium throughout the remainder of the novel (in much the same way as Petry's allegorization of the wounded body concretizes "fleshless" scars), for in moments that would suggest a confrontation with individuals hostile and invasive of Min's personal space, Min's table speaks for her, challenging the hostile individual and eliminating any chance of recourse.

Min's life, as described in the novel, is one of dependency on others who are often abusive. Jones, her present live-in companion, detests the sight of Min after Lutie Johnson moves into the building. His obsession

context of the Chandlers' home. Her distaste for Min's apparent dependency on men points up the fact that Lutie reads some black women's bodies the same way her *own* body was read by the female friends of Mrs. Chandler, and she overlooks (as these women did) the individuality of some black women's experiences. We will see later that Lutie recognizes inanimate signs of materialism, not the materiality of bodies. Min, moreover, may represent for Lutie the future she does not want to envision for herself.

27. Baker, *Workings of the Spirit,* 202, 77.

with Lutie dominates his narrative in the space of the novel, and it is this obsession and his feelings of inadequacy that cause him to abuse Min after Lutie rejects his advances. In one instance he brutally slaps and kicks Min after Lutie rejects him because Min is a readily available target. Min endured similar atrocities at the hands of her last husband, Big Boy, who would use her hard-earned money to fuel his drinking habit. It is at this time in Min's life that the table becomes her protector, because it contains a secret drawer that allows her to hide her money from her abusive partners. For Min, this table represents the site where she achieves independence within her dependent, co-addictive relationships. Min confronts Big Boy with the table because it frustrates him. With Jones, who does not ask for money but, instead, encourages Min to move in with him, the table epitomizes presence, for it creates its own space and identity within the small apartment he and Min share on 116th Street.

In assessing the intimate relationship Min shares with her table, one can see how the table encourages Min's development as a woman and as an individual. Through being able to hide her money from her abusive partners, Min gains the power to reverse her cycle of economic dependency. This relationship also facilitates Min's movement from silence to voice and from submission to self-confidence in some interesting ways. Initially, Min hopes to buy false teeth with the money she has saved, but her declining relationship with Jones forces her to reallocate those funds. "[T]he false teeth would just have to wait awhile longer, because she was going to spend her teeth money in order to stay in th[e] apartment" (118). Min's concerns about her future lead her to seek the advice of Mrs. Hedges, who directs her to a root doctor, Prophet David. This encounter is significant in that Min's efforts to rebuild her relationship with Jones also enable her to minister to her own personal wounds. This process begins when Min purchases conjuring materials from Prophet David, who is the first man to allow her the opportunity to speak: "'Tell me about it,' the prophet said again . . . his manner was so calm and so patient that without further thinking about it she started talking" (133).

The confidence Min gains from this encounter is twofold. Certainly the text frames a cultural dialogue between two aspects of spirituality found in the African American community: that of conjure (rooted in African culture) and that of Christian theology (rooted in Euro-American culture). These conversations do not imply that these religious practices are mutually exclusive nor that one is uninfluenced by the other. Rather, what these conversations make clear is that, in some cases, Christian theology is not only *privileged* over other forms of religious expression rooted in African culture, it may even *conflict* with the spiritual needs of the individual seeking assistance from the community. Min's struggle to reconcile herself to these two forms of religious expression underscores her internal conflict over whom she should go to for help. Initially, she feels guilty about seeking the aid of the prophet because she knows the preacher at her church would disapprove, for it implies that the church is ineffective in handling some spiritual matters.

Embedded in this guilt is Min's sense that her live-in relationship with Jones (a "sin" in the Christian theological sense) places her outside the reach of God's love, and outside the ark of safety of the church. Prophet David does not judge her. Min's relationship with him differs greatly from the ones she has had with preachers in the past. The few times she approached the minister to ask for his assistance he interrupted her and said, "We all got our troubles, Sister. We all got our troubles" (137), and then turned and walked away. Having the opportunity to speak to someone who will listen to her innermost fears empowers Min to think about her own well-being for the first time in a long while. It is this encounter that forces Min to *consciously* rethink the way she sees herself within her immediate environment. Her initial attempt to refigure this space, and claim the right *to be*, develops when she returns from her visit with the prophet. Normally, Min's disposition upon entering the apartment she shares with Jones is one of timidness and unassuredness. His volatile behavior has left her overwhelmed by the prospect of what she will find on the other side of the door. After her visit with the prophet, Min enters the apartment with a certain quiet dignity. Instead of timidly inserting her key in the lock, she thrusts her key in the door and pushes the door open with confidence. Jones frowns as he listens to her enter the room "because on top of that she slammed the door. Let it go out of her hand with a bang that echoed through the apartment and in the hall outside, could even be heard going faintly up the stairs" (139).

This pivotal scene marks the end of Min's desire to be invisible, voiceless, and submissive. Her actions transcend all spaces, those in the apartment and those in the hallway. Min is heard. Subsequently, Min's newly acquired voice and identity force her to leave Jones, for her presence in his apartment disrupts its previous order. Min realizes that staying with Jones would lead only to his wanting to physically suppress and violently extinguish her newfound voice, for her other relationships had followed a similar pattern: first, the threats to her body, then "the grip around the neck that pressed the windpipe out of position so that screams were choked off and no sound could emerge from her throat" (357). Thus Min escapes to the street that gave her voice, taking the table that safeguards her money, and with her few belongings she goes in search of somewhere she can breathe.

Min's absence has a profound effect on Jones. Obviously, he no longer has a person upon whom he can vent his anger. But more specifically, in light of the arguments proposed in this study, Min's table emphasizes her presence and then her absence in Jones's personal space. When Min was there the table held a prominent space in the apartment; when she leaves Jones has difficulty filling the void of the space where the table used to be. He tries placing other furniture in that spot, but that only "emphasized the absence of the gleam and shine of the table's length" (375). Even in her absence, Min "speaks" to Jones, altering his physical as well as his mental "space." This encounter reinforces Jones's own feelings of inadequacy within the larger social structure of the street as the emphasis is placed, in this instance, on the value of space and the importance of material possessions—two things Jones lacks in his own life. Disempowered and emasculated, Jones is left wandering the hallways of an apartment building he will never own, working toward a goal he will never achieve.

Min's table is intricately connected to her intimate space because it helps her create a voice and identity in *The Street*. With the action of hiding her money, Min gains not only economic independence but, in a small sense, also a self-assuredness that enables her to transform her abusive situation. Her movement from invisibility to visibility, submission to self-confidence, and finally voicelessness to voice provides an unsettling story of triumph and determination as a counter to Lutie's failure. Min creates her own identity and is seen and heard. Her narrative illustrates the contradictory impulses of the street as both a delimiting and an immeasurable space. Min reminds us that for Petry, in order to be recognized as a person, one must create a space where one can refashion one's self within the context of one's immediate milieu.

Seared Bodies

Place and space are also what define the life of Mrs. Hedges. Her narrative offers the most vivid illustration of obtaining voice and visibility through the social landscape of the body. Similarly, it is her rise to "overlord" of the street that presents the most compelling example of bodily scarring that is directly attributable to class mobility and economic gain. For Mrs. Hedges, these developments materialize because her body, as walking text, speaks to her indomitable spirit, and she, in turn, is able to use her body as a site for self-evaluation and self-redefinition.

Because the body as language functions under the auspices of the visual, how the body is viewed determines the process of self-creation. Mrs. Hedges understands the power of sight and how it relates to the concepts of invisibility and visibility. Doubly marked by her blackness and her disfigurement, Mrs. Hedges embodies two states of being—she is both seen (as a thing/object) and not seen (as a human being/subject). This dynamic is clearly evident when she visits the employment offices seeking work—the revulsion in the faces of the agents and the constant stares from others who don't always hide the disgust in their eyes make Mrs. Hedges feel like a prisoner in her own body. A similar experience occurred in Mrs. Hedges's hometown in Georgia—her enormous size and dark hue made her a novelty, and the townspeople never got used to her. For these reasons, she goes to the city, where she feels she can be indistinct. Although Mrs. Hedges distinguishes the *intent* of the reading of her body by the townspeople from that of the employment agencies (this is supported by the tone of the language used to describe each incident), the adverse effects of these experiences, coupled with her inability to fit into the normative model of womanhood, create for her a void that sends her prowling the streets for comfort, food, and acceptance. It is in the street that Mrs. Hedges finds inconspicuousness, and it is there that she redefines the boundaries of place, space, and the creation of identity.

In an effort to rend the veils that confine the meaning of her body to ambiguity and nonproductivity, Mrs. Hedges circumscribes what Bachelard terms *felicitous space*, the space of human value that "may be grasped, that may be defended against adverse forces, the space we love."[28] Because her potential for developing a viable economic identity has been shortchanged by the social languages and discourses that govern the spaces of ethnicity and gender, Mrs. Hedges goes to the street, whose economy is based on the fluidity of its boundaries. As a janitor and rent collector, Mrs. Hedges moves from the *space* of home-

28. *Poetics of Space*, xxxi.

lessness to a *place* of economic assuredness. Although not the owner of the building, she creates for herself an interesting relationship with Junto, who is able to buy two buildings based on the advice and encouragement he receives from her.

Mrs. Hedges's transformation to the voice that we hear over the sound of the wind in the street in the opening of the narrative stems from her economic prowess, which moves her into a space traditionally associated with men. What is ironic about this association is that her subsequent disfigurement in the basement of the apartment building that represents the business she helped create allows her the ability to reform what it means to be a woman economically, and this interrelationship grants her the power to design her own space on the street. As the narrative discloses, Mrs. Hedges was trapped in a fire in the basement of one of the buildings in which she slept. Unable to go through the door because of the flames, she sought an avenue of escape through the basement window, but the window was narrow. Fearing for her life, Mrs. Hedges forced her body through the small space. She could smell her hair and flesh burning and could feel her skin give way in the struggle. Determined, she continued to fight, making "the very stones of the foundation give until the window opening would in turn give way" (244).

In this illustration, Mrs. Hedges's body represents voice in action. The burning and tearing of her flesh allow her to physically turn herself inside out, creating a new being. These actions are similar to the ones she exhibits as a homeless person, turning bottles and pieces of metal into a profitable business. Her business partner, Junto, admires her actions in the fire, underscoring their common bond of ingenuity. It is during this juncture in her recovery, however, that Mrs. Hedges contemplates her future. Realizing that her scars from the fire have banished her to a life different from the one she imagined for herself, Mrs. Hedges, again, seeks to redefine how her bodily text is read as she moves into her position as overlord of 116th Street.

Mrs. Hedges's knowledge of the power she now possesses as the scarred partner of Junto is revealed in interesting ways. She is well aware that Junto will probably be the only man with whom she will have a close relationship. She also understands that his admiration for her stems from the actions she took during the fire. Junto considers her his equal. Armed with this ammunition, Mrs. Hedges develops another source of income for herself built on the bodies of others: a brothel that takes its customers from a space she knows well, the street. As she states, "the street would provide plenty of customers . . . men" who were disillusioned with their lives, "men who had to find escape from their hopes and fears . . . she would provide them with a means of escape in exchange for a few dollar bills" (250). Although Mrs. Hedges appears to be motivated by economic goals in starting this business, another desire also fuels her drive: other women's bodies. Mrs. Hedges is able to revision her own scarred body through her association with young, disenchanted women who blossom under her care. Moreover, just as Mrs. Hedges thought she could buy love, she foolishly believes that her association with the unscarred bodies of other young women will lessen the pain of her own scarring.

In contrast to Min and Lutie, whose subject and object positions cause them to operate within certain socially inscribed spaces, Mrs. Hedges's "lack" of femininity allows her to command spaces neither woman would. When Lutie is almost raped by the Super, for example, Min will not come into the hallway; instead, she opens the door and lets the dog out in an effort to rescue Lutie from the Super's vile attempts. Mrs. Hedges, on the other hand, commands the space of the hallway with power, using her enormous size as ally as she prevents the rape of Lutie.

Curiously enough, Mrs. Hedges's vocal and bodily repossession of this hallway differs greatly from her presence in the space into which she was relegated during her years of poverty, when she slept on a cot in the hall of the apartment of a friend. Although the hall and hallway may be viewed differently as sites of expression for Mrs. Hedges, her inability to find a job (which put her in the hall in the first place) and her ability to save Lutie from the grasp of Jones (an economic investment, in Mrs. Hedges's view) are related in that one action reverses the stigma of the other. In other words, Mrs. Hedges's ability to produce economic value in a space she has re-created serves to counteract the impact of her previous history as a homeless woman. This act, coupled with those exemplary efforts exhibited during the apartment fire that left her body scarred, amplifies the power Mrs. Hedges has within the space of the narrative, and it is *this* voice that occupies the space of the hallway with force, to the extent that "her rich, pleasant voice filled the hallway, and at the sound of it the dog slunk away, his tail between his legs" (237). The Super's failed rape attempt, metaphorically referred to in this passage through the reference to his dog's limp tail, contributes to the frustration he feels at being unable to contain the mystical reach Mrs. Hedges appears to have over the street, in particular over those who occupy *his* apartment building. Jones had hoped Mrs. Hedges's illegal prostitution business would put her in jail, thereby clearing the way for him to "have" Lutie. But as the Super finds out, Mrs. Hedges exists outside the reaches of the law. Junto has seen to that. Through her association with Junto, Mrs. Hedges is able to manipulate what Baker terms the "placeless place of law,"[29] creating for herself a distinct site for renewed bodily expression.

Thus, Mrs. Hedges's "felicitous space" becomes the street, and the window becomes the phenomenological venue through which she seizes this space. It is in this window facing the street that Mrs. Hedges becomes deified, heard, and recognized. She appears to possess godlike qualities: she warns Lutie of the arrest of her son before Lutie has knowledge of it; she reads Min's mind as she plans to move out of Jones's apartment; she tells Jones, before he sees his apartment, of Min's departure. In this respect, Mrs. Hedges's creation of place in her window—a place *earned* through her ability to force her bulky body through the small aperture in the basement of the previous building—allows her the privilege of occupying and transcending traditional mediums of expression. Her actions change the very foundation of that building and alter the very notion of what it means to *move* beyond one's immediate spatial confinements. In her space in the window, Mrs. Hedges is on display for all to see—her body bears the marks and tells her story.

This return to the site of the visual is an important thematic current in Mrs. Hedges's narrative. Because she has often been read by other characters in the novel as an Other in the extreme, it is not coincidental that her eyes become the focus of much discussion. Mrs. Hedges knows the power of sight. She has seen in the eyes of others exclusion, disgust, and hatred. For this reason, she shields her innermost self with the malignancy of her eyes. This helps her hide the pain she feels at being seen as a freak, a nuisance, a monstrosity. The immensity of the street aids her in developing this armor, so Mrs. Hedges watches the

29. I borrow this term from Baker's *Workings of the Spirit*. Baker defines the "placeless place of law" as the displacement and denial of African American viability within the Western economic community. Historically, people of African descent were denied their ability to claim commercial possession of their labor. Slavery provided the genesis of this way of thinking within North American society, but I argue that within certain urban centers such as Detroit, Chicago, and Harlem, this same displacement holds true today. If one considers, for example, Mrs. Hedges's role in *The Street*, it becomes evident that she has reinvented this space/place for her own benefit and has likewise co-opted the legal system in ways that tie economic viability to legal power.

street as though "if she stopped looking at it for a minute, the whole thing would collapse" (121). The street has given Mrs. Hedges the only source of comfort she has known—it is her spouse, her existence, her very being.

Barbara Christian concludes, "*The Street* marks a change in setting and tone in the literature of the black woman. After the publication of this novel, the black city woman could not be forgotten."[30] Indeed, *The Street* makes for compelling reading. Lutie, Min, and Mrs. Hedges offer startling portrayals of creation and re-creation as each woman uses the qualities she possesses to refigure her space and to define new ways of self-expression. Petry uses these characters to direct attention to the embodied experiences of African American women and the uncanny ways their identities are shaped by their interrelationships with their environments. In writing about the multiple systems of oppression that bind these women to the street, to their space and place in society, Petry encourages us to move the black woman's narrative to the forefront of urban literary studies, and in the process to reorder the way we view the value of material possessions within the context of the city.

Petry's exploration of the embodied experiences of African American women in *The Street* points up the cultural realities and spatial dynamics of body woundedness in the urban setting. As Slattery reminds us, the gestural body "in its woundedness or its disability is *the* 'essential metaphor' by which the 'sickening social order' can be displayed." While many of Petry's characters display maladies that disfigure them beyond the surface of the flesh, their "disabilities," be they economic, social, physical, or emotional, nonetheless lay bare the "sickening social order" that underlies their oppression. Perhaps, as Slattery suggests, it is through the blending of world and self (and author and text, I would argue) that "the body wounded, diseased, putrefied, pierced, marked, tattooed, bloated, or murdered" reveals something about the interactions of people and the world and, more specifically, about the individual and his or her destiny.[31]

This latter sentiment offers fertile ground for examining the embodied experiences of African American men. Specifically, I want to explore the most ritualized form of bodily marking—lynching—as presented in the other writings of Richard Wright and Ralph Ellison.

30. *Black Feminist Criticism*, 47.
31. *Wounded Body*, 99, 11.

Keeping in mind that lynching and other forms of disfigurement have been an ever-present threat to black men at various moments in our social history, I will demonstrate that the rhetorical legacy of Ellison and Wright speaks to these concerns vis-à-vis the inscribed black male body/psyche, and their examinations inevitably influence the creative processes of writers such as John Edgar Wideman, Michael S. Harper, and James Alan McPherson, who answer "the call" of their literary predecessors. The creative acts of these authors bind that which has been wounded literally and figuratively as they invite those who hear the voices of the ancestors to connect to that part of themselves where life still speaks.

Six

Fingering the Fissures of the Black Male Psyche

Wright and Ellison Revisited

There are no dry bones
Here in this valley. The skull
Of my father grins
At the Mississippi moon
From the bottom
Of the Tallahatchie,
The bones of my father
Are buried in the mud
Of these creeks and brooks that twist
And flow their secrets to the sea.
But the wind sings to me
Here the sun speaks to me
Of the dry bones of my father.

—Etheridge Knight, "The Bones of My Father"

In the introduction to the 1996 edition of Richard Wright's *Eight Men*, Paul Gilroy observes that the republication of this volume coincides with "one of those lengthy periods in African-American political culture when the integrity of the race as a whole is being defined exclusively as the integrity of its menfolk." Indeed, the integrity of an entire people has rested, in recent years, on the public's perception of men such as O. J. Simpson, Rodney King, Darryl Strawberry, and Marion Barry. Nestled in the social profiles of these highly visible persons are

138

the sexual, criminal, and racial voyeurisms of a nation viscerally obsessed with the image of the black man. According to Sandra Gunning the black male body "hypersexualized and criminalized has always functioned as a crucial and heavily overdetermined metaphor in an evolving national discourse."[1] This discourse, predicated on maintaining certain racial, political, and sexual boundaries, is rooted in a desire for power—in the form of economic and political supremacy. History has demonstrated that whenever this power is threatened, reconfigured, or socially realigned, violence—be it literal or rhetorical—is the method of defense. As D. W. Griffith determined more than one hundred years ago, the birth of a nation, indeed the genesis of America's national identity, rests in conjuring malignant images of the African American male.

But America's fascination with the ways of black men has archetypal roots that go far beyond their most recent manifestations. As this study has demonstrated, the legal and social discourse of slavery created a national language for the propagation of mythological half-truths and socially sanctioned phobias about African men. Their progeny, descendants of this legacy, inherited a birthright unlike any other group. As Ralph Ellison puts it, "Being 'highly pigmented,' as the sociologists say, it was our Negro 'misfortune' to be caught up associatively in the negative side of this basic dualism of the white folk mind, and to be shackled to almost everything it would repress from conscience and consciousness. The physical hardships and indignities of slavery were benign compared with this continuing debasement of our image." Ellison's halting reference to the "indignities of slavery" and the "continuing debasement" of African American people in American culture points up the materiality—indeed the cultural commodification—of the African American body within America's sociosymbolic realm. As Ellison would state elsewhere, American society has actively created a system of corporeal inscriptions that continues to disfigure the image of African American people. In particular, this "racial ritual of keeping the Negro 'in his place'" has played itself out in repetitious formulations centered on "maleness"—formulations that continue to serve as a chief mechanism for defining relations of power in American society.[2] These vary from portrayals of black men as oversexed criminals in print media and film[3] to, in their most insidious forms, economic, social, and polit-

1. Gilroy, introduction to *Eight Men* by Richard Wright, xx; Gunning, *Race, Rape, and Lynching*, 3.
2. "Change the Joke and Slip the Yoke," 48; "The Shadow and the Act," 276.
3. Two films readily come to mind: D. W. Griffith's *Birth of a Nation* and the 1923

ical disenfranchisement and, to a haunting degree, the racially coded practice of penalization. This latter form of legal "enslavement" not only ensures the surveillance of black male bodies—as young as twelve years old—but also carries with it a social penalty that includes a loss of voting privilege, a loss of legitimate avenues for economic productivity, and a social stigma reminiscent of slavery that marks the children and grandchildren of these individuals.[4] Within the larger context of African American history, these cultural interplays mimic historical and ideological mappings of centuries past that mask the violent reappropriation of black male bodies, bodies viewed as "strange fruit" within the American body politic.

Thus, the return to the masculine is a restorative effort, steeped in the tradition of repairing the much beleaguered image of African American men, for many believe the race's ability to act in its own best interests, be they political or otherwise, hinges on the systematic restructuring of the African American male identity. As Gilroy explains, "an elaborate literature of self-help, self-analysis, and self-worth has grown up around the idea that black masculinity can, in redeeming itself, transform the plight of those who have undergone procedures of symbolic castration that deny them access to the personal and political benefits of authentic maleness."[5] It is Gilroy's attention to the interventionist measures of African American writing—and more specifically his allusions to the ritualistic "procedures of symbolic castration"—that allows for a return to the writings of authors such as Richard Wright who, in a need to unlayer the complicated process of sexualization and engenderment that accompanies the transformation of "flesh" to "body" or more specifically of chattel to citizenry, refocus the social discussions of African Americans' claims to economic and political equality at the site of the black male body.

King Kong. For excellent discussions of the cultural ramifications of these films see chapter 1 of Ed Guerrero's *Framing Blackness* or Michael Rogin's "'The Sword Became a Flashing Vision': D. W. Griffith's *The Birth of a Nation.*"

4. In the American chattel system the child of a slave mother had the social and legal status of the mother, regardless of patriarchy. These loopholes in the legal system gave slavemasters unbridled access to black bodies, to the extent that it would take the 1954 decision of *Brown vs. Board of Education* to undo the damage of *Plessy vs. Ferguson* (1894), which sanctioned the separate but equal treatment of African American citizens. Key to this decision was the judge's contention that descendants of slaves *were not* American citizens and should therefore not be granted the full legal rights of citizens. African Americans, to this day, live under this shadow of a de facto citizenry rooted in the primacy of the masculine.

5. Introduction to *Eight Men*, xxi.

When we view their work in terms of the landscape of the body, we can see how these writers testify to the perverse and varied meanings associated with the articulations of white male supremacy within the American context. Often, these discussions revolve around the ritual of lynching, which represents the most grotesque form of "disciplinary action" enacted against those who "transgress" the racial and sexual borders of American society. "Lynchings were carefully designed to convey to black persons in this country that they had no power or nothing else whites were obligated to respect," argues Trudier Harris. "Black males were especially made to feel that they had no right to take care of their families to any degree beyond that of bare subsistence, and no right to assume any other claims to manhood as traditionally expressed in this country. Lynchings became, then, the final part of an emasculation that was carried out every day in word and deed." Robyn Wiegman restates Harris's premise another way: "Lynching figures its victims as the culturally abject, monstrosities of excess whose limp and hanging bodies function as the specular assurance that the threat has not simply been averted, but negated, dehumanized, and rendered incapable of return. . . . It is this that lynching and castration offer in their ritualized deployment, functioning as both a refusal and a negation of the possibility of extending the privileges of patriarchy to the black man."[6]

Thus, in returning to these moments of ritualized torture, writers such as Wright refigure the dynamic of the castrated and dismembered black male body through a literary ritual of mourning and evocation that allows them to re-member this body—physically and psychologically inscribed—in the African American literary imagination. It is also through the written testimonies of these authors that the black male body takes on symbolic proportions as the lynched and castrated figure—silenced during the ritual itself—is again given a voice.

Initiation Rites: Marking the Black Male Psyche

Our bones are dried, and our hope is lost: we are cut off for our parts.
—Ezekiel 37:11

The social challenge of establishing a literary tradition around the fear of castration usually associated with lynching can be seen in an ex-

6. Harris, *Exorcising Blackness*, x; Wiegman, "The Anatomy of Lynching," 446, 450.

amination of the works of Ralph Ellison and Richard Wright. While these authors are routinely viewed as ambassadors of the "forgotten age"—that period roughly following the Harlem Renaissance up to the civil rights movement—the work of each is usually reduced to one text: for Ellison, it is *Invisible Man*; for Wright, it is *Native Son*. The critical focus on these two texts has all but negated any real investigation into the literary significance of other thematic currents apparent in their other writings. This dynamic can be seen, for example, in the critical examinations of Wright's *Native Son*. While numerous studies attempt to rescue Bigger from his urban and "critical" hell—a hell prescribed and inscribed by his poverty, his blackness, his murderous intentions, his misogynistic tendencies—few if any have discussed the obsessive manner in which Wright attempts to recoup the disfigured black male body, often returning to the "site of the crime," as he does in his 1935 poem "Between the World and Me," in an effort to re-member "textually" the lynched figure in the woods. This rhetorical strategy not only allows Wright to "inhabit" the body of the lynched victim; it also allows him to revisit his own precarious status as a black man in America's southern Black Belt. Trudier Harris believes that both Wright and Ellison were preoccupied with the subject of lynching early in their writing careers due to the increased concern in the 1920s and 1930s over the nature of lynching and the brutal manner in which African Americans were being killed. In 1930, a few years before Wright's work appeared in print, twenty people were lynched. Although small, this number represented an increase of almost 200 percent from the total for the previous two years.[7] This increase served as a notice to some African American writers who saw shadows of a former historical pattern. Wright, Ellison, and others such as Langston Hughes and Sterling Brown redirected attention to the sadistic tendencies evident in this practice as nationally recorded incidents such as the brutal lynching of Claude Neal in Florida in 1934 provided further evidence that African Americans had not yet gained equal protection under the law.

Wright would touch upon figurative manifestations of this theme in *Native Son* through his portrayal of Bigger Thomas, but it is in his poem "Between the World and Me" that we can most clearly see the culturally symbolic uses of lynching in his work. Those familiar with the poem

7. See Arthur F. Raper's *The Tragedy of Lynching* and Robert L. Zangrando's *The NAACP Crusade against Lynching, 1909–1950* for more information on the increase of lynchings specific to this time period.

will recall that the speaker, during a morning walk in the woods, stumbles upon the charred remains of a sapling and an assemblage of white bones resting on a pile of ashes. Unable to name "the thing" he has just found, the speaker suddenly finds himself thrust back in time and space as he assesses the disturbing circumstances of the scene before him—torn tree limbs, burnt leaves, an empty shoe and hat, and a pair of blood-soaked pants. The callousness with which this act was carried out is reflected in the objects left at the site. There are discarded cigarette butts, peanut shells, and an abandoned liquor canister. Overwhelmed by what he knows to be true, the speaker is gripped with fear as the dry bones start to stir and rattle, melting themselves into his flesh, entering his own bones as the speaker and victim become one. It is at this moment that the speaker relives the victim's nightmare, feeling his pain and experiencing his agony as the voices of the past drown out his own. In the end, the speaker, now altered by this experience in the woods, becomes the dry bones, his face a stony representation of the horror he has witnessed.

Wright's vivid depiction of the horrific details of this incident is at once a testament of a cultural haunting and a remembrance of his own exposure to incidents of racial violence and poverty during his childhood. His use of religious imagery—baptism by gasoline and fire—and his reference to the very popular sermonic text "Valley of Dry Bones" not only amplify the general effect of African American martyrdom but also demonstrate how, like the dry bones in the valley, each victim will rise and reassemble himself within the consciousness of other African Americans. In the words of David P. Demarest Jr., Wright's "philosophy" on violence was that "racial violence done to any single black involves all blacks, a compelling consciousness, a pity and fear, that is unavoidably involving, that can become an obsession. Such a consciousness of violence and threat must stand forever between the speaker and the world. No black can escape awareness of white violence; no black can avoid an identification with the victims." According to Melvin Dixon, "situating this poem in Wright's career helps us to understand how his voice emerges from a reaction to racial violence as well as from 'the ethics' of surviving de facto segregation." Thus Wright's attention to lynching, both as a subtext that underwrites the cultural narrative of black male identity and as a wandering wound that afflicts the formation and development of individual identity within the American body politic, allows him to rhetorically dis-member to re-member the effectual emasculation of black men. Wright would return again and

again to this theme in his other writings, expounding on what he considered the fundamental reality of "the extreme situation"—a situation
that finds a man's essential dignity challenged, as Nathan Scott argues,
by the "unconscionable subversion of justice."[8] These symbolic acts of
castration deny an individual the ability to act in his own behalf.

Ralph Ellison explores similar themes of bodily inscription in his
little-known short story "The Birthmark" (1940). The narrative centers
on the lynching of a young black man named Willie whose badly disfigured body is found in a clearing beneath trees and pine needles. The
brother and sister of this young man, Matt and Clara, are told that a car
has hit their brother. But there is evidence to the contrary: Willie's flesh
appears to have been "hacked and pounded as though it had been beat-
en with hammers"; his jaw is found "hanging limply against the shoulder, the mouth gaping" as if to acknowledge the horror of the last moments of his life. These chilling "signatures" of lynching hasten Matt's
need to confirm his brother's identity based on a birthmark that lies beneath Willie's navel. But in searching for the birthmark Matt discovers
his brother has suffered the ultimate act of emasculation—castration—
for "where [the birthmark] should have been was only a bloody mound
of torn flesh and hair." Matt's response to this discovery mimics the response of the speaker in Wright's poem "Between the World and Me":
"Matt went weak. He felt as though he had been castrated himself."
Matt's symbolic castration, amplified by the white patrolman's insistence that Willie had indeed been hit by a car—"Nigger, we told you
that boy was hit by a car, understand?"—signals a reinscription of the
bodies of both Willie and Matt as it simultaneously points up the cir-
cuitous relationship of the spoken and unspoken rules of social law that
subtend the power relations of blacks and whites.[9]

The objectification of this relation—signified in the torn and battered flesh of Willie—lays bare the ideological investments underlying
the rituals of lynching and castration. As Wiegman keenly observes,
"the story's final image of the body of the castrated black man lying
bloody and brutalized, 'between the white men's legs,' . . . is figured in
its relation to the power and privilege of white masculinity, and the
body of the dismembered 'other' takes its place as bearer of the white
phallus's meaning." Thus the "birthmark," the indelible mark of black

8. Demarest, "Richard Wright: The Meaning of Violence," 237; Dixon, *Ride Out
the Wilderness: Geography and Identity in Afro-American Literature*, 57; Nathan A.
Scott Jr., "The Dark and Haunted Tower of Richard Wright," 149.
9. "The Birthmark," 16, 17.

skin, not only refers to the visibility/invisibility of black skin; it also activates, as Wiegman points out, "the narrative's symbolic structure, allowing us to read castration as the remedy for the symbolic birthmark—the penis—that 'flaws' black men" according to the discursive consignment of the black male body in America's cultural consciousness.[10]

Ellison's examination of not only the dynamics of these power relations but also the impact of these acts of violence on the lives of everyday people is realized in Matt's shocking reacclamation to these brutal realities and his inability to circumvent them. His futile effort to comfort his sister, Clara, who knows that her cries for redress will be met only with denial and vicious retribution, heightens Matt's dismay. As the white patrolman explains to them both for the final time, "you better remember that nigger . . . and your sister better remember that, too. 'Cause a car might hit *you*. Understand what I mean?" Such an acknowledgment of the negation of black life and the worthlessness of this human life within the context of America's legal system comes at a great cost to Matt's own personal well-being as his silence and his eventual acquiescence—"'I'll remember,' he said bitterly, 'he was hit by a car'"—are the last haunting words of Ellison's short narrative.[11]

Harris rightfully argues in her analysis of Wright and Ellison that, within the literary history of black writers, the figure of the emasculated black male has occupied a secondary if not primary role for "the antithesis of all protest and discontent." This tradition, spanning some one hundred years, details in painful acuity the unwritten rules that govern black and white interaction—rules that, by their very nature, question the humanity of African American men and reaffirm, through word and deed, the myths of inferiority associated with "antiblack" attitudes and practices solidified in political and social forums. According to Ellison, "the anti-Negro image is a ritual object," used to promote the "ethics," as Wright would call them, of living within the margins of American society and outside the realm of economic and social empowerment. These ethics created an atmosphere of fear and resentment among southerners in particular and *demanded* from black men compliance, making them "willing" participants in their own emasculation and disenfranchisement.[12] A black man in the South knew, for example, that he was not allowed to look a white man in the face or challenge his authority in any way, even if that man was in error. A black

10. Wiegman, "The Anatomy of Lynching," 450, 449.
11. "The Birthmark," 17, 16.
12. Harris, *Exorcising Blackness*, 31.

man was also supposed to look the other way if he witnessed or heard of the sexual violation of a black woman, even if that woman was his mother or wife. Nor could he give the vaguest inclination that he wished to defend her honor. Such infractions carried deadly consequences.

Wright recalls an incident in which he and a female fellow employee were walking home after work and a white night watchman slapped the woman on her buttock as he passed them in the street. "I turned around, amazed," remembers Wright. "The watchman looked at me with a long, hard, fixed-under stare. Suddenly he pulled his gun and asked: 'Nigger, don't yuh like it?'" Wright's initial hesitation was met with another command from the watchman—"I asked yuh don't yuh like it?"—as he stepped forward, presumably in a threatening way. Wright mumbled his response, "yes sir," and was asked to repeat his answer in a manner "appropriate" for southern decorum. "'Oh, yes sir!' I said with as much heartiness as I could muster."[13] Wright's figurative castration, symbolized in this encounter, illustrated to him the limitations placed on his personhood. Such acts would leave lasting scars on Wright's psyche, and, almost in a ritualistic form of literary exorcism, he would reopen these wounds again and again in an effort to rid himself of the stigma that shadowed his early southern upbringing.

Although Wright began by exploring social practices he witnessed in the South, he, like other writers, knew that such practices were not confined to the South. As early as the midnineteenth century, men from Douglass to Griggs were exploring the dehumanizing practice of symbolic castration in the North. They were likewise determining that the maturation process for African American men centered on such instances of social effacement. These acts marked the black male psyche and created a historical pattern of black male behavior. As William H. Grier and Price M. Cobbs determine:

> Under slavery, the black man was a psychologically emasculated and totally dependent human being. Times and conditions have changed, but black men continue to exhibit the inhibitions and psychopathology that had their genesis in the slave experience. . . . The black man . . . is regarded as socially, economically, and politically castrated, and he is gravely handicapped in performing every other masculine role.[14]

13. "The Ethics of Living Jim Crow," 1395.
14. William H. Grier and Price M. Cobbs, *Black Rage*, 60.

Thus, these "acts" of symbolic castration create the essence of "the shadow" that becomes part of the black man's reality—and part of the African American imagination. It is this reality that Wright returns to in *Eight Men*.

Shadowy Existence: Variations on the Theme

In the beginning was not the shadow, but the act.
—Ralph Ellison, *Shadow and Act*

The focus of *Eight Men* is on black masculinity. Published in 1961, after Wright's premature death, the collection was conceived and assembled during his European exile. It has met with some resistance from critics who find his existential forays into the North American political and social systems debilitating and didactic. Many critics have also argued that Wright's quest for a habitable space in which to explore his spiritual and inner selves left him cut off, as Saunders Redding and Nick Ford claim, from his cultural roots. Harold T. McCarthy suggests that the subhuman caricature of Wright's Bigger Thomas appears in various configurations throughout Wright's later works. Wright's reliance on this image demonstrates that the "monstrosity," the pathos of Bigger's mental and spiritual evolution, stemmed from "the sordid cultural objectives of white America." Regardless of the extremeness of Wright's critical perception of man—in his "sordid" and pathetic manifestation—McCarthy and others have concluded that the trajectory of Wright's work carried him through many ideological encounters. "That the record he left behind is uneven is beyond dispute," point out Richard Macksey and Frank E. Moorer. "At times the writing can be labored, the symbolism forced, the arguments tendentious. . . . But at its best, [Wright's] voice has a unique authenticity and power to engage his readers, a rare courage to grasp the fear and rage that the creator shared with the 'many thousands gone' who suffered these emotions inarticulately—the courage, in short, to acknowledge himself in his creations."[15]

This creative vision is extended in the portraits developed in *Eight Men*. The eight stories record the coming-of-age experiences of African

15. Redding (quoting Ford), "The Way It Was," 328–29; McCarthy, "Richard Wright: The Expatriate as Native Son," 73; Macksey and Moorer, eds., *Richard Wright: A Collection of Critical Essays*, 20.

American men who, treated like "boys" in every aspect of their lives, try to assert their manhood in futile and often tragic ways. These encounters, artistic manifestations of the interplay of race, class, and gender, reveal, to a lesser degree, the naturalistic tendencies prevalent in urban living. On a larger scale, these vignettes expose the migratory impulse of the African American experience—an experience sensitive to the fundamental restlessness of a people in search of a more nourishing environment for the development of community and self. Often, these pilgrimages are spurred by a sense of fear or a need to avoid impoverishment or even death. Dave, the protagonist in "The Man Who Was Almost a Man," wishes to flee the stifling conditions of his sharecropping existence. His affinity for a Sears Roebuck catalog and a two-dollar gun that brings nothing but trouble sends him on the run. When the Illinois Central rounds the curve near his house, he hops on the train, "away to somewhere, somewhere where he could be a man."[16] This story, the first in the collection, sets the framework for the remainder. Each story builds upon the ones that precede it, so that when we get to the last story, "The Man Who Went to Chicago," the unnamed protagonist becomes everyman, not only alienated from himself and his family, but totally disenchanted with the material conditions of his new life in Chicago. These literary forays into the cultural forces that shape black life in the new South—Chicago's urban slums—demonstrate that Wright never strayed far from his cultural roots or the literary aesthetic that marked his earlier works, but instead found more fitting ways to convey the political and social estrangement of African American people in light of the civil rights movement of the 1950s.

As in Dunbar's *Sport of the Gods* or Ellison's *Invisible Man*, the North is figured in *Eight Men* as a paradoxical space of freedom and limitation. "In my novel the narrator's development is one through blackness to light . . . from ignorance to enlightenment: invisibility to visibility," notes Ellison. "He leaves the South and goes North; this, as you will notice in reading Negro folktales, is always the road to freedom—the movement upward."[17] But this movement is not without cost. For Dunbar's characters, the loss is one of morality and spiritual identity. For Dorothy West's characters in *The Living Is Easy*, the movement north can lead to an excessive and materialistic lifestyle that compromises the moral ethics of those who make the journey. And for Toni Morrison, as

16. *Eight Men*, 18.
17. "Shadow and Act," 173.

seen in *The Bluest Eye* and *Jazz*, the North—as a symbol of alienation and cultural displacement—leaves the individual disconnected from traditional values necessary for communal life. For Wright, all of these factors converge in a symphony of voices in *Eight Men*. Each of the eight men featured in this collection is a shadow of the others, a wounded man who feels alienated from himself and from his family.

Although many critics have concentrated on the character of Fred Daniels, the protagonist in "The Man Who Lived Underground," a literary kin to Ellison's *Invisible Man*, it is the character of Saul Saunders, in Wright's "The Man Who Killed a Shadow," who best exemplifies the threat of figurative and literal castration for black men. Saul is a southern black who ever since childhood has been fearful of living with "shadows." These are not just any shadows but the "subtler shadows which he saw and which others could not see: the shadows of his fears." In distinguishing these shadows from those "innocent" shadows of Saul's childhood, those shadows whose silhouettes served as companions for him as he played along the dirt roads of his hometown, Wright demonstrates that as young children, African Americans are made to see the world "split in two, a white world and a black one, the white one being separated from the black by a million psychological miles." Thus, from the very beginning, children such as Saul "look timidly out from [their] black world," seeing only "the shadowy outlines of a white world" that is unreal to them and not their own.[18]

This cultural initiation translates into social anxiety for Wright's character Saul. His name, a reference to the biblical Saul who is transformed by his contact with a force greater than himself, leads the reader to reconsider the ways in which shadows haunt the African American psyche. In this instance, "shadows" are not only the progenitors of those anxieties—racist white people "who would some day claim him," as Saul explains, "as he had seen them claim others"[19]—but also stereotypes themselves, which serve as social extensions of this racist ideology. In Wright's narrative, this ideology is revisited in a symbolic exchange between Saul and a white "shadow-woman" in charge of the small library Saul cleans every day. Although the shadow-woman never speaks to him, except to begrudgingly extend to him an occasional and curt "good morning," Saul catches her staring at him at various intervals during the day. This woman's apparent interest in Saul takes on

18. *Eight Men*, 185–86.
19. Ibid., 188.

sexual connotations when Saul is told to clean under her desk by his boss. Left alone in the library with this woman one evening, Saul discovers her true intentions:

> "Why don't you clean under my desk?" she asked him in a tense but controlled voice. "Why, ma'am," he said slowly, "I just did." "Come here and look," she said, pointing downward. He replaced the book on the shelf. She had never spoken so many words to him before. He went and stood before her and his mind protested against what his eyes saw, and then his senses leaped in wonder. She was sitting with her knees sprawled apart and her dress was drawn halfway up her legs. He looked from her round blue eyes to her white legs whose thighs thickened as they went to a V clothed in tight, sheer, pink panties; then he looked quickly again into her eyes. . . . Saul was so startled that he could not move.[20]

Wright's critical assessment that black men are not only sexualized but also *projected* as superior sexual beings is realized in the interaction of these two characters. Perhaps out of a need to remove the stigma of chastity (she is still a virgin at forty years of age), or perhaps out of a need to exert her white privilege (a privilege she can exercise conveniently when Saul rejects her advances), the librarian relies upon her stereotypical notions of the black man's sexual prowess in order to force Saul to submit to her. This graphic illustration of sexual racism underscores the vulnerability of black men as the hunted and the haunted. As Gilroy reiterates, "The Man Who Killed a Shadow" bears the imprint of Wright's investigation into "the social issues that arose from thinking about black mental health in the United States." Thus, this discomforting tale "introduces the interrelation of racism and sexuality in a striking reversal of some stereotypical notions of predator and quarry." That Wright chose to address this issue within the confines of America's most sensitive subject—the interracial coupling of black men and white women—demonstrates how, historically, black men have felt simultaneous uneasiness and degradation in the presence of white women. Saul's paralysis at the initial moment of the shadow-woman's fleshly exposure to him, and his subsequent murder of her because of what he knows will be alleged of him based on their encounter, underscores this point: "The woman was screaming continuously . . . in her scream he heard the sirens of the police cars that hunted down black

20. Ibid., 192–93.

men and he heard the shrill whistles of white cops running after black men and he felt again in one rush of emotion all the wild and bitter tales he had heard of how whites always got the black who did a crime and this woman was screaming as though he had raped her."[21]

The racial memory this woman's screams evoke in Saul leads him to murder her. His reaction to this impossible situation—a situation ostensibly associated with being caught in an uncompromising position with a white woman—unearths the emotional responses associated with crossing the racial divide—a divide tenuously occupied by both the librarian and her sexual counterpart, Saul Saunders. As Earle V. Bryant argues, "both Saul and the shadow-woman are victims of racism's sexualization. In essence, both have been victimized through conditioning. . . . [G]iven the *forma mentis* of each character, their encounter could not have ended any other way than it does." The violence with which Saul kills his victim is mirrored only by the fear Saul has of the world of shadows that has consumed his natural life. Saul's predicament underscores the plight of all black men who suffer under the weight of history and custom. As Bryant concludes, "the stereotypical conception of black male sexuality is one of the most prevalent stereotypes in America's racial mythology." Thus the race-sex nexus that is so effectually incorporated into white America's social fabric provides a backdrop against which to explore the disfigurement of the black male psyche; as Gilroy attests, "the supposed beneficiaries of white supremacy are no less likely to be unhinged by its operations than its black victims."[22]

Wright's allegorization of the shared experiences of African American men is key to understanding the distinct psychological factors governing the economic and social conditions of black Americans. His examinations, when viewed in tandem with those of Ellison and others, weave a cultural tapestry of literary gesturing that suggests that even on the "lower frequencies" there is a need to be heard, and this need— whether primal or not—is directly connected to ways in which the black male body, in this instance, is disfigured—imagined if you will— within the primary cultural discourses of the society.

Yet the irony of this gesturing is that these writers, when placed in the context of America's competing discourses, must recognize their

21. Gilroy, introduction to *Eight Men*, xiii; Wright, *Eight Men*, 194.
22. Bryant, "The Sexualization of Racism in Richard Wright's 'The Man Who Killed a Shadow,'" 121, 119; Gilroy, introduction to *Eight Men*, xiii.

own disfigurement and refashion the language from which to speak the body's wounds. Although lynching renders its victims speechless— nonverbal entities within the sexually charged dynamic of patriarchal rule—Ellison and Wright both demonstrate that the "body of evidence," disemboweled and castrated, *speaks* on multiple levels. This evidence, whether in the form of a dry skeleton as in Wright's poem or in the form of a birthmark as in Ellison's short story, makes these acts of lynching *real* in the collective racial memory of African Americans as it simultaneously foregrounds and unveils the *imagined* circumstances under which these acts take place.

Because of the threat of castration, black males have invariably had a physical part of themselves identified with their powerlessness. This vulnerability and its accompanying psychological identification ties many contemporary writers such as Michael S. Harper, James Alan McPherson, and John Edgar Wideman to the rhetorical legacy scripted by their literary predecessors. These writers nonetheless attempt to address, through symbolic reversals and aesthetic revoicing, the unresolvedness evident in these works. Harper, for example, exposes the ironic influences of lynching as a disciplinary practice for racial control in his poem "Grandfather." In it, Harper explains the circumstances of one black man, the grandfather of the title, who, in 1915, found his house surrounded by neighbors who intended to burn him and his family out of their home, just like

> in a movie they'd just seen
> and be rid of his kind:
> the death of a lone black
> family is the *Birth*
> *of a Nation*
> or so they thought.

Harper's rearticulation of the symbolic association of violence and nationhood is obvious here, but unlike the ending in the movie *Birth of a Nation*, which has its central character, Gus, submit (if you can call it that) to the whims of the Klan, Harper's protagonist, who is all of "5'4," with a "waiter gait" and a "white jacket smile," asks his neighbors

> up on his thatched porch
> for the first blossom of fire
> that would burn him down.

His direct response to their threat, unscripted in the movie's text, reverses the social order:

> They went away, his nation
> spittooning their torched necks
> in the shadows of the riverboat
> they'd seen, posse decomposing.

This image of the grandfather early in the poem is later juxtaposed with the image of the same grandfather

> stitched up after cancer,
> the great white nation immovable
> as his weight wilts.

The fragility of a man able to withstand a threat to family and home exposes the nature of humanity trapped among the shadows of America's racial drama. Like those neighbors unable to tell the difference between the "imagined" black family in films and the "real" black family present in their community, the grandson's image of his grandfather is unable to sustain him against the steady assault of racial prejudice. The grandfather's wilting figure embodies the spiritual fragility of the grandson as he imagines his grandfather

> on a porch
> that won't hold my arms,
> or the legs of the race run
> forwards, or the film
> played backwards on his grandson's eyes.[23]

Harper's poetic exploration of the tension inherent in remembering the past and moving forward toward a different, if uncertain, future reflects his primary interest in exploring the dual consciousness of African Americans. As Joseph A. Brown argues, Harper participates in the time-honored tradition seemingly devoted to the sharing of "images" of his kin, what Robert Stepto has called elsewhere, an "articulate kinsman[ship]." In sharing these images, Harper exposes "a world where the souls of black folk are continually threatened with dreams which turn

---

23. Harper, "Grandfather," 2281.

into nightmares." These nightmares have generational significance as "the film played backwards on his grandson's eyes" in the previously mentioned poem redirects attention to the "film" played backward in the collective racial memory of African Americans everywhere. This "dead zone," a space of reflection created by the dual image of wounds and wings, of death and regeneration, allows Harper to explore death in all its manifestations. This poetic impetus, as Brown concludes, gives Harper ample space to demonstrate how "he has fought a way for himself out of the tomb, the temptation to eternally reside in nightmares."[24] His literary performance becomes a way to reimagine death, not as a final destination but as an open-ended journey.

Harper is not the first writer to use the subject of death as a means of exploring possible transformations within the African American literary imagination, but when viewed within the larger context of lynching, Harper's creative forays into the existential awareness of African Americans' condition within the broader historical configuration of sexual and gendered relations provide an interesting window into the symbolic uses of lynching in postmodern literature. Specifically, the significance of lynching as coterminous with the move to cultural freedom or spiritual resurrection, as can be seen in John Edgar Wideman's "Damballah," centers on the moment when words fail and the past becomes present in the disembodied spirits of the ancestors. Sheri I. Hoem argues that one of the hallmarks of "minority" literature is the material production of some form of the ancestor in establishing a creative link between the varying perspectives of historical time presupposed in African American fiction.[25] These instances of cultural "rememoration" mediate the corrective measures of literary exploration as they simultaneously revise the past in a gesture that confirms and subverts the power of historical representation. John Edgar Wideman's artistic conjuration of the ancient African divinity Damballah sustains such an analysis in a way that allows him to explore the long-term effects of lynching on the African American male psyche by returning to the moment of initial subjugation: slavery.

Wideman's narrative follows the spiritual journey of Orion, a slave who, renamed Ryan within the slave community, detaches himself from the suffocating confines of slavery by immersing himself in a river, a

24. "Their Long Scars Touch Ours: A Reflection on the Poetry of Michael Harper," 209, 211.

25. "'Shifting Spirits': Ancestral Constructs in the Postmodern Writing of John Edgar Wideman," 249.

symbolic gesture of baptism meant to connect him to the distant past of his ancestors. Orion's experience is a physical one as "all things seemed to come these past few months, not through the eyes or ears or nose but entering his black skin as if each pore had learned to feel and speak." This spiritual connection between the internal and external selves allows Orion to connect to the ancestral world, "his skin becoming like that in-between place the priest scratched in the dust—the sacred *obi*." Wideman's brilliant representation of the doubleness of black skin, not as a burden but as a "talking text" intuitively drawn by racial memory "across the sea," reinvests the flesh with omnipotent power. Orion's ability to reclaim this part of himself that has been taken away stems from his need to keep the "outside forces" from affecting his internal being. "When he walked the cane rows and dirt paths of the plantation," Wideman tells us, Orion "could feel the air of this strange land wearing out his skin, rubbing it thinner and thinner until one day his skin would not be thick enough to separate what was inside from everything outside." Thus, Orion's decision not to speak the language of his oppressor comes from the fact that "his skin whispered that he was dying." Clearly, the narrative of lynching underwrites Wideman's subtle pronouncements that black skin—that which is intimately connected to African American identity—is "rubbed thinner and thinner" through a series of torturous "rituals" that not only separate the slave from his native land but also disembody him from his very self. Thus, the "air of the plantation" becomes, in this instance, the kerosene, the tar that slowly boils Orion's skin away on a daily basis. That Wideman has his central character vow never to speak the language of his oppressor redirects attention to the *ritual* of lynching itself, particularly the sense in which the victim reinscribes language through a series of moans and hollers or through the medium of silence. Orion's "behavior" frustrates his owner to this extent as his "leatherish back . . . receives the stripes constant misconduct earn him."[26] Orion's scarred back becomes a testament, a written "transcription" of his willingness to return, in spirit, to his village across the sea.

The final "transcription" occurs when Orion is dragged across the yard to the barn to be lynched. The young boy witnessing this action, the one who would later rewrite the story of Orion through oral and written testimony, recalls hearing "one scream that night. Like a bull when they cut off his maleness." This reference to lynching is followed

26. "Damballah," 2336–37.

by a more detailed description of the ritual as the reader is made aware of Orion's fate when the young boy enters the interior of the barn only to find "Orion there, floating in his own blood," covered by a blanket of flies. The young boy scatters the flies. He then sinks to the dirt floor, crossing his legs where he stood. "He moved only once, ten slow paces away from Orion and back again . . . to see again how the head had been cleaved from the rest of the body, to see how the ax and tongs, branding iron and other tools were scattered around the corpse, to see how one man's hat and another's shirt, a letter that must have come from someone's pocket lay about in a helter-skelter way as if the men had suddenly bolted before they had finished with Orion."[27]

Wideman's decision to have this young boy find the dismembered and viciously tortured body of his ancestor is key to understanding the *genealogical* repercussions of lynching on the developing black male psyche. Only twelve years earlier Wideman had explored this same premise in his 1973 novel *The Lynchers,* which follows the exploits of four black men who plot the lynching of a white police officer. The failure of their attempt does not deny the brilliance of this ironic reversal as a means of making a daring political (and legal) statement. It does reveal, however, the horror of the act of lynching itself and likewise ties these young men to the very characters in history they seek to expose and undermine. This history, stunningly presented in a nineteen-page preface to the narrative, graphically details the brutality African Americans have suffered at the hands of mob violence. Wideman's philosophical examination of the historical effects of mob violence on the racial memory of African Americans in *The Lynchers* is represented in "Damballah" through the relationship of Orion and the young boy as he becomes the carrier of Orion's legacy, his untold and misunderstood story. In theory, this young boy personifies the reader as Wideman presents us with "a complex grafting of historical/fictional performance," according to Hoem, "situated in a field of moral and political struggle" that, in the end, asks us "to define ourselves in the present." Hence, we become the young boy who sees the disfigured body of his ancestor and sitting with crossed legs listens to him tell the stories again and again until his "eyes rise up through the back of the severed skull . . . and the wings of the ghost measure out the rhythm of one last word."[28]

---

27. Ibid., 2340–41.
28. Hoem, "Shifting Spirits," 225; Wideman, "Damballah," 2341.

"Necessary Bread"

We are the subjects of our own narrative, witnesses to and participants in our own experience, and in no way coincidentally, in the
experiences of those with whom we have come in contact. . . . And
to read imaginative literature by and about us is to choose to examine centers of the self and to have the opportunity to compare
these centers with the "raceless" one with which we are, all of us,
most familiar.
—Toni Morrison, "Unspeakable Things Unspoken"

The literary journey to find those "centers of the self" that both empower and liberate us rests in the regenerative experiences of the soul.
The writers considered in this volume have searched for this spirit
through their own narratives or in the creative explorations of their literary characters. For those artists writing before the turn of the century, the politics of their situation required them to distinguish themselves
from the perceptions of dehumanization that were implicit in their writings. In this way, they hoped to prove their common humanity with the
readers to whom their narratives were directed. For those writing after
the turn of the century, the struggle to find a voice and shape a literature tied to the larger struggle of African American freedom meant that
often they had to inhabit the very body they wrote about discursively
in order to create a new, regenerative body—one that both presented
the scars on the body and absorbed these same wounds in a simultaneous gesture of rhetorical healing. As such, their struggle is a complicated one. While Wright and Ellison present characters seemingly bound
by their predicament, Wideman, Petry, Morrison, and Williams present
memorable portraits of regenerative spirits. But their portraits are remnants of a prior existence that reaches back across the century, across
the waters to those whose voices have been silenced by the rhythms of
time. The old must be placed in context with the new so that we, as
black writers and critics, understand why ritualistically we write out of
a need to rescue our bodies, our minds, our very souls. For us, writing is
"necessary bread."[29]

29. For this phrase, see Cheryl Clarke quoted in the introduction to Cheryl A.
Wall, ed., *Changing Our Own Words: Essays on Criticism, Theory, and Writing by
Black Women*.

Coda

Awakenings

A Personal Odyssey

Before Emmett Till's murder, I had known the fear of hunger, hell and the Devil. But now there was a new fear known to me—the fear of being killed just because I was black. This was the worst of my fears.

—Anne Moody, *Coming of Age in Mississippi*

I don't know why the case pressed on my mind so hard—but it would not let me go.

—James Baldwin, *Blues for Mister Charlie*

It's like a jungle sometimes, it makes me wonder
How I keep from going under.

—Grandmaster Flash and the Furious Five, "The Message"

I conclude this work with a personal odyssey, one that has served as a backdrop to some of the investigations undertaken in this study. It began rather innocently. "Mommie, what's lynching?" I remember that question well, and as I looked into my young son's face, I had to decide whether to preserve his innocence, or tell him about the history of African American men.

My son's question reacquainted me with my own haunting experience with the history of lynching. I wasn't even born when Emmett Till

158

was killed, but I remember seeing the photograph at some point during my childhood. I recall being repelled by and likewise drawn to his image. I remember well the before and after pictures. His face whole and recognizable in one; in the other his eye gouged out, a big hole in his head, a missing ear, and a distorted and disfigured face ten times its normal size. It was horrifying to think that people were actually capable of doing this to a child. Although time and region separated me from Emmett's experience, my awareness of his murder came from knowing that he was just a child, a young boy of fourteen who had gone south to visit family and friends for the summer. I had also spent many summers in the South, visiting grandparents and relatives for months at a time, often oblivious to the regional and cultural differences.

I never really feared gangs growing up in Los Angeles; never thought much about the surrounding turf wars allegedly consuming the neighborhood I once lived in; never thought much about becoming another victim of the war called poverty. But the Till murder was different. That murder frightened me. Maybe it was the vengeance with which two grown men exercised their right over the body of a "free" black youth. Maybe it was the historical proximity, a murder twenty years young at that time in my life. As I was completing the work for this project, I experienced the same twisted anxiety of my childhood. I could not look at Till's photograph for any length of time. I remember covering up the image with other pages from the article in which it appeared so that I could concentrate on the cultural implications of his murder, devoid of any emotional attachment or personal reactions to child murder and its aftermath.

But that's hard to do when you're a mother, particularly when you're the mother of an African American child whose gender alone causes others to prejudge him. I have a beautiful son—he's smart, intelligent, and considerate. One of the things I love about him is his inquisitiveness. As I have been writing this book, we've shared interesting conversations about African American history and literature. I think of him as an "old soul," for he seems wise beyond his eleven years.

One of these conversations centered on the topic of lynching. It is customary in my house during black history month for my son to read to me (usually while I'm cooking) from a book of his choice so that we can share information about someone important to African American culture. During this particular session, my son chose to read about Ida B. Wells. His attraction to her was simple: they have the same birth date, and I'm sure he was aware of the fact that I had included her in my study on bodies and scars. Given this kinship, he seemed fascinated by her influence on history and her diligence in extolling the virtues of all men. After reading her brief biography, my son asked me that question, "Mommie, what's lynching?" He was all of nine years old then. I have to admit I was taken aback by the question at first, a little unprepared for addressing such a sensitive and weighty subject. Children usually let you know when they are ready to talk, and this question was my obvious signal. I answered his question directly and truthfully. "There used to be a time, honey, when men could come in our house and take you, and string you up to a tree, and hang you, and I would be powerless to prevent it." Silence. "There once was a time when white men would castrate you during that same act because you were who you were." "What's castration, Mommie?" I sighed deeply at this question, but took a deep breath and answered. "Castration is when your private parts are cut off." There was a pained look in his eyes. "Why?" he asked. "Because they are afraid, honey. Afraid of who they are *not*, and afraid of what you represent," I told him.

Explaining to my son the realities of African American history was as painful as telling him that there is no Santa Claus or Tooth Fairy. More telling is the fact that I did not have to explain to him who the "they" were. He knew. Just like he knew at three years old to scream when he saw the white male police officer approaching my mother's car. He had seen Rodney King's beating on television. I had tried in all honesty to shield him from that experience, but it takes only one time. My son was so terrified that his grandmother was going to be harmed that I had to physically remove him from the car and take him inside the house (my mother was being cited for double-parking in front of my house on a Sunday afternoon). It is uncanny how the unlayering of one wound reveals the contours of another whose festering flesh must be cut away so that, as Sherley Anne Williams explains, the wound can heal completely.

The legacy of Rodney King's beating will always be those haunting images of his assault. My son recognized at once his own black face in those images—not as a criminal but as a wounded body. This primal reaction to black male pain resonates a sounding chord in the cultural memory of African American people. Sandra Gunning is correct when she theorizes that the present-day impulse to map out the history, meaning, and consequence of the figure of the criminalized black male body inevitably leads us back to slavery and post-Reconstruction American culture. My son's early experience with the brutalization of black men led me to tell him my view of the truth about lynching. I had to tell him so that he knows *I* know of the veil that exists around him. But I also had to tell him so that he knows why *he* must continue on, why he must do well in school, why he must set an example for those other young brothas who seem unmotivated in life. "Thank goodness we don't live in that time honey," I explained to him. "Black men can't be hung from trees anymore, cannot be lynched anymore because of fear or racial paranoia."

But then three young white men made a liar out of me in some small town in Texas that same year. They dragged an African American man to his death behind an old pickup truck, separating his body from his head, his shoulder from his body, and in the process grinding off kneecaps and testicles. They even stopped to change a tire with James Byrd still attached to the truck by that chain, barely alive but alive. The crime was so heinous I had to look at my calendar again to make sure I hadn't traveled back in time, like Octavia Butler's character Dana, in her novel *Kindred*, to a period I had only read about in books. And then there was that incident in New York where four white officers emptied their guns into a young African immigrant entering his own apartment complex. Now how do I explain that to an eleven year old?

This is a concern I grapple with daily. It is an awesome experience to be raising an African American child today, particularly if he's a young man. I don't want to end up like Petry's Lutie Johnson, disenchanted and frustrated, leaving my child to the whims of a system that would love to add him to its list of casualties for this century. I don't have to worry about that, though. I have a good support system, like the one Sethe has in Morrison's *Beloved*, good praying women who surround me with their love and beseech the Creator every day on my and my son's behalf, asking for his protection, praying for our strength and his guidance in our lives. "We need you," they tell me, "for our babies coming up." "Yes, Ma'am," I answer. And their smiles give me that extra strength I need when it seems like "our babies" just ain't gettin it.

I began this study with a personal experience, one that shaped, if not the theoretical focus, then the spiritual focus of this endeavor. I complete this project with an equally challenging prospect: my own "call and response" that centers around the continuous wounding of the African American mind, body, and spirit. I still see that woman in that church, with her scars, with her children. This is the woman I've been speaking for, the one whose name I'll never know. She represents the nameless, wounded spirits I walk among every day. Empty eyes. Soulless. Seeking salve for their wounds, their pain. How, I ask, can the body heal, when the spirit, the very essence of humanity, is continually under attack?

It heals because we write, we tell our stories, we ritualistically "lay bare" before the nation our own communal pain—and theirs. We have to, if not for us, then for our children. They must see that the ancestors have paved the way for us, and it is on their shoulders that we stand. And so I tell my son the legacy of lynching. I open that historical wound again so that I may close it once more with a new understanding of the way things used to be, and with an inspired hope of the way things can be.

Bibliography

Alexander, Elizabeth. "'Can You Be BLACK and Look at This?': Reading the Rodney King Video(s)." *Public Culture* 7 (1994): 77–94.

American Anti-Slavery Society. *American Slavery As It Is: Testimony of a Thousand Witnesses.* 1839. Reprint. New York: Arno, 1968.

Anderson, Benedict. *Imagined Communities: Reflections on the Origin and Spread of Nationalism.* London: Verso, 1983.

Andrews, William L. "The Representation of Slavery and the Rise of Afro-American Literary Realism, 1865–1920." In *Slavery and the Literary Imagination,* ed. Deborah E. McDowell and Arnold Rampersad, 62–80. Baltimore: Johns Hopkins University Press, 1989.

———. *To Tell a Free Story: The First Century of Afro-American Autobiography, 1760–1865.* Urbana: University of Illinois Press, 1986.

Andrews, William L., ed. *The Oxford Frederick Douglass Reader.* New York: Oxford University Press, 1996.

Angelo, Bonnie. "The Pain of Being Black: An Interview with Toni Morrison." *Time* 133.21 (May 22, 1989): 120–23.

Anzaldúa, Gloria. *Borderlands/La Frontera: The New Mestiza.* San Francisco: Aunt Lute Books, 1987.

———. *Making Face, Making Soul, Haciendo Caras: Creative and Critical Perspectives by Women of Color.* San Francisco: Aunt Lute Books, 1990.

Aptheker, Herbert. *American Negro Slave Revolts.* New York: International Publishers, 1963.

Atwood, Margaret. "Haunted by Their Nightmares." In *Critical Essays on Toni Morrison's* Beloved, ed. Barbara H. Solomon, 39–42. New York: G. K. Hall and Co., 1990.

Armitage, C. H. *The Tribal Markings and Marks of Adornment of the Natives of the Northern Territories.* London: Harrison, 1924.

Awkward, Michael. *Inspiriting Influences: Tradition, Revision, and Afro-American Women's Novels.* New York: Columbia University Press, 1989.

————. *Negotiating Difference: Race, Gender, and the Politics of Positionality*. Chicago: Chicago University Press, 1995.

————. "Race, Gender, and the Politics of Reading." *Black American Literature Forum* 22 (spring 1988): 5–27.

Bachelard, Gaston. *Air and Dreams: An Essay on the Imagination of Movement*. Dallas: Dallas Institute Publications, 1988.

————. *On Poetic Imagination and Reverie: Selections from the Works of Gaston Bachelard*. Indianapolis: Bobbs-Merrill, 1971.

————. *The Poetics of Space*. Boston: Beacon Press, 1964.

Baker, Houston. *Blues, Ideology, and Afro-American Literature: A Vernacular Theory*. Chicago: University of Chicago Press, 1984.

————. *A Journey Back: Issues in Black Literature and Criticism*. Chicago: University of Chicago Press, 1980.

————. "The Promised Body: Reflections on Canon in an Afro-American Context." *Poetics Today* 9.2 (1988): 339–55.

————. *Workings of the Spirit: The Poetics of Afro-American Women's Writing*. Chicago: University of Chicago Press, 1991.

Baldwin, James. *Blues for Mister Charlie*. New York: Dial Press, 1964.

————. *Fire Next Time*. 1962. New York: Vintage Books, 1993.

Barrett, Lindon. "African-American Slave Narratives: Literacy, the Body, Authority." *American Literary History* 7.3 (fall 1995): 415–40.

————. *Blackness and Value: Seeing Double*. New York: Cambridge University Press, 1999.

————. "(Further) Figures of Violence: *The Street* in the American Landscape." *Cultural Critique* 25 (fall 1993): 205–37.

Bassard, Katherine Clay. "'Beyond Mortal Vision': Harriet E. Wilson's *Our Nig* and the American Racial Dream-Text." In *Female Subjects in Black and White: Race, Psychoanalysis, Feminism*, ed. Elizabeth Abel, Barbara Christian, and Helene Moglen, 187–200. Berkeley: University of California Press, 1997.

Bell, Bernard. "Ann Petry's Demythologizing of American Culture and Afro-American Character." In *Conjuring: Black Women, Fiction, and Literary Tradition*, ed. Marjorie Pryse and Hortense J. Spillers, 105–15. Bloomington: Indiana University Press, 1985.

————. "*Beloved*: A Womanist Neo-Slave Narrative; or 'Multivocal Remembrances of Things Past.'" *African American Review* 26.1 (1992): 7–15.

Bell, Derrick. *Faces at the Bottom of the Well: The Permanence of Racism*. New York: Basic Books, 1992.

Bennett, Lerone, Jr. *Before the* Mayflower: *A History of Black America.* New York: Penguin Books, 1993.

———. "Nat's Last White Man." In *William Styron's Nat Turner: Ten Black Writers Respond,* ed. John Henrik Clarke, 3–16. Boston: Beacon Press, 1968.

Benston, Kimberly W. "I yam what I am: The Topos of (Un)naming in Afro-American Literature." In *Black Literature and Literary Theory,* ed. Henry Louis Gates Jr., 151–72. New York: Routledge, 1984.

Berlant, Lauren. "National Brands/National Body: *Imitation of Life.*" In *Comparative American Identities: Race, Sex, and Nationality in the Modern Text,* ed. Hortense Spillers, 110–40. New York: Routledge, 1991.

Berlin, Ira. *Many Thousands Gone: The First Two Centuries of Slavery in North America.* Cambridge: Harvard University Press, 1998.

Bhabha, Homi K. "The Other Question: The Stereotype and Colonial Discourse." *Screen* 24.6 (November–December 1983): 18–36.

Bibb, Henry. *Narrative of the Life and Adventures of Henry Bibb, an American Slave, Written by Himself.* 1849. In *I Was Born a Slave: An Anthology of Classic Slave Narratives,* ed. Yuval Taylor, 2:1–101. Chicago: Lawrence Hill Books, 1999.

Billops, Camille, James Van Der Zee, and Owen Dodson. *Harlem Book of the Dead.* Dobbs Ferry, N.Y.: Morgan and Morgan, 1978.

Blassingame, John. *The Slave Community: Plantation Life in the Antebellum South.* Oxford: Oxford University Press, 1979.

Bragg, Rick. "Mother of 'Carjacked' Boys Held in Their Deaths; Police Say Woman Admits to Killings as Bodies of 2 Children Are Found inside Her Car." *New York Times,* November 4, 1994, A1.

Breeden, James O., ed. *Advice among Masters: The Ideal in Slave Management in the Old South.* Westport: Greenwood Press, 1980.

Brent, Linda [Harriet Jacobs]. *Incidents in the Life of a Slave Girl.* 1851. Ed. Walter Teller. San Diego: Harcourt Brace, 1973.

Broad, Robert L. "Giving Blood to the Scraps: Haints, History, and Hosea in *Beloved.*" *African American Review* 28.2 (summer 1994): 189–96.

Brody, Jennifer DeVere. "Effaced into Flesh: Black Women's Subjectivity." In *On Your Left: Historical Materialism in the 1990s,* ed. Ann Kibbey, Thomas Foster, Carol Siegel, and Ellen E. Berry, 184–205. New York: New York University Press, 1996.

Brown, Joseph A., S.J. "Their Long Scars Touch Ours: A Reflection on the Poetry of Michael Harper." *Callaloo* 26 (winter 1986): 209–20.

Brown, Marshall, ed. *The Uses of Literary History*. Durham: Duke University Press, 1995.

Bryant, Earle V. "The Sexualization of Racism in Richard Wright's 'The Man Who Killed a Shadow.'" *Black American Literature Forum* 16.3 (autumn 1982): 119–21.

Butler, Robert. *Contemporary African American Fiction: The Open Journey*. Madison, N.J.: Fairleigh Dickinson University Press, 1998.

Carby, Hazel. "Policing the Black Woman's Body in an Urban Context." *Critical Inquiry* 18 (summer 1992): 738–55.

―――. *Reconstructing Womanhood: The Emergence of the Afro-American Woman Novelist*. New York: Oxford University Press, 1987.

Christian, Barbara. *Black Feminist Criticism: Perspectives on Black Women Writers*. New York: Pergamon Press, 1985.

Clark, Keith. "A Distaff Dream Deferred? Ann Petry and the Art of Subversion." *African American Review* 26.3 (1992): 495–505.

Coffin, Levi. *Reminiscences of Levi Coffin*. Cincinnati: Western Tract Society, 1876.

Collins, Patricia Hill. *Black Feminist Thought: Knowledge, Consciousness, and the Politics of Empowerment*. New York: Routledge, 1990.

Conrad, Earl. *Harriet Tubman*. Washington: Associated Press, 1943.

―――. "I Bring You General Tubman." *Black Scholar* 1.3–4 (January–February 1970): 4–5.

Cooey, Paula. *Religious Imagination and the Body: A Feminist Analysis*. New York: Oxford University Press, 1994.

Cripps, Thomas. "The Reaction of the Negro to the Motion Picture *The Birth of a Nation*." In *Focus on* The Birth of a Nation, ed. Fred Silva, 114–24. New York: Prentice Hall, 1971.

Curry, George E. "The Death That Won't Die: Memories of Emmett Till 40 Years Later." *Emerge* 6.9 (July/August 1995): 24–32.

Curtin, Philip D. *The Atlantic Slave Trade: A Census*. Madison: University of Wisconsin Press, 1969.

Cutler, James E. *Lynch-Law: An Investigation into the History of Lynching in the United States*. New York: Longmans, Green, and Co., 1905.

Darling, Marsha. "In the Realm of Responsibility: A Conversation with Toni Morrison." *Women's Review of Books* 5 (March 1988): 5–6.

Davis, Angela Y. "Reflections on the Black Woman's Role in the Community of Slaves." *Black Scholar* 3.4 (December 1971): 3–15.

―――. *Woman, Race, and Class*. New York: Random House, 1981.

Davis, Cynthia J. "Speaking the Body's Pain: Harriet Wilson's *Our Nig*." *African American Review* 27.3 (1993): 391–404.

Dayan, Joan. "Romance and Race." In *The Columbia History of the*

American Novel, ed. Emory Elliott, 89–109. New York: Columbia University Press, 1991.

Delbanco, Andrew. "An American Hunger." In *Critical Essays on Richard Wright's* Native Son, ed. Keneth Kinnamon, 138–46. New York: Twayne Publishers, 1997.

Demarest, David P., Jr. "Richard Wright: The Meaning of Violence." *Negro American Literature Forum* 8.3 (autumn 1974): 236–39.

Dewey, John. "The Act of Expression." In *The Critical Tradition: Classic Texts and Contemporary Trends*, ed. David W. Richter, 486–99. New York: St. Martin's Press, 1989.

Dixon, Melvin. *Ride Out the Wilderness: Geography and Identity in Afro-American Literature*. Urbana: University of Illinois Press, 1987.

Douglass, Frederick. *My Bondage and My Freedom*. 1855. Reprint. With an introduction by Philip S. Foner. New York: Dover, 1969.

———. *Narrative in the Life of Frederick Douglass, an American Slave*. 1845. New York: Anchor-Doubleday, 1989.

Doyle, Laura. *Bordering on the Body: The Racial Matrix of Modern Fiction and Culture*. New York: Oxford University Press, 1994.

Du Bois, W. E. B. *Black Reconstruction in America*. New York: Harcourt, Brace and Co., 1935.

———. *The Souls of Black Folk*. 1903. Reprint. New York: Bantam Books, 1989.

duCille, Ann. "The Occult of True Black Womanhood: Critical Demeanor and Black Feminist Studies." In *Female Subjects in Black and White: Race, Psychoanalysis, Feminism*, ed. Elizabeth Abel, Barbara Christian, and Helene Moglen, 21–56. Berkeley: University of California Press, 1997.

Dunbar, Paul Laurence. *The Sport of the Gods*. 1902. Reprint. With an introduction by William L. Andrews. New York: Penguin Books, 1999.

———. "We Wear the Mask" and "Sympathy." In *Call and Response: The Riverside Anthology of the African American Literary Tradition*, ed. Patricia Liggins Hill et al., 614–15. Boston: Houghton Mifflin, 1998.

Ellison, Ralph. "The Birthmark." *New Masses*, July 2, 1940, pp. 16–17.

———. "Change the Joke and Slip the Yoke." In his *Shadow and Act*, 45–59. New York: Random House, 1964.

———. *Invisible Man*. 1947. Reprint. New York: Vintage Books, 1995.

———. "The Shadow and the Act." In his *Shadow and Act*, 273–81. New York: Random House, 1964.

Ellmann, Richard. *The Consciousness of Joyce*. New York: Oxford University Press, 1977.

Equiano, Olaudah. *Equiano's Travels*. 1789. Reprint. Ed. Paul Edwards. London: Cox and Wyman, 1989.

Ervin, Hazel. *Ann Petry: A Bio-Bibliography*. New York: G. K. Hall, 1993.

Evans, James H., Jr. *Spiritual Empowerment in Afro-American Literature: Frederick Douglass, Rebecca Jackson, Booker T. Washington, Richard Wright, Toni Morrison*. New York: E. Mellen Press, 1987.

Fabre, Genevieve, and Robert O'Meally, eds. *History and Memory in African-American Culture*. New York: Oxford University Press, 1994.

Feldstein, Ruth. "'I Wanted the Whole World to See': Race, Gender, and Constructions of Motherhood in the Death of Emmett Till." In *Not June Cleaver: Women and Gender in Postwar America, 1945–1960*, ed. Joanne Meyerowitz, 263–303. Philadelphia: Temple University Press, 1994.

"First Novel." *Ebony*, April 1946, pp. 35–39.

Foner, Eric. *Reconstruction: America's Unfinished Revolution, 1863–1877*. New York: Harper and Row, 1988.

Foreman, P. Gabrielle. "Manifest in Signs: The Politics of Sex and Representation in *Incidents in the Life of a Slave Girl*." In *Harriet Jacobs and* Incidents in the Life of a Slave Girl: *New Critical Essays*, ed. Deborah Garfield and Rafia Zafar, 76–99. Cambridge: Harvard University Press, 1996.

Foster, Frances Smith. *Witnessing Slavery: The Development of Antebellum Slave Narratives*. Madison: University of Wisconsin Press, 1994.

Foucault, Michel. *Discipline and Punish: The Birth of the Prison*. Trans. Mark Hurley. New York: Vintage, 1980.

———. "Nietzsche, Genealogy, History." In *The Foucault Reader*, ed. Paul Rabinaw, 76–100. New York: Pantheon, 1984.

Franklin, John Hope. *From Slavery to Freedom: A History of Negro Americans*, 5th ed. New York: Knopf, 1980.

Freud, Sigmund. "The Uncanny." In his *From the History of an Infantile Neurosis*, 217–52. London: Hogarth Press, 1955.

Fuss, Diana. *Essentially Speaking: Feminism, Nature, and Difference*. New York: Routledge, 1989.

Gaspar, David Barry, and Darlene Clark Hine, eds. *More than Chattel: Black Women and Slavery in the Americas*. Bloomington: Indiana University Press, 1996.

Gates, Henry Louis, Jr. *Loose Canons: Notes on the Culture Wars*. New York: Oxford University Press, 1992.

——. *The Signifying Monkey: A Theory of African-American Literary Criticism*. New York: Oxford University Press, 1988.

——. "Thirteen Ways of Looking at a Black Man." *New Yorker*, October 23, 1995, pp. 56–65.

——, ed. *Bearing Witness: Selections from African American Autobiography in the Twentieth Century*. New York: Pantheon, 1991.

Gates, Henry Louis, Jr., and Nellie Y. McKay, eds. *The Norton Anthology of African American Literature*. New York: W. W. Norton and Co., 1997.

Genovese, Eugene. *From Rebellion to Revolution: Afro-American Slave Revolts in the Making of the New World*. Baton Rouge: Louisiana State University Press, 1979.

Giddings, Paula. *When and Where I Enter*. New York: William Morrow, 1984.

Gilbert, Sandra, and Susan Gubar. *Madwoman in the Attic: The Woman Writer and the Nineteenth-Century Literary Imagination*. New Haven: Yale University Press, 1979.

Gilman, Sander. "Black Bodies, White Bodies: Toward an Iconography of Female Sexuality in Late Nineteenth-Century Art, Medicine, and Literature." *Critical Inquiry* 12.1 (autumn 1985): 205–43.

——. *Difference and Pathology: Stereotypes of Sexuality, Race, and Madness*. New York: Cornell University Press, 1985.

Gilroy, Paul. *The Black Atlantic: Modernity and Double-Consciousness*. Cambridge: Harvard University Press, 1993.

——. *There Ain't No Black in the Union Jack*. London: Hutchinson, 1987.

Goldman, Anne E. "'I Made The Ink': (Literary) Production and Reproduction in *Dessa Rose* and *Beloved*." *Feminist Studies* 16.2 (summer 1990): 313–30.

Goldsby, Jacqueline. "The High and Low Tech of It: The Meaning of Lynching and the Death of Emmett Till." *Yale Journal of Criticism* 9.2 (1996): 245–82.

Gomez, Michael A. *Exchanging Our Country Marks: The Transformation of African Identities in the Colonial and Antebellum South*. Chapel Hill: University of North Carolina Press, 1998.

Graham, Renee. "Stuart Dies in Jump off Tobin Bridge after Police Are Told He Killed His Wife; Image Proved Unjust; The Stuart Murder Case." *Boston Globe*, January 5, 1990, Metro/Region, 1.

Grandmaster Flash and the Furious Five. "The Message." In *The Norton Anthology of African American Literature*, ed. Henry L. Gates Jr. and Nellie Y. McKay, 62–65. New York: W. W. Norton and Company, 1997.

Greene, Marjorie. "Ann Petry Planned to Write." *Opportunity: Journal of Negro Life* 24.2 (April–June 1946): 78–79.

Grier, William H., and Price M. Cobbs. *Black Rage*. New York: Basic Books, 1968.

Griffin, Farah Jasmine. *"Who Set You Flowin'?": The African American Migration Narrative*. New York: Oxford University Press, 1995.

Griggs, Sutton Elbert. *The Hindered Hand: or The Reign of the Repressionist*. Nashville: Orion Publishing Co., 1905.

———. *Imperium in Imperio*. 1889. Reprint. Miami: Mnemosyne Publishing, 1969.

Gross, Theodore L. "Ann Petry: The Novelist as Social Critic." In *Black Fiction: New Studies in the Afro-American Novel since 1945*, ed. Robert Lee, 41–53. New York: Vision Press, 1980.

Guerrero, Ed. *Framing Blackness*. Philadelphia: Temple University Press, 1994.

Gunning, Sandra. *Race, Rape, and Lynching: The Red Record of American Literature, 1890–1912*. New York: Oxford University Press, 1996.

Hakutani, Yoshinobu, and Robert Butler, eds. *The City in African-American Literature*. Madison, N.J.: Fairleigh Dickinson University Press, 1995.

Halasz, Nicholas. *The Rattling of Chains: Slave Unrest and Revolt in the Ante-bellum South*. New York: D. Mckay, 1966.

Harper, Michael S. "Grandfather." In *The Norton Anthology of African American Literature*, ed. Henry L. Gates Jr. and Nellie Y. McKay, 2280–81. New York: W. W. Norton and Co., 1997.

Harris, Middleton A. *The Black Book*. New York: Random House, 1974.

Harris, Trudier. "*Beloved*: Woman, Thy Name Is Demon." In *Toni Morrison's Beloved: A Casebook*, ed. William L. Andrews and Nellie Y. McKay, 127–57. New York: Oxford University Press, 1999.

———. *Exorcising Blackness: Historical and Literary Lynching and Burning Rituals*. Bloomington: Indiana University Press, 1984.

———. *Fiction and Folklore: The Novels of Toni Morrison*. Knoxville: University of Tennessee Press, 1991.

———. *From Mammies to Militants: Domestics in Black American Literature*. Philadelphia: Temple University Press, 1982.

Hartman, Saidiya. *Scenes of Subjection: Terror, Slavery, and Self-Making in Nineteenth-Century America.* New York: Oxford University Press, 1997.

Henderson, Carol E. "Borderlands: The Critical Matrix of Caste, Class, and Color in *Incidents in the Life of a Slave Girl.*" *Legacy* 16.1 (1999): 49–58.

———. "The 'Walking Wounded'": Rethinking Black Women's Identity in Ann Petry's *The Street.*" *Modern Fiction Studies* 46.4 (winter 2000): 849–67.

Henderson, Mae G. "Speaking in Tongues: Dialogics, Dialectics, and the Black Woman Writer's Literary Tradition." In *Changing Our Own Words,* ed. Cheryl A. Wall, 16–37. New Brunswick: Rutgers University Press, 1991.

———. "Toni Morrison's *Beloved:* Re-membering the Body as Historical Text." In *Comparative American Identities: Race, Sex, and Nationality in the Modern Text,* ed. Hortense Spillers, 62–86. New York: Routledge, 1991.

Hernton, Calvin C. *The Sexual Mountain and Black Women Writers.* New York: Anchor Press, 1987.

Herskovits, Melville. "Problem, Method and Theory in Afroamerican Studies." *Phylon* 7 (1946): 337–54.

Higginbotham, A. Leon, Jr. *In the Matter of Color: Race and the American Legal Process, the Colonial Period.* New York: Oxford University Press, 1978.

———. *Shades of Freedom: Racial Politics and Presumptions of the American Legal Process.* New York: Oxford University Press, 1996.

Hine, Darlene Clark. "Rape and the Inner Lives of Black Women in the Middle West." *Signs: Journal of Women in Culture and Society* 14.4 (summer 1989): 912–20.

Hodges, Graham Russell, and Alan Edward Brown, eds. *"Pretends to Be Free": Runaway Slave Advertisements from Colonial and Revolutionary New York and New Jersey.* New York: Garland, 1994.

Hoem, Sheri I. "'Shifting Spirits': Ancestral Constructs in the Postmodern Writing of John Edgar Wideman." *African American Review* 34.2 (summer 2000): 249–61.

Holladay, Hilary. *Ann Petry.* New York: Twayne Publishers, 1996.

Holloway, Karla. "*Beloved:* A Spiritual." In *Toni Morrison's Beloved: A Casebook,* ed. William L. Andrews and Nellie Y. McKay, 67–78. New York: Oxford University Press, 1999.

———. *Codes of Conduct: Race, Ethics, and the Color of Our Character.* New Brunswick: Rutgers University Press, 1995.

———. *Moorings and Metaphors: Figures of Culture and Gender in Black*

Women's Literature. New Brunswick: Rutgers University Press, 1992.

Homans, Margaret. "'Racial Composition': Metaphor and the Body in the Writing of Race." In *Female Subjects in Black and White: Race, Psychoanalysis, Feminism*, ed. Elizabeth Abel, Barbara Christian, and Helene Moglen, 77–101. Berkeley: University of California Press, 1997.

hooks, bell. "Feminism Inside: Toward a Black Body Politic." In *Black Male: Representations of Masculinity in Contemporary American Art*, ed. Thelma Golden, 127–40. New York: Whitney Museum of American Art, 1994.

———. *Talking Back*. Boston: South End Press, 1989.

Hopkins, Pauline. *Contending Forces: A Romance Illustrative of Negro Life North and South*. 1899. Reprint. Carbondale: Southern Illinois University Press, 1978.

Hubbard, Dolan. *The Sermon and the African American Literary Imagination*. Columbia: University of Missouri Press, 1994.

Hughes, Langston. "Harlem." In *Call and Response: The Riverside Anthology of the African American Literary Tradition*, ed. Patricia Liggins Hill et al., 897. Boston: Houghton Mifflin, 1998.

Ivy, James. "Ann Petry Talks about Her First Novel." *Crisis* 53 (1946): 48–49.

Jacobs, Sally, and Diego Ribadeneira. "No Wallet, So Killer Opens Fire." *Boston Globe*, October 26, 1989, Metro/Region, 1.

Jameson, Fredric. *The Political Unconscious: Narrative as a Socially Symbolic Act*. Ithaca: Cornell University Press, 1981.

Jones, Gayl. *Corregidora*. Boston: Beacon Press, 1975.

Jones, Jacqueline. *Labor of Love: Black Women, Work, and the Family from Slavery to the Present*. New York: Basic Books, 1985.

Jordan, Shirley M., ed. *Broken Silences: Interviews with Black and White Women Writers*. New Brunswick: Rutgers University Press, 1993.

Jordan, Winthrop. *White over Black: American Attitudes toward the Negro, 1550–1812*. Boston: Harvard University Press, 1968.

Joyce, Joyce Ann. *Richard Wright's Art of Tragedy*. Iowa City: University of Iowa Press, 1986.

Kinnamon, Keneth, ed. *New Essays on* Native Son. Cambridge: Cambridge University Press, 1990.

King, Martin Luther, Jr. "The Current Crisis in Race Relations." In *A Testament of Hope: The Essential Writings and Speeches of Martin Luther King, Jr.*, ed. James M. Washington, 85–90. New York: HarperCollins, 1986.

King, Nicole. "Meditations and Mediations: Issues of History and Fiction in *Dessa Rose*." *Soundings* 76.2–3 (summer–fall): 351–68.

Knight, Etheridge. "The Bones of My Father." In *Call and Response: The Riverside Anthology of the African American Literary Tradition*, ed. Patricia Liggins Hill et al., 1488. Boston: Houghton Mifflin, 1998.

Kogawa, Joy. *Obasan*. 1981. Boston: D. R. Godine, 1982.

Kolchin, Peter. *American Slavery, 1619–1877*. New York: Hill and Wang, 1993.

Krumholz, Linda. "The Ghosts of Slavery: Historical Recovery in Toni Morrison's *Beloved*." *African American Review* 26 (fall 1992): 395–408.

Lawrence, David. "Fleshly Ghosts and Ghostly Flesh: The Word and the Body in *Beloved*." *Studies in American Fiction* 19.2 (autumn 1991): 189–201.

Lerner, Gerda, ed. *Black Women in White America: A Documentary History*. New York: Random House, 1971.

Littlefield, Daniel C. *Rice and Slaves: Ethnicity and the Slave Trade in Colonial South Carolina*. Baton Rouge: Louisiana State University Press, 1981.

Lovejoy, Arthur. *The Great Chain of Being: A Study in the History of an Idea*. New York: W. W. Norton, 1977.

Lovell, Thomas B. "By Dint of Labor and Economy: Harriet Jacobs, Harriet Wilson, and the Salutary View of Wage Labor." *Arizona Quarterly* 52.3 (1996): 1–32.

Mabee, Carleton. *Sojourner Truth: Slave, Prophet, Legend*. New York: New York University Press, 1993.

Macksey, Richard, and Frank E. Moorer, eds. *Richard Wright: A Collection of Critical Essays*. Englewood Cliffs, N.J.: Prentice-Hall, 1984.

Marshall, Paule. *Daughters*. New York: Maxwell Macmillan International, 1991.

May, Samuel J. "Margaret Garner and Seven Others." 1856. In *Toni Morrison's Beloved: A Casebook*, ed. William L. Andrews and Nellie Y. McKay, 25–36. New York: Oxford University Press, 1999.

McCarthy, Harold T. "Richard Wright: The Expatriate as Native Son." In *Richard Wright: A Collection of Critical Essays*, ed. Richard Macksey and Frank E. Moorer, 68–85. Englewood Cliffs, N.J.: Prentice-Hall, 1984.

McDowell, Deborah. "Negotiating between Tenses: Witnessing Slavery after Freedom—*Dessa Rose*." In *Slavery and the Literary Imagination*, ed. Deborah E. McDowell and Arnold Rampersad, 144–63. Baltimore: Johns Hopkins University Press, 1989.

McDowell, Deborah E., and Arnold Rampersad, eds. *Slavery and the Literary Imagination*. Baltimore: Johns Hopkins University Press, 1989.

McGovern, James R. *The Anatomy of a Lynching: The Killing of Claude Neal*. Baton Rouge: Louisiana State University Press, 1982.

McKay, Nellie Y. "Ann Petry's *The Street* and *The Narrows*: A Study of the Influence of Class, Race, and Gender on Afro-American Women's Lives." In *Women and War: The Changing Status of American Women from the 1930s to the 1950s*, ed. Maria Diedrich and Dorothea Hornung Fischer, 127–40. New York: Berg, 1990.

———. Introduction to *Toni Morrison's Beloved: A Casebook*, ed. William L. Andrews and Nellie Y. McKay, 3–19. New York: Oxford University Press, 1999.

McKissack, Patricia C., and Fredrick L. McKissack. *Rebels against Slavery: American Slave Revolts*. New York: Scholastic, 1996.

McLaurin, Melton A. *Celia, a Slave*. New York: Avon Books, 1991.

McPherson, James Alan. "The Story of a Scar." In his *Elbow Room*, 118–36. New York: Fawcett Crest, 1993.

Mercer, Kobena. "Looking for Trouble." In *Lesbian and Gay Studies Reader*, ed. Henry Abelove, Michele Aina Barale, and David Halperin, 350–59. New York: Routledge, 1993.

Mintz, Sidney W., and Richard Price. *An Anthropological Approach to the Afro-American Past: A Caribbean Perspective*. Philadelphia: Institute for the Study of Human Issues, 1976.

Mobley, Marilyn Sanders. "Ann Petry." In *African American Writers*, ed. Lea Baechler and A. Walton Litz, 347–59. New York: Charles Scribner's Sons, 1991.

Moody, Anne. *Coming of Age in Mississippi*. New York: Dell, 1976.

Morrison, Toni. *Beloved*. New York: Penguin Books, 1987.

———. *The Bluest Eye*. 1970. Reprint. New York: Pocket, 1972.

———. *Dancing Mind*. New York: Alfred Knopf, 1996.

———. *Jazz*. New York: Penguin Books, 1993.

———. "Nobel Lecture 1993." *World Literature Today* 68 (1994): 5–8.

———. *Playing in the Dark: Whiteness and the Literary Imagination*. Cambridge: Harvard University Press, 1992.

———. "Rootedness: The Ancestor as Foundation." In *Black Women Writers, 1950–1980*, ed. Mari Evans, 339–45. New York: Anchor-Doubleday, 1984.

———. "Unspeakable Things Unspoken: The Afro-American Presence in American Literature." *Michigan Quarterly Review* 28 (1989): 1–34.

Morton, Patricia. *Disfigured Images: The Historical Assault on Afro-American Women*. New York: Greenwood Press, 1991.

Mullin, Michael. *Breaking the Chains: African American Slave Resistance*. New York: Atheneum Books, 1990.

Naylor, Gloria. "A Conversation: Gloria Naylor and Toni Morrison." *Southern Review* 21.3 (1985): 567–93.

Nelson, Dana D. *The Word in Black and White: Reading "Race" in American Literature, 1638–1867*. New York: Oxford University Press, 1993.

Nichols, Charles H. *Many Thousand Gone: The Ex-Slaves' Account of Their Bondage and Freedom*. Leiden, Netherlands: E. J. Brill, 1963.

Painter, Nell Irvin. *Sojourner Truth: A Life, a Symbol*. New York: W. W. Norton, 1996.

Park, You-Me, and Gayle Wald. "Native Daughters in the Promised Land: Gender, Race, and the Question of Separate Spheres." *American Literature* 70.3 (September 1998): 607–33.

Perez-Torres, Rafael. "Knitting and Knotting the Narrative Thread: *Beloved* as Postmodern Novel." *Modern Fiction Studies* 39.3–4 (fall/winter 1993): 689–707.

Peterson, Carla L. *"Doers of the Word": African-American Women Speakers and Writers in the North (1830–1880)*. New York: Oxford University Press, 1995.

Peterson, Nancy J. "Introduction: Canonizing Toni Morrison." *Modern Fiction Studies* 39.3–4 (fall/winter 1993): 461–79.

Petry, Ann. "Ann Petry." In *Contemporary American Autobiography Series*, 6:253–69. Detroit: Gale Press, 1988.

———. "My Most Humiliating Jim Crow Experience." *Negro Digest*, June 1946, pp. 63–64.

———. *The Street*. 1946. Reprint. Boston: Houghton Mifflin, 1991.

Peyton, Thomas. Poem. 1620. In Alden T. Vaughan, "From White Man to Redskin: Changing Anglo-American Perceptions of the American Indians." *American History Review* 87 (1982): 917–53.

Prince, Mary. *The History of Mary Prince, a West Indian Slave, Related by Herself*. 1831. Reprint. Ed. Moira Ferguson. Ann Arbor: University of Michigan Press, 1997.

Pryse, Marjorie. "'Pattern against the Sky': Deism and Motherhood in Ann Petry's *The Street*." In *Conjuring: Black Women, Fiction, and Literary Tradition*, ed. Marjorie Pryse and Hortense J. Spillers, 116–31. Bloomington: Indiana University Press, 1985.

Rampersad, Arnold. Introduction to *Native Son* by Richard Wright, i–xxi. New York: HarperCollins, 1998.

Raper, Arthur F. *The Tragedy of Lynching*. Chapel Hill: University of North Carolina Press, 1933.

Rawick, George, ed. *The American Slave: A Composite Autobiography*. 41 vols. Westport, Conn.: Greenwood, 1973.

Rawley, James A. *The Transatlantic Slave Trade: A History*. New York: W. W. Norton and Co., 1981.

Redding, Saunders. "The Way It Was." In *Richard Wright: The Critical Reception*, ed. John M. Reilly. 325–50. New York: Burt Franklin, 1978.

Richardson, Robert, and Toni Morrison. "A Bench by the Road." *World* 3.1 (January/February 1989): 4, 5, 37–41.

Roberts, Dorothy E. *Killing the Black Body: Race, Reproduction, and the Meaning of Liberty*. New York: Pantheon Books, 1997.

Rogin, Michael. "'The Sword Became a Flashing Vision': D. W. Griffith's *The Birth of a Nation*." *Representations* 9 (winter 1985): 150–95.

Rushdy, Ashraf. "Daughters Signifyin(g) History: The Example of Toni Morrison's *Beloved*." In *Toni Morrison's Beloved: A Casebook*, ed. William L. Andrews and Nellie Y. McKay, 37–66. New York: Oxford University Press, 1999.

Sale, Maggie. "Call and Response as Critical Method: African-American Oral Traditions and *Beloved*." *African American Review* 26.1 (1992): 41–50.

Sanchez, Marta E. "The Estrangement Effect in Sherley Anne Williams' *Dessa Rose*." *Genders* 15 (winter 1992): 21–37.

Sanchez, Sonia. *Wounded in the House of a Friend*. Boston: Beacon Press, 1995.

Sanchez-Eppler, Karen. "Bodily Bonds: The Intersecting Rhetorics of Feminism and Abolition." *Representations* 24 (fall 1988): 28–59.

———. *Touching Liberty: Abolition, Feminism, and the Politics of the Body*. Berkeley: University of California Press, 1993.

Scarry, Elaine. *The Body in Pain: The Making and Unmaking of the World*. New York: Oxford University Press, 1985.

Scott, Nathan A., Jr. "The Dark and Haunted Tower of Richard Wright." In *Richard Wright: A Collection of Critical Essays*, ed. Richard Macksey and Frank E. Moorer, 149–62. Englewood Cliffs, N.J.: Prentice-Hall, 1984.

Shange, Ntozake. *Sassafrass, Cypress and Indigo*. New York: St. Martin's Press, 1982.

Silverblatt, Michael, and Toni Morrison. "The Writing Life: A Conversation between Michael Silverblatt and Toni Morrison." *Los Angeles Times Book Review*, November 1, 1998, pp. 3, 9.

Simpson, William M. "Reflections on a Murder: The Emmett Till Case." In *Southern Miscellany: Essays in History in Honor of Glover Moore*, ed. Frank Allen Dennis, 177–200. Jackson: University Press of Mississippi, 1981.

Sitter, Deborah Ayer. "The Making of a Man: Dialogic Meaning in *Beloved*." *African American Review* 26.1 (1992): 17–29.

Slattery, Dennis Patrick. *The Wounded Body: Remembering the Markings of Flesh*. Albany: State University of New York, 2000.

Smith, Billy G., and Richard Wojtowicz, eds. *Blacks Who Stole Themselves: Advertisements for Runaways in* The Pennsylvania Gazette, *1728–1790*. Philadelphia: University of Pennsylvania Press, 1989.

Smith, Felipe. *American Body Politics: Race, Gender, and Black Literary Renaissance*. Athens: University of Georgia Press, 1998.

Smith, Valerie. "Black Feminist Theory and the Representation of the 'Other.'" In *Changing Our Own Words*, ed. Cheryl A. Wall, 38–57. New Brunswick: Rutgers University Press, 1989.

———. *Self-Discovery and Authority in Afro-American Narrative*. Cambridge: Harvard University Press, 1987.

Solomon, Barbara H., ed. *Critical Essays on Toni Morrison's* Beloved. New York: G. K. Hall and Co., 1990.

Spillers, Hortense J. "Cross-Currents, Discontinuities: Black Women's Fiction." In *Conjuring: Black Women, Fiction, and Literary Tradition*, ed. Marjorie Pryse and Hortense J. Spillers, 249–61. Bloomington: Indiana University Press, 1985.

———. "Mama's Baby, Papa's Maybe: An American Grammar Book." *Diacritics* 17.2 (summer 1987): 65–80.

Stampp, Kenneth. *The Peculiar Institution: Slavery in the Antebellum South*. New York: Vintage Books, 1964.

Starling, Marion Wilson. *The Slave Narrative: Its Place in American History*. Boston: G. K. Hall, 1981.

Stepto, Robert B. *From behind the Veil: A Study of Afro-American Narrative*. Urbana: University of Illinois Press, 1979.

———. "I Thought I Knew These People: Richard Wright and the Afro-American Literary Tradition." In *Chant of Saints: A Gathering of Afro-American Literature, Art, and Scholarship*, ed. Michael S. Harper and Robert B. Stepto, 195–211. Chicago: University of Illinois Press, 1979.

Stewart, Maria. *Productions of Mrs. Maria W. Stewart*. 1835. Reprint in *Spiritual Narratives*, with an introduction by Sue Houchins. New York: Oxford University Press, 1988.

Stuckey, Sterling. *Slave Culture: Nationalist Theory and the Foundations of Black America*. New York: Oxford University Press, 1987.

Takaki, Ronald. *A Different Mirror: A History of Multicultural America*. Boston: Little, Brown and Co., 1993.

———. *Iron Cages: Race and Culture in Nineteenth Century America*. Seattle: University of Washington Press, 1979.

Tate, Claudia. *Domestic Allegories of Political Desire*. New York: Oxford University Press, 1992.

———. "Toni Morrison." In *Black Women Writers at Work*, ed. Claudia Tate, 1117–31. New York: Continuum, 1983.

Taylor-Guthrie, Danille, ed. *Conversations with Toni Morrison*. Jackson: University Press of Mississippi, 1994.

Thelwell, Mike. "Back with the Wind: Mr. Styron and the Reverend Turner." In *William Styron's Nat Turner: Ten Black Writers Respond*, ed. John Henrik Clarke. Boston: Beacon Press, 1968.

Thomson, Rosemarie Garland. "Ann Petry's Mrs. Hedges and the Evil, One-Eyed Girl: A Feminist Exploration of the Physically Disabled Female Subject." *Women's Studies* 24.6 (September 1995): 599–614.

Trapasso, Ann E. "Returning to the Site of Violence: The Restructuring of Slavery's Legacy in Sherley Anne Williams's Dessa Rose." In *Violence, Silence, and Anger: Women's Writing as Transgression*, ed. Deirdre Lashgari, 219–30. Charlottesville: University Press of Virginia, 1995.

Truth, Sojourner [Olive Gilbert]. *Narrative of Sojourner Truth, a Bondswoman of Olden Time: With a History of Her Labors and Correspondences Drawn from Her "Book of Life."* With an introduction by Jeffrey C. Stewart. New York: Oxford University Press, 1991.

———. *The Narrative of Sojourner Truth*. Ed. Margaret Washington. New York: Vintage Books, 1993.

Van Deburg, William L. *Slavery and Race in American Popular Culture*. Madison: University of Wisconsin Press, 1984.

Vansina, Jan. *Paths in the Rainforests: Toward a History of Political Tradition in Equatorial Africa*. Madison: University of Wisconsin Press, 1990.

Walker, Alice. *In Search of Our Mothers' Garden: Womanist Prose*. San Diego: Harcourt Brace, 1983.

Wall, Cheryl A., ed. *Changing Our Own Words: Essays on Criticism, Theory, and Writing by Black Women*. New Brunswick: Rutgers University Press, 1989.

Washington, Mary Helen, ed. *Black-Eyed Susans / Midnight Birds: Stories by and about Black Women*. New York: Anchor-Doubleday, 1990.

———. "Taming All That Anger Down: Rage and Silence in Gwendolyn Brooks's *Maud Martha*." *Massachusetts Review* 24.2 (summer 1983): 453–66.

Weisenburger, Steven. *Modern Medea: A Family Story of Slavery and Child-Murder from the Old South*. New York: Hill and Wang, 1998.

Wells-Barnett, Ida B. *Crusade for Justice: The Autobiography of Ida B. Wells-Barnett*. Ed. Alfreda M. Duster. Chicago: University of Chicago Press, 1970.

———. *Selected Works of Ida B. Wells-Barnett*. Comp. Trudier Harris. New York: Oxford University Press, 1991.

———. *Southern Horrors and Other Writings: The Anti-Lynching Campaign of Ida B. Wells, 1892–1900*. Ed. Jacqueline Jones Royster. Boston: Bedford Books, 1997.

Welter, Barbara. "The Cult of True Womanhood: 1820–1860." *American Quarterly* 18 (summer 1966): 151–74.

West, Cornel. *Race Matters*. New York: Vintage Books, 1993.

West, Dorothy. *The Living Is Easy*. 1948. Reprint. With an afterword by Adelaide M. Cromwell. New York: Feminist Press, 1982.

White, Deborah Gray. *"Ar'n't I a Woman": Female Slaves in the Plantation South*. New York: W. W. Norton, 1985.

White, Hayden. "The Value of Narrativity in the Representation of Reality." *Critical Inquiry* 7 (1980): 5–27.

White, Walter F. *Rope and Faggot: A Biography of Judge Lynch*. New York: Knopf, 1929.

Whitfield, Stephen. *A Death in the Delta: The Story of Emmett Till*. New York: Free Press, 1989.

Wideman, John Edgar. "Damballah." In *The Norton Anthology of African American Literature*, ed. Henry Louis Gates Jr. and Nellie Y. McKay, 2335–41. New York: W. W. Norton and Co., 1997.

Wiegman, Robyn. "The Anatomy of Lynching." *Journal of the History of Sexuality* 3.3 (1993): 445–67.

Williams, Juan. *Eyes on the Prize: America's Civil Rights Years, 1954–1965*. New York: Viking Press, 1987.

Williams, Patricia J. *The Alchemy of Race and Rights*. Cambridge: Harvard University Press, 1991.

Williams, Sherley Anne. *Dessa Rose*. New York: William Morrow, 1986.
———. *Give Birth to Brightness: A Thematic Study in Neo-Black Litera-ture*. New York: Dial Press, 1972.
———. "The Lion's History: The Ghetto Writes B[l]ack." *Soundings* 76.2–3 (summer–fall): 245–59.
———. "Meditations on History." In *Black-Eyed Susans, Midnight Birds: Stories by and about Black Women*, ed. Mary Helen Washington, 223–79. New York: Anchor-Doubleday, 1990.
Wilson, Harriet E. *Our Nig: or, Sketches from the Life of a Free Black*. 1859. Reprint. New York: Vintage Books, 1983.
Wood, Peter H. *Black Majority: Negroes in Colonial South Carolina from 1670 through the Stono Rebellion*. New York: Alfred A. Knopf, 1974.
Wright, Richard. "Between the World and Me." In *The Heath Antholo-gy of American Literature*, 3d ed., ed. Paul Lauter et al., 2:1959–60. New York: Houghton Mifflin Co., 1998.
———. *Eight Men*. New York: HarperCollins, 1996.
———. "The Ethics of Living Jim Crow." In *The Norton Anthology of African American Literature*, ed. Henry L. Gates Jr. and Nellie Y. McKay, 1388–96. New York: W. W. Norton and Co., 1997.
———. "How 'Bigger' Was Born." In his *Native Son*, ed. Arnold Ram-persad, 431–62. New York: HarperCollins, 1998.
———. *Native Son*. 1940. Reprint. New York: Harper and Row, 1966.
———. *Uncle Tom's Children*. 1936. Reprint. New York: Signet Books, 1947.
Wyatt, Jean. "Giving Body to the Word: The Maternal Symbolic in Toni Morrison's *Beloved*." *PMLA* 108.3 (May 1993): 474–88.
Yellin, Jean Fagan. *Women and Sisters: The Antislavery Feminists in Amer-ican Culture*. New Haven: Yale University Press, 1989.
Zangrando, Robert L. *The NAACP Crusade against Lynching, 1909–1950*. Philadelphia: Temple University Press, 1980.

Index

African American body, 2, 3, 7, 24; marked or wounded, 4, 7, 111, 112; as sign/language, 4, 9, 94, 95; as voice, 6, 69, 95; as metaphor, 8, 128; as flesh, 9, 23–24; rituals of marking, 15, 16; in pain, 37, 38, 82, 85, 90, 91; rhetorical strategies of, 38–42, 69, 116; as "speaking" text, 39, 40

African American culture, 2, 5; Los Angeles street culture, 2, 159; civil rights movement, 3; folk/oral history, 5, 68, 82; call and response, 11, 12, 58; signifyin', 12; "begetting of wounds," 14; and black dialect, 68; ancestral memory, 81; spiritual purification, 91–93; healing rituals, 126, 127; migration from South to North, 148, 149

African American identity, 6, 7, 11; criminalization of, 5, 6, 23; cultural markers of, 10; blacks as offsprings of Satan, 22, 23; black womanhood and disfigurement, 44; black manhood, 103, 104, 105, 106, 107, 138, 139, 140, 145–46, 160–61; in film, 140

African American institutions: church religion, 1, 2; Baptist church culture 2; and African religions, 93

African American writers: reclaiming the black body, 6, 8, 9, 12, 82, 151, 152; as respondents to culture, 7, 16, 58, 81, 82, 114, 157; reclaiming the black self, 11, 69, 162; and American history, 62

Africans: as indentured servants, 10, 20; as racial Other, 11, 19, 20, 21; as

property, 23, 25, 26; and ceremonial tribal markings, 30, 31, 32; and the Middle Passage, 33; and ethnic origins, 33, 34

American body politic, 3, 4, 8; cultural identities, 10; formations of race, 19–20; national disremembering of slavery, 87, 88; and black male stereotypes, 139, 140

American legal system: and slavery, 21; black women and rape, 21, 22; and master's rights, 22; Fugitive Slave Act of 1850, 40; Fugitive Slave Law of 1793, 40; and African Americans' displacement, 135n29

Anzaldua, Gloria: "borderlands," 9, 13

Bachelard, Gaston: and phenomenology of space/body, 126, 132, 133

Baker, Houston: and black women's expression, 72, 73, 126, 128, 135n29

Benston, Kimberly W.: and literary self-creation, 6

Bibb, Henry: and public flogging, 36

Brent, Linda. *See* Jacobs, Harriet

Brown vs. Board of Education (1954), 140n4

Carby, Hazel, 49, 72

Christian, Barbara: and Petry's *The Street*, 136

Cooey, Paula: and religion and the body, 3

Davis, Angela: and slave rebellion, 65, 66

De facto slavery, 20

181

Sanchez-Eppler, Karen: and abolition-
ism, 4; and embodied identities, 10,
39, 50
Scarry, Elaine, 90–91, 94, 96
Scars, 2, 9, 10, 27; dual functionality
of, 7, 15; as wounds, 8; as "signatures
of slavery," 23–25; meanings in runaway slave ads, 24, 27, 28, 33, 34;
whip-scarring vs. branding, 26;
teleology of scarring, 27; "country
marks," 32, 33, 34; literary treatment
of, 71–74, 75, 77–79, 85, 89, 97
Slattery, Dennis: and the gestural
body, 15; and wounded body as symbol, 112, 113
Slavery: significance to scarring, 9–10;
neo-slavery aesthetic, 14, 113, 114;
social costs of, 15, 16; legal and social formation of, 19, 20, 21, 82; and
class distinctions, 20; slave testimonies, 23, 39; and Ben Franklin's
Pennsylvania Gazette, 24, 25; fugitive slave ads, 24–27; slavemasters'
anxieties, 26, 28; medical conditions, 28–29; auction block, 36;
slave punishment, 36–37; initiation
rites, 37–38; whip as speech act,
43–44, 98; as national wound, 61;
slave resistance to, 65, 66, 67, 68,
105, 106; national recognition of,
84, 85
Spillers, Hortense: "high crimes against
the flesh," 9; "Mama's Baby, Papa's
Maybe," 13, 14; and language of scar
("American Grammar"), 33, 34
State of Missouri vs. Celia, 21–22
Stereotypes of blackness, 4–5; national fears, 5; in visual and print media,
5, 24–29

Thelwell, Mike: and "para-language,"
68

Truth, Sojourner: and sexual disfigurement, 45, 47–48; famous speech,
46–47; and cult of true womanhood, 47
Tubman, Harriet, 45, 66

Wells-Barnett, Ida B.: and the Moss-
McDowell-Stewart Incident, 54, 55;
and lynching, 54, 56, 57
West, Cornel: *Race Matters*, 15, 16
White, Hayden: and the value of narrative, 76
Wideman, John Edgar, 16, 156;
"Damballah," 154, 155
Wiegman, Robyn, 16, 141,
Williams, Sherley Anne: literary treatment of slavery, 61, 63; and *Confessions of Nat Turner*, 62, 63; "Meditations on History," 63; rhetorical
use of body, 63–65, 69–71; *Dessa
Rose*, 63–81, 111; rhetorical use of
scars, 71, 72, 73, 74, 75, 76, 77, 78,
79, 80; treatment of slave resistance,
67, 68, 75; mistress/slave relationship, 72
Wilson, Harriet, 114; and disfigurement in *Our Nig*, 115–17
Wounding ideology: body woundedness, 8; social "disabilities," 15;
"walking wounded," 15; psychologi-
cal/physical, 35–36, 82, 85, 111,
112, 162
Wounds: dual function of, 15. *See also*
Scars
Wright, Richard: *Native Son*, 113,
120–23; and scarred male psyche,
120, 121, 123; *Uncle Tom's Children*,
122; *Eight Men*, 138, 147–48; "Between the World and Me," 142–43;
"Ethics of Living Jim Crow," 145,
146; "The Man Who Killed a Shadow," 149–51

Permissions

Passages from *Dessa Rose* by Sherley Anne Williams, copyright © 1986 by Sherley Anne Williams, reprinted by permission of HarperCollins Publishers Inc. and Time Warner Books UK.

Passages from *The Street* by Ann Petry, copyright 1946, renewed 1974 by Ann Petry, reprinted by permission of Houghton Mifflin Company. All rights reserved.

Lines from "The Bones of My Father" from *The Essential Etheridge Knight,* by Etheridge Knight, copyright © 1986, reprinted by permission of the University of Pittsburgh Press.

Passages from *Beloved* by Toni Morrison, copyright © 1987 by Toni Morrison, reprinted by permission of International Creative Management, Inc.

Passages from *Wounded in the House of a Friend* by Sonia Sanchez, copyright © 1995 by Sonia Sanchez, reprinted by permission of Beacon Press, Boston.

Passages from "Grandfather" by Michael S. Harper, copyright © 1975 by Michael S. Harper, reprinted by permission of the author.